UNIVERSITY COLLEGE LIBRARY
CARDIFF

This book must be returned on or before
the last date stamped below.   Borrowers

Two week
loan

Please return on or before the last
date stamped below.
Charges are made for late return.

IS 239/0799

INFORMATION SERVICES PO BOX 430, CARDIFF CF10 3XT

Soldiers and students

International Library of Sociology

Founded by Karl Mannheim
Editor: John Rex, University of Warwick

Arbor Scientiæ
Arbor Vitæ

A catalogue of the books available in the **International Library of Sociology** and other series of Social Science books published by Routledge & Kegan Paul will be found at the end of this volume.

Soldiers and students

A study of right- and left-wing radicals

Rob Kroes
American Institute,
University of Amsterdam

Routledge & Kegan Paul
London & Boston

First published in 1975
by Routledge & Kegan Paul Ltd
Broadway House, 68–74 Carter Lane,
London EC4V 5EL and
9 Park Street,
Boston, Mass. 02108, USA
Set in 10 on 11pt Times New Roman
and printed in Great Britain by
Western Printing Services Ltd, Bristol
© Rob Kroes 1975
ISBN 0 7100 8089 1 (c)
ISBN 0 7100 8090 5 (p)

Contents

Introduction

I hesitate to suggest that this book is an exercise in the sociology of conflict. The reproach, heard repeatedly over the past fifteen years, that established academic sociology has exclusively focused on problems of order, stability, equilibrium, and harmony, has led some sociologists to come up with the alternative perspective of a sociology of conflict.[1] The German sociologist Dahrendorf, for one, suggested that one should consider conflict and harmony as disparate phenomena each of which needs an explanatory framework of its own. He invokes the Janus face of social reality: harmony and conflict can each be discerned, depending on what perspective one chooses. A theory meant to explain the one phenomenon cannot possibly refute a theory touching upon the other. The explanatory reaches of the theories do not intersect.[2]

An approach along these lines, however, would restore conflict as a proper subject of sociological analysis at the expense of problems concerning the relationship between order and conflict. Only if we manage to develop a perspective on social life that would allow us to conceive of order and conflict as divergent outcomes of one and the same *game* between groups in society, may we hope to acquire insight into the conditions causing order to give way to conflict or conflict to be transformed into order. The game concept has been used before as a metaphor to demonstrate the artificiality of a rigid separation of conflict and order. In an essay on soccer,[3] Norbert Elias pointed out that whatever changing configurations the game displays, conflict and co-operation are concurrent aspects. The chain of configurations cannot be properly understood unless one conceives of the game as co-ordinated conflict. This is one of the basic insights we have wished to insert into the perspective from which this book has been written.

Usually, conflict and co-ordination tend to evoke divergent

1

associations as to the impact of each on the persistence of a specific game pattern. Co-ordination is usually conceived of as a contribution to the structuring of a game, to the emergence of a set of rules, whereas conflict tends to be seen mostly as a disorganizing force, a constant source of threat to persistence and order. In that sense, both concepts are more than just references to concurrent aspects of the game: they point out the forces which can organize or disorganize it. They can, therefore, be used in an historic or diachronic analysis of how specific games have come about. They can serve to highlight the permanent tension between the forces of 'coagulation'—leading towards the emergence of order and regularity—and those of fluidization and disorganization. This summarizes one more insight that will guide the analysis throughout this book. However, fallacious implications may be lurking here, which again, however inadvertently this time, the work of Elias may illustrate. Notwithstanding the almost ideal view of the constantly shifting forces of coagulation and fluidization of forms of social life which the perspective, as outlined above, offers, the observer may be tempted to stress the forces of co-ordination and order, thus reducing the on-going alternation of order and conflict to a finite process. Open alternation has then become subject to a definite entelechy. The clearest example here may be Elias' classic study on the process of civilization.[4] The dominant picture to emerge from this analysis is one of an unfolding, almost pre-ordained development towards a situation where, in the end, the disorganizing potential of conflict has been checked by a gradual build-up of counter-forces such as the monopolization of the means of violence in the hands of a central state authority or the gradual growth of psychological forces of impulse restraint. The misleading suggestion emanating from a similar entelechian perspective would leave us fully unprepared for the analysis of the vulnerability and actual breakdown of these counter-forces.

Therefore, I have carefully attempted to keep teleology from interfering with the analytic perspective. Indeed, throughout the book, a main effort has been to bring out and highlight the potential for disruption of whatever institutionalized order has taken shape. The most general definition of those forces, as well as of the factors constantly supporting them, will be given in the first chapter. The following chapters can best be thought of as illustrations—comparative studies of how to recognize the general model in specific historical situations. *Qua* illustrations, the chapters inevitably may seem arbitrary. They are handpicked from the universe of situations differing in time and locale which the researcher would need for a methodologically impeccable, comparative approach.

The fanning-out of conflict into the emergence of oppositional camps, outlined in the first chapter, renders the overall picture of the breakdown of a given established order. Both rival camps in this context can be thought of as embodying the forces of maintenance and upheaval of that order. What we shall call the left-radical camp represents the forces of upheaval; what we shall call the right-radical camp represents the attempts at reaction and restoration.

A curious paradox is involved here. In the conflict both parties tend to grow alike in so far as both increasingly tend to resort to those means of organization and violence which in themselves signify the disruption of established order. The disruptive potential of conflict tends to be multiplied in the process. This offers one more reason for conceiving and analysing forces of conservation and disruption as interdependent. Yet, in the analysis of concrete, historical cases, we may choose to accentuate either force, without, however, neglecting the other. For indeed the oppositional camps that take shape when conflict runs its course have strategic options of their own which deserve separate attention. Therefore, two chapters are devoted to the right-radical camp in action, under the heading of 'Right-wing radicalism and the military'. The following two chapters deal with the left-radical camp under the title of 'Left-wing radicalism among students'. Notwithstanding this focus, however, time and again the other camp—be it left- or right-radical—is introduced in the analysis, true to the perspective that we have outlined above. It is our conviction that the analysis of student radicalism in particular, usually treated as a separate left-wing phenomenon by other authors, in total neglect of its interplay with adversaries, has stood to gain by our approach.

In the final chapter we return once more to the perspective in its full scope and bearing. This chapter, in a sense serves as counterpoint to the first chapter. There, an upward movement may be noticed; based on surmises and intuitions, disparate theoretical insights are interwoven, resulting in a concise statement of what we hold might be a fruitful process model of conflict and the rise of radicalism. The endeavour, in its lifting itself up from vague intuition on to a clearer perspective, unhampered by empirical vicissitudes, may seem reminiscent of the baron of Munchausen who managed to pull himself from the swamp by his own hair. In contrast to this, the final chapter shows a downward movement; the confrontation of model and empirical fact in the preceding chapters had illustrated the need for delimitation of the perspective, or rather the specification of what, in the first chapter, may have seemed, however briefly, to aim at general validity.

In addition to this, the final chapter presents some theoretical reflections on the perspective which, throughout the preceding analysis, has been brought to bear on problems of order, conflict and radicalism. Here we may briefly point out that the overall perspective represents the fusion of structuralist and interactionist or phenomenological approaches. Thus the analysis of the impact of underlying structures of interests, arising in a setting of social competition, and of normative structures, regulating competition, proceeds by way of the definitions accorded these patterns by the actors involved in the situations under study. Specific patterns of incongruity of interests as well as of normative conflict—referred to as the interference of criteria of achievement and ascription—are shown to give rise to specific patterns of redefinition and re-orientation for the various parties involved in competition. Thus processes are set in motion which, summarily, can be taken to range from competition to confrontation. An additional advantage of the approach may be that it allows the synthesis of sociological perspectives which are commonly presented as disjunct alternative views of society. They are, respectively, the consensus view, the exchange view and the coercion view of society. In our perspective they can be taken to represent the actors' dominant outlook on society during different stages of conflict. Thus exchange and consensus may be taken to represent the main ingredients of social integration in conditions of competition. Latent functions, in the Mertonian sense, of processes of mobility and piece-meal social change may, however, spur the processes of conflict and radicalization which, in the end, may be reflected in the dominance of a coercion view of society under conditions of confrontation. Although we propose to reserve the finer implications for separate treatment in the final chapter, it may be good to keep these theoretical considerations in mind when reading the preceding chapters.

1 Conflict and radicalism: a two-stage model[1]

1 Introduction

Two seemingly incompatible models of conflict generation can be found in studies of social conflict. In this chapter we shall attempt to delineate both models and to explore possible ways of reconciling them. It will be shown that one such way is a re-interpretation of the models in social-psychological terms. This will allow us to perceive the models in their proper time sequence and to conceive of one model as fulfilling an 'ignition function' for the second. We shall refer to the two models as the rank equivalence model and the rank *in*equivalence model respectively.

The models are similar in several respects. Both relate the occurrence of conflict to certain socio-structural factors. Both focus on the criteria according to which scarce goods such as political and economic power, prestige, income, and education are distributed. Both involve a multi-dimensional conception of society, the members of which can be ordered according to their share of social goods. Aside from similarities, several differences can be mentioned.

One model, organizing insights that can be traced back to Marx, and, more recently, to Dahrendorf,[2] relates conflicts to a distribution of social goods where each individual's shares of each of the goods tend to grow equivalent. The other model, the incipience of which can perhaps be found in de Tocqueville's analysis of the *ancien régime*, directs the analysis rather towards an inequivalence of shares of social goods which individuals have managed to acquire for themselves.

An early example of the rank equivalence model is Marx's analysis of the contradictions inherent in a society with a capitalistic system of production, though we need to remind ourselves of the fact that there the pattern of equivalence derives partly from a tautology. Positions on non-economic dimensions fall in line with the distinction

5

between proprietors and non-proprietors of capital goods on the basis of definitions rather than empirical regularities.[3]

An example of the rank *inequivalence* model is de Tocqueville's analysis of the *ancien régime*. His insight that the chance for social conflicts to arise increases after a period of improvement in economic conditions, rather than being contingent upon any absolute standards of living, or a downright decline therein, can be translated in terms of our pattern of inequivalence. The improvement in economic conditions can be conceived as a collective ascent of groups in the society along the dimension of, say, income. When on other dimensions the positions remain unchanged at their previous low level, we are able to recognize the pattern of the second conflict model.

The impression of mutual incompatibility of the models, accentuated by our use of the words equivalence and inequivalence, may be deceiving. We shall have to interpret the models in order to trace what, particularly in recent use of the models, the precise links are thought to be between structural data and the occurrence of conflicts. Thus we may hope to arrive at a more precise statement of possible inter-relations between the models.

2 The concepts of conflict and radicalism

Because we are dealing with the way conflicts can be related to structural data, these will be our focus in the definition of the concepts. Stuctural data, in our analysis, are thought to refer to the different positions occupied by the members of a society on a number of dimensions on the basis of their different shares of certain social goods. As a general rule, we state that a given distribution entails different interests for groups that hold different shares. The ones best-off are assumed to be actively striving to maintain or enlarge their share. We might call these interests *objective* in the sense Marx uses the term. We thereby grant the possibility that groups in a society can behave in a way which deviates from their objective interests— the possibility, that is, that objective interests may fail to be transformed into clear guides for action. Thus the empirical problem arises as to which factors cause objective interests to become self-conscious. We shall come back to this later. At the moment, however, we shall try to designate the logical categories describing a 'field' which consists of two rival parties under the conditions of a zero-sum game[4] in which a gain by one party causes an equally large loss to the other party and in which both parties may or may not act in accordance with their objective interests. See table 1.1.

The situation $(- -)$ indicates the extreme case in which neither of the parties is guided by its objective interests as defined above. In this category belongs the type of society in which neither the criteria

TABLE 1.1   *Objective interests and subjective awareness*

Objective interests of the worst-off		Objective interests of the ones best-off	
		not self-conscious −	self-conscious +
not self-conscious	−	− −	− +
self-conscious	+	+ −	+ +

of distribution nor the factual distribution which results from these is in dispute, a situation which can either be the result of the power estimates of the parties involved, or, on the other hand, can result from an effective value consensus.

The situation (− +) could be one of exploitation in the Marxist sense: the ones best-off are up to enlarging their shares at the expense of the ones worst-off who fail to show signs of realizing their objective interests. The situation (+ −) is one in which the worst-off realize what their objective interests are and act accordingly; the positions of the best-off are attacked without the latter reacting as might have been expected on the basis of their objective interests. In the situation (+ +), finally, both parties confront each other, bringing to bear the opposing strategies which we assume them to display on the basis of their objective interests. Given our additional assumption of zero-sum conditions, it is impossible for both of the parties to attain their goals. Therefore we term this situation one of *conflict*.[5]

In this connection one may note that our definition of objective interests and the assumption of zero-sum conditions imply a conflict situation. However, it is only when both parties are self-consciously aware of their objective interests that a situation of actual conflict arises.[6]

In situations of both the (+ −) and the (− +) variety, the party that acts on self-conscious interests is able to reach its goals. The acquiescence of the opposing party is, as in the (− −) case, evidence of an effective consensus, or the result of power estimates of the parties involved. These two alternatives have been suggested by both Parsons and Etzioni in their (remarkably consonant) analyses of the concept of power.[7] Attempts at either establishing societal consensus or maintaining it, can be considered as a useful means in the defence of or the attack at a given distribution of social goods. As such, these attempts can be taken to signal the stage where one of the parties has become aware of its objective interests. For either the (+ −) or (− +) situations, however, the appeal to common values will issue in starkly divergent ideologies. The characteristic ideology justifying the (− +) situation may be called *conservative*; the ideology for the (+ −) situation *egalitarian*.

The confrontation of both the egalitarian and the conservative ideologies in a (++) situation where, under zero-sum conditions, they advocate conflicting goals, may have specific consequences for each of them. The fact that each party is thwarted in reaching its goal by the adverse policy of the opponent, lends a particular character to the ideologies that we choose to call *radical*. We seem justified in doing so in so far as radicalism is generally understood to combine a set of cognitions and beliefs regarding a drastic change in a social structure with conceptions of the identity and the aims of a malicious adversary blocking the road to the cherished goal. Radicalism in that sense focuses on the militant strategies that are advocated in an ideology.

3 The rank equivalence model

As we said earlier, the rank equivalence model is marked by the maximum inter-correlation between separate dimensions of social distribution. It allows us to conceive of this model as a limiting case of a continuum of patterns of increasingly lower correlations. The second limit, then, is the pattern that shows zero-intercorrelations; here the position that an individual holds on one dimension does not warrant predictions as to his positions on other dimensions. This latter type can be taken to represent a pluralistic society[8] in which, characteristically, individuals on the basis of their divergent interests find themselves alternatively aligned with the ones best-off and with the ones worst-off. This society is marked by a dispersion of interest groups and, consequently, of individual solidarities, which clearly contrasts with the pattern of polarized interest groups that was found at the other extreme of the continuum. Grossly synonymous with the term pluralist society[9] are such labels as multiple loyalties and multiple role-playing,[10] criss-cross,[11] multiple group affiliations,[12] interlocking memberships.[13]

In order to analyse the possible relevance for a general theory of conflict of these different patterns of interconnections between dimensions of social distribution, we shall consider a simplified example of society which has only two distributive dimensions, which, in turn, have only two positions each—a top position T and a low position L.[14]

We assume that the goods distributed along these lines, are respectively economic power and political power. All possible combinations of positions can be shown in a simple 2 × 2 matrix. See table 1.2. The actual distribution of members of this imaginary society within this matrix determines the rank of this society on the continuum, ranging from pluralism to polarization, that we referred to above.

1 The polarized type can be easily identified. When the members

TABLE 1.2 *Two dichotomous dimensions of social distribution*

Economic power	Political power	
	T	L
T	TT	TL
L	LT	LL

of the society are distributed in such a way as to leave the LT- and TL-cells empty, the situation reflects the pattern of our model of rank equivalence.

2 It may seem slightly more complicated to define the conditions for pluralism as an extreme case. However, if we recall what we said earlier, that a pluralistic pattern does not warrant predictions as to combinations of positions, the different dimensions being independent of each other, we can define a pluralist society as one in which the distribution of the entire population within the matrix does not differ from its distribution along the separate dimensions. In such a case neither the T-, nor the L-group on one dimension are over- or under-represented in taking T- or L-positions on the other dimension.[15] An example may illustrate this point (see table 1.3).

TABLE 1.3 *The limiting case of pluralism*

Economic power	Political power		
	T	L	Total
T	20	20	40
L	30	30	60
	50	50	100

Both dimensions are completely independent. In other words, the TT and LL cells do not show any heavier concentrations than the TL and LT cells. A simple measure may be as follows:

$$\frac{[(TT)+(LL)] - [(TL)+(LT)]}{N}$$

For the above case of perfect pluralism the measure would have a value of zero, which in fact would indicate the absence of polarization. Indeed, the opposite case of perfect polarization would cause the measure to show a value of 1, as Table 1.4 illustrates.[16]

9

TABLE 1.4 *The limiting case of polarization*

Economic power	Political power		
	T	L	Total
T	20	—	20
L	—	80	80
	20	80	100

3   There is one situation which deserves separate mention. One can imagine the case where all political top positions are held by the wielders of economic power but where the number of political top positions is not sufficiently large to equal the number of those who hold economic power, as Table 1.5 is meant to illustrate.

TABLE 1.5 *An intermediate case*

Economic power	Political power		
	T	L	Total
T	20	20	40
L	—	60	60
	20	80	100

Although a strong tendency towards polarization is evident—all political subjects happen to be excluded from economic power—a category of people has emerged, due to numerical inequalities between the political and economic dimensions of power, which shares an economic top position with the TT-group and the position of political subject with the LL-group. Thus a group with potential *multiple loyalties* has entered the scene and thereby reduces the measure of polarization to 0·6.[17]

We now want to deal more specifically with the issue of what consequences different structural types in our continuum may have for the occurrence of conflicts. The interpretation of rank equivalence models of conflict as an extreme type in a continuum ranging from pluralism to polarization allows us to analyse its explanatory value within a wider context. For one thing, we should beware of viewing the extreme types of pluralism and polarization as models of societies respectively lacking in conflict or abounding with it. On the contrary, our basic assumption that the differential distribution of each separate social good entails intrinsically conflicting objective interests implies that conflicts can focus on just one hierarchical dimension. The pluralist model, therefore, does not represent a society without conflict, but rather one in which the dispersion of interests prevents a conflict from transcending its initial bounds. Authors such as Coser and Dahl dwelt extensively upon this impact of a pluralist structure on the course of conflicts.[18] As Coser says:[19]

> The multiple group affiliations of individuals makes them participate in various group conflicts so that their total personalities are not involved in any single one of them. Thus segmental participation in a multiplicity of conflicts constitutes a balancing mechanism within the structure.

This view of pluralism as an antidote against the potentially disintegrating effects of conflicts upon a society is even more clearly expressed by Ross:[20]

> A society, therefore, which is ridden by a dozen oppositions along lines running in every direction may actually be in less danger of being torn with violence or falling to pieces than one split just along one line. For each new cleavage contributes to narrow the cross conflicts, so that one might say that society *is sewn together* by its inner conflicts.

Between these quotations there is a definite shift in the claims made for the case of pluralism, in that Coser conceives of pluralism as a check on the disruptive potential of conflict, while Ross, much more positively, holds that conflicts actually integrate a pluralistic society. It is especially this last point of view that brings out the specific use that can be made of the rank equivalence model of conflict. Focusing on polarization in a society, the model shows how people's interests regarding a plurality of social goods become increasingly homogeneous and how, consequently, conflicts about one social good tend to spark off conflicts about other goods. The rank equivalence model, therefore, lends itself in particular for the study of escalation of conflicts in which the opposing parties are aligned on the basis of a plurality of interests. Conflicts, in this case, are increasingly intense and violent.[21] Implicit in the use of this model is the consideration that only through the process of escalation do conflicts tend to become disruptive for the society as a whole. It is this consideration that allows us to add one more aspect to the antithetical nature of the concepts of pluralism and polarization in so far as conflicts within these opposed types of society are either potentially integrating or disruptive in their effects. One final remark needs to be made. The structural given of a pluralist pattern need not be *per se* the unfailing check that prevents conflicts from dividing society into two opposing camps. The matrix of Table 1.2 may serve to illustrate this. Even in

11

the case in which a population is distributed within the matrix in such a way as to make the resulting pattern pluralistic, there is no compelling reason why, for instance in a political conflict, the TT- and LT-groups would not unite in defending their political top position against a coalition of TL- and LL-groups, *unless at the same time the distribution of economic power represents a dimension of conflict.*

Only in the case in which all objective interests in this two-dimensional model are activated are we warranted in making the conflict-theoretical predictions that follow from the pluralist model.[22]

4 An excursion: the case of the Netherlands

Some aspects of the related concepts of pluralism and polarization have still to be mentioned, and we suggest they may come out most clearly through a discussion of a recent application of the concept of pluralism. The book we propose to deal with is *The Politics of Accommodation, Pluralism and Democracy in the Netherlands,* by A. Lijphart.[23] The pivotal question which the author deals with is how the Dutch political system, although allegedly deviating from the pluralistic model due to its organizational principle of *verzuiling,* could possibly have defied the theory by its apparent stability over the years. The author suggests that the conscious policies of the political elite may have served as a functional alternative for the integrative functions that pluralism purportedly fulfils. In the following discussion we shall examine the argument used to sustain Lijphart's contention that the Dutch political system is a deviant case in terms of pluralist theory.

Verzuiling is Lijphart's central evidence. He notes that Dutch society is divided into four large blocks which, on the basis of one shared characteristic, have each sought strength through isolation—an organizational device which pervades all spheres of life. The four blocks consist of two religious ones—the Catholic and the Calvinistic blocks—and two secular ones—the liberal and the socialist blocks. According to Lijphart, no *overlapping membership* occurs, one of the several labels for a pluralistic pattern,[24] as we noted earlier. This contention, however, holds true only in part. Neither are all workers contained within the socialist block, nor all employers within the liberal block. As the author himself correctly points out, *verzuiling* implies two different organizational criteria which work at cross-purposes, the one criterion being the secular/religious dichotomy, the other the liberal/socialist one. However, in order to buttress the case for the disruptive tendencies inherent in such a situation, the author goes on to state:[25] 'After all, when one cuts a pie crosswise one gets four separate pieces rather than a single whole pie.' That, however, is a misleading metaphor. The simultaneous effects of both dimensions can be shown in a matrix in order to illustrate our argument (see Table 1.6).

TABLE 1.6   *The two dimensions of* verzuiling

Socio-economic position	Religion secular	religious
employers	a	b
employees	c	d

This matrix differs in one important respect from the one we used earlier. There, reduced to dichotomies, the distribution was shown of two social goods, irrespective of the criteria for distribution, whereas here, especially in the religious/secular dichotomy, those social characteristics are shown which actually serve as criteria for distribution. We shall leave this distinction between a given distribution and its criteria for more systematic treatment in the next part of this chapter.

Lijphart himself gives the relevant information about how the Dutch population is distributed over the cells of the matrix.[26] The dimensions are mutually independent—employers and employees are represented among the religious and secular blocks in about the same proportions as in the total population, though Catholics still tend to be under-represented in the higher positions in society. Our measure of degree of polarization would have a value approaching zero—in other words: the situation as represented by these two dimensions tends towards the pluralist extreme.[27]

In addition, the historical fact of emancipatory movements, of both religious and working-class varieties, as well as the actual strength of organization based on religion or class, may serve to suggest that both dimensions are 'activated'. Both preconditions for a pluralist pattern to be effective have thus been fulfilled and we may expect, consequently, that the conflict-theoretical predictions apply to the case of the Netherlands.

The question arises, then: what could have led Lijphart to represent the Dutch situation as tending towards the disruptive other extreme of the continuum? It may be due to semantic ambiguities. We did mention earlier the alternative labels which are used by students of pluralism. Our point now is that some of these labels express less fully the crucial characteristic of a pluralist pattern and, therefore, can lead to incorrect conclusions. The term *overlapping membership* seems to be one such label. It focuses exclusively on the phenomenon of organization on the basis of just one particular dimension. The very fact of such organization, however, in a situation

13

where several cross-cutting dimensions are activated, has two simultaneous effects: divergent interests become united while shared interests become divided. For instance, an organization based on religion brings together the b- and d-groups (see Table 1.6) which have divergent socio-economic interests, and thereby jeopardizes its strength and unity of action on issues that are not related to the basis of organization: the shared interest. Such an organization separates, on the other hand, the d-group from the c-group, though both have economic interests in common. However, as long as those common interests too are activated—which is to say that they are an independent factor of solidarity—we may expect coalitions to emerge, for the sake of strengthening their strategic position in economic conflicts, between d- and c-groups (or, to borrow more extensively from the alphabet, between the NKV and the CNV, both religious labour unions, and the NVV, the secular labour union).

Membership in formal organizations based on one single dimension is only one of the corollaries of a pluralist pattern that is relevant to a theory of conflict. As Galtung points out, any position on a single dimension that otherwise different groups have in common can be viewed either as a link—a basis of organization—or as a common loyalty—a basis for temporary coalitions and common strategies.[28]

Finally, we want to stress once more that any assertion about the Dutch case as significantly deviating from the pluralist model would have been justified only if evidence had shown that the cells (a) and (d) of the matrix were improportionally loaded—if, for example, all economic underdogs were Catholic. Lijphart seems to have projected the integrating role of the political elite against the background of a social structure that is one-sidedly represented as inherently tending towards disintegration.[29]

5 The rank inequivalence model

On the basis of the continuum stretching from pluralism to polarization, all non-polarized types of society are, strictly speaking, rank inequivalent due to the fact that individuals can be identified that hold non-equivalent ranks on certain dimensions, ranks such as are exemplified by the TL- and LT-cells of the matrix of Table 1.2. It is this particular constellation of ranks that some students of conflict contend is the conflict-generating element of the rank inequivalence model. Varying labels are used such as status incongruence, status discrepancy and rank (in)equivalence. A survey of different approaches and empirical findings is given by Berting and Galtung.[30]

About a quarter of a century ago, Benoit-Smullyan[31] had already pointed out that the discrepancy can be eliminated in two different ways: either by bringing the lower ranks onto a par with the higher or, in the case where such an upward movement is thwarted, by embracing radicalism, aimed at reshaping the status structure as a whole. The tendency to eliminate the discrepancy is, in the first place, a recurrent postulate in analyses of status incongruence and has been, more recently, related to general social-psychological balance theories as developed by Heider, Festinger, Cartwright and Harary, or Newcomb.[32]

The process can also be accounted for in terms of reference group behaviour and a theory of social justice, as formulated, for example, by Homans and Runciman:[33] the T position, which the TT group and the LT group have in common, may provide an element of equality on the basis of which the inequality along the other dimension may be perceived as unjustified.

We shall return to this point shortly. However, whatever the explanation suggested for the recurrent attempts at overcoming an inequivalence of ranks, it will be evident that, from the point of view of a theory of conflict the situation in which these attempts are thwarted is of crucial relevance. Therefore, in the following, we propose to focus on that situation and to review a number of potential blockings.

Blockings

A first category might be called structural blockings. In Table 1.5 we referred to the case of a society which, although characterized by a strong tendency towards polarization, for structural reasons did not allow all holders of economic power to occupy positions of political power. Here the blocking cannot be traced to normative notions defining the legitimacy of claims on certain positions; it should, rather, be causally connected with what we might call a structural gap. The claims on certain positions, inspired by the taking of other positions, are frustrated because of an insufficient 'supply' of the desired positions. The incapacity of a society to create sufficient highly valued positions in order to meet the legitimate demand of its members can be enough reason for the emergence of political radicalism. The situation of present-day England might serve to illustrate such a structural gap; the specific variety of social mobility commonly called the 'brain drain' might serve, however, as a safety-valve to prevent internal tension from building up.[34]

A second category consists of blockings that can be traced to normative notions defining the legitimacy of claims on certain positions—notions concerning the criteria according to which social goods ought to be distributed. We can distinguish between, on the one hand, distributive criteria that are particularly well suited to aspirations of upward mobility and those, on the other hand, which make for high rigidity of one's share of social goods. A distinction in this vein is similar to the one, commonly made, between *achieved* ranks and *ascriptive* ranks. Each of these is based on essentially different consensual notions among members of a society concerning the basis on which claims on certain shares of social goods are rested.

One such basis is individual achievements, such as a person's level of education. Differences in achievement correspond to differences in the claims that, according to the normative consensus, a person is justified in holding.

A different distributive principle, similarly based on a normative consensus, uses a different set of criteria, such as race, religion, social background, that are hard, if not impossible, to change by individual effort. Normative expectations exist, internalized or held by others, concerning the concurrence of such attributes and particular shares in the distribution of social goods.[35]

The very fact that both principles can be operating simultaneously in a society represents a crucial dynamic factor for our analysis. Each principle can interfere with the way the other operates so as to undermine the very consensus on which each is based, *under the assumption of the tendency towards rank equilibration* that we mentioned above. A rise in position on any particular dimension on the basis of individual achievement engenders the aspiration to move positions on other dimensions to a similar level. Such aspirations represent claims on rewards that may conflict with current notions about the legitimacy of such claims according to ascriptive attributes—a situation which may be exemplified by the worker who has worked his way up one ladder through schooling and education but finds no acceptance in higher social *milieux* on account of his social background.

The consequences of such a situation have been analysed, among others, by Lenski, Jackson, Goldthorpe and Lockwood, and Galtung.[36] The reaction to the frustration of newly risen claims tends to be *extra-punitive*, as Jackson calls it: society is blamed for the obstruction of aspirations; the reaction leads to political radicalism and association of those who share this particular grievance.

An issue which recurs in the analysis of radicalism and status discrepancy is the distinction between right and left radicalism.[37] In the area of conceptualization of the problem, there appears to be a beginning of agreement. Both shades of radicalism are connected with the ascriptive principle of distribution in society. The radical-left protest, however, is thought to be induced by the impossibility of leaving low ascriptive positions whereas positions on non-ascriptive dimensions have risen, with all this entails in terms of changes in reference group behaviour, expectations and claims on rewards. The radical right, by contrast, is thought to be essentially *reactionary*; it is composed of those who on the basis of ascriptive criteria hold high positions that they perceive to be threatened by the rising expectations of those of low ascriptive status. It tends to gain in strength and intensity the lower the positions are that the threatened elite holds on non-ascriptive dimensions. It can be conceived of as an attempt at reactivating ascriptive principles of distribution of social goods.

According to a conceptualization in this vein, radicalism is linked with a competitive model which shows social groups competing in order to maintain or increase their share of those social goods which are subject to zero-sum conditions. These conditions are essential; as long as an increase in the share of one social group does not *ipso facto* reduce the share of other groups, the different claims are not conflicting. In an expanding economy, for instance, wage demands can be met to a certain extent, because the very fact of expansion mitigates the zero-sum conditions. It is these conditions, it should be remembered, that cause the conflict of claims and make radicalism of the right and of the left into inter-related phenomena.

Referring back to what was said in section 2 of this chapter where we defined the concepts of conflict and radicalism, we can bring out more fully this inter-related character of both shades of radicalism by saying that the situation of conflict $(++)$ is reflected in the emergence of opposing radical ideologies.

So far, the argument has served to relate the concept of blockings to the sphere of normative systems; it has allowed us to point out which rival parties can be expected to emerge in the on-going process of distribution of social goods. Before proceeding, we will briefly examine some implications of this argument.

It would be fallacious to assume that the appeal to either of the alternative normative systems by the rival parties occurs automatically. Rather, we should conceive of this as an option—a strategic opportunity open to both parties. The so-called right-radical group may refrain from reference to attributive criteria or, in so far as it does resort to them at all, can choose to apply them with greater or lesser rigorousness to a larger or smaller number of opponents. Therefore we shall move on to the subject of the strategic alternatives of which the contending parties can avail themselves in their struggle for shares of social goods.

Strategies

The problem which confronts us here is to analyse more closely the zero-sum conditions; evidently they are pivotal in that it takes those conditions for claims on social rewards to acquire their conflict-generating potential. First, we want to point out that the zero-sum concept serves the purpose of unambiguously bringing out the

17

attributes of a situation that we judge relevant on the basis of theoretical considerations. We use the concept in an ideal-typical way so that we may expect no more than a loose fit with real-life situations, especially so where the macro-sociological distribution of social goods is concerned. No distribution, not even the most rigid one, turns out to leave individuals without the possibility, however small, of moving upwards. Even for rigid, estate-like structures, individual but notable exceptions can be found to illustrate this possibility.[38] Therefore the problem should rather be taken to be how many individuals may manage to 'slip through'—to 'pass', so to speak—without being experienced as a threat to the established distribution. The problem is not so much whether zero-sum conditions actually exist, as whether relevant actors define a particular situation in ways which we may fruitfully describe with the zero-sum concept.

These considerations lead us to ponder the possibility of there being a critical threshold value, which, moreover, may differ according to the nature of the social good to be distributed, beyond which social mobility is experienced as an encroachment upon established positions. Thus we can conceive of the situation where, as in the case of the working class in Europe, entire sections of a population experience an increase in real income without thereby alerting higher income groups to deploy their defensive strategies. Such a case we might define as one of collective improvement in positions on the income dimension. The threshold value in this case is relatively high. It might, however, be considerably lower for the dimension of, say, social prestige in the sense that the upward mobility of even a small number of individuals may be perceived as undermining the prestige of those higher on the scale, as in the case of the negro family that moves into a white neighbourhood and thereby causes an exodus of white families.

What we have formulated here is a strategic option of the dominant party. It is at this party's discretion to set the threshold value—to determine what quota of the underlying party it is willing to accept into its ranks. It can allow limited upward mobility in the hope of robbing the underlying party of its potential leadership. The price it is willing to pay may vary; the threshold value, in other words, can be higher or lower. However, once this threshold value is exceeded, the dominant party will stop tolerating upward mobility and start to deploy protectionist strategies. Whatever the outcome, however, processes of this kind in general are apt to flow from the confrontation of the dominant party and the group of upwardly mobile.

In addition to this, related developments may be perceived in the relations between the upwardly mobile and those that are left behind. In a systematic elaboration of suggestions taken from Stouffer's *The American Soldier*, Runciman[39] points out that the rate of upward social mobility has a non-lineary effect upon the degree of relative deprivation of those that stay behind. As long as the rate of mobility is low, relative deprivation decreases—though the possibility of the upward way out clearly exists and may serve to alleviate feelings of relative deprivation, its rate is small enough not to make a person's lack of mobility seem humiliating. When, however, the rate of mobility, in terms of numbers of persons, increases up to a certain point, one may expect a simultaneous upsurge in relative deprivation of the non-mobile.

When we attempt to spell out the combined impact, both upward and downward, of social mobility, we might come out with the following proposition: *under zero-sum conditions, an increase in upward mobility from a particular social stratum leads to an increase in the obstruction of mobility and an increase in relative deprivation among the non-mobile.* Should this proposition bear the test, it may clearly turn out to be of central importance for a theory of conflict: the upwardly mobile persons will in the increased blocking of their aspirations find sufficient cause to turn radical, while, on the other hand, the deprived non-mobile persons constitute the potential recruiting base for a radical movement. An analysis along these lines contains suggestions as to who will constitute the leadership of such a movement and who will be the followers that are to be mobilized.[40]

The increased blocking effects a shift in the pattern of reference group behaviour on the part of the upwardly mobile. Different theoretical formulations of the relationship between a process of blocking of mobility and reference group behaviour may serve to support this.[41] The thrust of the argument is that a 'vertical' reference is replaced by a 'horizontal' one—the stratum that the upward aspirers wanted to leave becomes a basis for identification and solidarity. Individual intentness on upward mobility within a given distributive order is abandoned for a more collective orientation on changing the established order.

As a final point, we should like to make some suggestions as to the differences in what we called threshold values for mobility along different distributive dimensions. We might, to that end, subsume the different dimensions under the captions of *class, status* and *power* and define them somewhat along the lines suggested by Lockwood, Dahrendorf and Runciman.[42] The concept of class we may take to represent such attributes as external market position, differences in income and in 'life chances', status is thought to refer to social prestige and a certain life-style; and power, finally, to the structured access to positions of decision-making.

The empirical findings on which Runciman reports bear some relevance on our problem. Although his study focuses on the relative deprivation with regard to these goods and does not go into the possibilities of increased blocking caused by mobility along one of these respective dimensions, the tentative conclusion may be warranted that status is the most precarious and delicate of the three goods in the sense that it most easily inspires a feeling of relative deprivation on the one hand and radical-right attempts at thwarting mobility from below on the other.[43]

There is yet another way to formulate the special position of the social good of status. Unlike power or class, status, for its very incidence, requires inequality of distribution. As soon as the distribution of status, according to one criterion or other, tended to become more equal, the criterion would thereby lose its usefulness for measuring the superiority or inferiority of individuals or groups *vis-à-vis* other individuals or groups. In other words: even the zero-sum concept would be too loose to describe this situation appropriately. Mobility from below, measured in terms of one specific status criterion, not only threatens to reduce the shares of the ones better-off—it would reduce *the total sum* of the good, in terms of that criterion. This provides us with yet another reason why the undercutting of an established distribution of status may have far wider impact than is the case for power or class.

6   A tentative reconciliation of the two models

A convenient starting-point in our quest for a way to reconcile the two models may be provided by an evident weakness of the rank equivalence model. Only those dimensions of social distribution are admitted in the construction of the model that help project the image of equivalence that we discussed earlier. The problem, then, would be if no relevant actors could be found in situations under study who apparently oriented their behaviour towards distributive dimensions that would disturb the equivalence. One expedient way out might be to indicate explicitly which specific dimensions in which specific situations should be deemed relevant for an analysis of conflict and, on that basis, to inquire whether those dimensions, taken together, show the rank equivalence pattern.

Dahrendorf, for one, has selected the distribution of power in social organizations as the crucial dimension to be inserted in his model of conflict-generation. His position is that a conflict about the particular distribution of power within one organizational context tends to spill over into different contexts as soon as the original conflicting parties are again opposed, though in different roles, in these other contexts.[44] In this strategy of analysis, Dahrendorf leaves out other attributes of social contexts, however relevant they might appear from the vantage point of a different theoretical approach. We mentioned above that a conflict about the distribution of power can be conceived as one specimen of a wide range of conflicts centering on such social goods as can be subsumed under the labels of class, status or power. There is no *a priori* reason why we should refrain from studying class and status conflicts as such along with power conflicts in terms of a more general theory of conflict.

Therefore we would advocate a different approach. We mentioned earlier, in our analysis of the rank equivalence pattern, the fact that a re-orientation occurs among those individuals that experience a blocking of their aspirations for upward mobility, to the effect that they actually abandon their aspirations of moving upwards within the established system of distribution. In other words: *they de-activate the dimension(s) on which they have risen highest and activate, instead, those dimensions on which they share low ascriptive positions with a potential following of relatively deprived individuals.*

Again, the matrix of Table 1.2 may serve to illustrate this point. Assuming that in this matrix the economic dimension is achieved and the political dimension is ascriptive, we may expect, once there is increased blocking of mobility, the TL-group to shift orientation from the TT-group which served as reference group on account of the shared T-position, and to stress solidarity with the LL-group on the basis of the shared L-position. A radical movement with a radical leadership is thus in the process of emerging.

Now, we want to point out emphatically that the process of de-activating the economic dimension and the resultant reduction in incongruence of positions, *as defined by the individuals themselves,* has the important consequence that *the overall picture increasingly acquires the traits of our rank equivalence model.* All shared L-positions (L_1, L_2, . . . L_n) are being activated, which is a different way of saying that the conflict is subject to the expansion of scale which, on the basis of the rank equivalence model, might have been predicted.

We might summarize this whole process by saying that the dimension which brought about the initial incongruence, under conditions of increased blocking, serves as an 'ignition' function for the rank equivalence model to become operative.

In this way we have suggested a temporal sequence between the two models that may have the additional asset of replacing the 'causal-functional' character of the rank equivalence model with a 'logico-meaningful' analysis that makes conflict and its escalation 'understandable' in terms of the strategies, goals and expectations of all relevant actors.

7 Elaboration and formalization of the model

The model which we have been developing so far projects the image

21

of a finite movement, starting from a situation where objective interests are becoming manifest guides for action and potential conflict groups have emerged as actual conflict groups. The process issued in a situation where conflict has fanned out across a wide array of areas of dispute and two camps find themselves opposed in an outright confrontation. However 'open' the outcome of the confrontation, the model itself is 'closed' in so far as it is limited to this single fanning out. It would be possible, however, to elaborate the model in such a way as to bring out a dialectical movement where, in an alternation of opposite developments, the model would keep refuelling itself. The course of conflict outlined thus far does indeed show pivotal moments where the process might be 're-cycled', and again processes are set off that can be understood in terms of the model. To elaborate this point more fully, it may be useful to return to the simple two-dimensional scheme used before. See Figure 1.1.

		Interest I	
Interest II		T	L
T		TT	TL
L		LT	LL

FIGURE 1.1

We have used the conflict model thus far for an outline of the conditions which might lead the TL- or LT-groups to present themselves as the leadership of a combatant organization; in this view, the LL-group can be thought of as constituting the rank-and-file support. The crucial point is now that, as soon as this organization has taken shape, with decision-making and control structures of its own, a novel structure has arisen that forms yet another arena within which social goods are distributed. Still in terms of our two-dimensional model, the leadership of such an organization can be thought of as an LT- or TL-group, this time, however, on grounds different from above. On the one hand, the leaders have small shares in common with their following, namely those shares for the increase in which the organization has been set up in the first place; on the other hand, this very organizational objective has resulted in bestowing a large share of power upon the leadership. Equipped with this transfer of power, the leadership engages in the confrontation with societal groups whose shares of social goods are in dispute. In so doing, however, the leadership may become subject to the danger of what we may call a gratification effect. One such gratification may be the increase in power that leadership positions bring, or the improvement of the leadership's class position due to its higher income. Other gratifications may be offered the leadership in its intercourse with the opponent in the way of a strategy of pay-offs. The opponent may revert to tactics of skimming the cream of the combatant organization, through awarding high status to the leadership *and the leadership alone*, in the hope of creating a split between leaders and followers. Yet another bait can be in the sphere of class rewards—alluring career opportunities may be opened to the leadership by desertion to the opposing camp.

These seductions to which the leadership is subject can be described as the possibility of giving up collective for individual orientations in the jockeying for larger shares of social goods. Once more the idea of a threshold value, set for mobility along the respective distributive dimensions, can be fruitfully used here.[45] The desertion, and subsequent insertion of a radical leadership into the ranks of the opposing party, does bring real mobility to the leadership, without, however, the opposing party defining it as a threat to its entrenched position.

Quite the contrary: the luring-away of emergent or established radical leadership leaves the combatant organization badly weakened. The leadership has betrayed its following.[46] This possibility of 'class treason' adds a new dynamic factor to the model. The paralysis inflicted on the radical organization by the desertion of its leadership implies an increase in the blocking which the deserted rank-and-file has to face—an increase which will exert an even stronger radicalizing influence on the movement. Rival leadership groups which thus far had not managed to penetrate to the power centre of the movement, will move to fill the vacuum and steer the movement in more radical directions. This can be simply illustrated by adding a third dimension to our two-axes model. See Figure 1.2.

		Interest II			
		T		L	
		Interest III		Interest III	
Interest I		T	L	T	L
T		TTT	TTL	TLT	TLL
L		LTT	LTL	LLT	LLL

FIGURE 1.2

If we assume that all incongruent groups are potential leadership groups, they can be distinguished according to two categories: leadership groups with two T-positions and leadership groups with only one such position. The first category can be most easily lured away by the opponent, who has to tolerate mobility along one dimension only. The following layer of leadership groups is farther removed from the opponent and harder to lure—it has two lowly positions in common with its following and only one top position in common with the opponent. The price to be paid for desertion is higher—the

23

rival camps are more clearly set apart and therefore more militantly opposed. An example in this context might be the trade unions in modern industrial societies. The composition of their membership is far from homogeneous—the organization is called upon to serve the interests of membership groups as divergent as white-collar office workers, middle-ranking administrative personnel, skilled and un-skilled workers. What may be effective advocacy of its interests in the eyes of the white-collar constituency can strike the most deprived members (the group with the largest amount of L-positions) as an outrageous forsaking of the mandate given the leadership. Thus, a wide rift may develop between that segment of the leadership with the most T-positions and those members with the most L-positions. Or, in other words, a large difference is apt to arise in access to pro-cesses of decision-making and day-to-day administration within the organization. This very experience of powerlessness can come to constitute the main component of alienation among the most de-prived members. The actions of the leadership will come to be per-ceived as treason and sell-outs, even in the absence of an actual desertion of the leadership.

Developments may take a different course as well. A potential, more radical, leadership grouping may attempt to break through the state of blocking within the organization by leaving it and setting up more radical organizations, aimed at the recruitment of the most deprived groups.[47]

Whatever the actual course of events, what we have just described renders the picture of a dialectical oscillation of conflict reduction and conflict eruption—both of them movements which can be under-stood in terms of the model. The fading of radical energy among an initial leadership group tends to fan the flames of radicalism among other groups. In other words, the model contains a description of energies on which it can continually feed.

As to the process where more radical vanguards take over, we may recall one of Dahrendorf's propositions,[48] that an increased blocking will cause conflicts to increase in both their intensity and violence. Thus we may expect a newly-risen, more radical, vanguard to choose more forceful or violent means in the recruitment of its following and in the pursuit of its objectives than the group from which it has parted or than the leadership whose place it has taken.

Developments along these lines, moreover, do have an impact on what we have so far considered as the environment of the model —the institutional characteristics of the arena. We can now insert these environmental variables in our model and treat them as endo-genous, guided by the consideration that a course of conflict, as out-lined in the model, tends to influence the institutional character of the arena. Once processes, as described above, cause conflict groups to grow more radical in both attitude and action, this will imply a drastic change in the institutional structure of the arena. In terms that we will elaborate more extensively in the next chapter, the institutional character of the arena will tend to grow praetorian rather than civic. For indeed, the very institutional characteristics prevailing at the outset of the conflict were instrumental in causing the alienation of parts of the following, potential or manifest, and in awakening the sense that available institutional means were insufficient for pursuing one's interests. To the extent that such an impairment of an institutional structure occurs, it implies that interest groups will tend increasingly to neglect precepts concerning legitimate means and, will opt, rather, for an unleashing of their naked power potential. The means they will resort to will increasingly be those of physical force and violence with all it entails in the way of disruption of orderly societal processes.

The model, in this elaboration, will serve as a guide—or, if one prefers, as a conceptual framework—for the analysis in the following chapters. To that effect it will be fruitful to come up with a concise formulation of both the central concepts of the model and of its central propositions. This procedure may, however, seem to accord a deceivingly apodeictic character to the statements, and convey the (false) impression that the single endeavour of reaching greater conciseness has managed to enhance the correctness, or truth, of the statements. If we do, in fact, convey this suggestion, the procedure would indeed acquire something Munchausen-like; then indeed it would seem as if sociological insight has managed to pull itself, as if by the tuft of its hair, from the bewildering muddle of hazy views and vague intuitions. We should like, therefore, to point out emphatically the hypothetical character of the model constructed in this chapter. Its main purpose is to serve as a concise statement of a surmise as to how certain phenomena might conceivably and possibly inter-relate.

In so far as the statements which together comprise the model are derived from more general points of departure, we shall preserve this distinction in the summary of the model and refer to *postulates* where the conceptual points of departure are concerned, and to *propositions* where the model itself is concerned. With a view to emphasizing the process character of the model, we shall indicate what different phases in the course of conflict might be discerned.

As regards the definition of basic concepts, the problem arises as to how specific we have to be. We have chosen a rather high degree of specificity, as may appear, for instance, from the connection of the concept of class with a given occupational structure, and, more generally, from connecting the concepts of class, status, and power to a structured arena of competition. As the need arises, we shall use less specific versions of the definitions in the following analyses. General problems of the degree of specificity of definitions will be dealt with in the final chapter.

8 Postulates, definitions, and propositions

Postulate I—Individuals who in the process of social distribution acquire inequivalent shares of different social goods will attempt to make the shares equivalent by bringing the initially smaller shares onto a par with the initially larger shares.

Definitions

(1) The social goods that are distributed in a society will be subsumed under the labels of class, status and power.

(1.1) Class, or class position, refers to a set of investments and economic rewards associated with a person's occupation at a certain time.[49]

(1.1.1) Investments refer to the education and knowledge required for or acquired in a person's occupation, his skill and experience, and finally his seniority.

(1.1.2) Economic rewards refer to the income that an occupation brings as well as to its career opportunities.

(1.1.3) In so far as a class position results from the mechanism of a labour market and therefore represents a certain market position, this market position can be thought to consist of an internal and an external market position.

(1.1.3.1) The internal market position represents the economic rewards within an organization of which a given occupation forms an integral part, for the investments that an individual has made or will make.

(1.1.3.2) The external market position represents the economic rewards that are offered outside the organization for the investments that an individual has made or will make.

(1.2) Status refers to the esteem which a person thinks is accorded him by relevant reference groups, on the basis of some of his qualities and characteristics.

(1.3) Power refers to the structured access to positions of decision-making which individuals or groups perceive within relevant hierarchical social structures.

26

(2) Any increase in the share of social goods of an individual can be considered as an instance of social mobility. The process from which a set of inequivalent ranks arises may be called primary mobility, while the process of rank equilibration, postulated above, may be called induced mobility.

(3) The process as outlined in the propositions leads to what we term a situation of conflict. The party that increasingly turns to ascriptive criteria of distribution in the defence of its threatened position will be called the radical right: the opposing party that has come to advocate a fundamental change in the criteria of distribution will be called the radical left.

(4) The range of alternative actions that are open to the opposed parties in a situation of conflict will be called strategies. These imply an evaluation of the resources at the disposal of both parties and a consideration of possible actions and reactions of the opponent party. The resources include both the use of violence and the threat of violence.

Postulate II—The distribution of social goods is in a greater or lesser degree subject to zero-sum conditions to the effect that an increase in the share of social goods of some individuals implies the reduction of the shares of others to a greater or lesser extent.

Postulate II.1—The actual degree to which a distribution is subject to zero-sum conditions is contingent upon the way social actors define their situation.

Postulate II.2—The social good of status may even be perceived as subject to diminishing-sum conditions.

Postulate III—Social goods are distributed on the basis of criteria that are either associated with social characteristics—commonly referred to as ascriptive criteria—or with personal achievements.

Postulate IV—The relation between the degree of upward mobility, as measured by the number of persons who increase their share of some social goods, and the degree of relative deprivation among the non-mobile, is non-linear. While an initial increase in mobility produces a decrease in relative deprivation, a further increase in mobility will lead to an increase in relative deprivation.

Propositions

Phase I   (1) Unlike primary mobility according to criteria subscribed to by all participants, induced mobility (a consequence of primary mobility which, by definition, is

27

not foreseen by all participants) may carry a threat to established criteria of distribution. Those that hold large shares will tend increasingly to define the distribution of the goods concerned as subject to zero-sum conditions.

Phase II (2) Individuals who consider their shares to be threatened will increasingly tend to assert ascriptive criteria of distribution, the more forcefully so, as their initial non-ascriptive shares are smaller.

(3) As ascriptive criteria of distribution become activated, upward mobility will be increasingly blocked.

Phase III (4) As upward mobility becomes blocked, those subject to this blocking will increasingly tend to give up their claims on the basis of their larger shares of social goods and, instead, opt for a radical re-orientation, aimed at changing the existing criteria of distribution.

(5) The effective amount of primary mobility, and the claims of induced mobility which it generates, will cause the relative deprivation of the non-mobile to grow.

Phase IV (6) The individuals whose upward aspirations are thwarted will increasingly seek to align themselves with the relatively deprived groups with which they have small shares in common.

Phase V (7) Once a militant organization of the radical left has emerged, this in itself will change the context of the distribution of status, class and power, which can cause reference group behaviour of the radical leadership to shift back from 'horizontal' to 'vertical'. This shift may then trigger processes as outlined above.

part one

Right-wing radicalism and the military

2 Military intervention in domestic politics: a framework for analysis[1]

1 Introduction

This chapter, along with the following, will be devoted to various aspects of right radicalism. The general definition of interests and strategies of right radicalism, as presented in the first chapter, will be brought to bear on the structural context of the military in its relation to the body politic. In this chapter our focus will be on one strategy in particular which is open to the military: the military coup. In the following chapter we will more specifically deal with alternative strategies of military intervention in politics.

Although the model which we constructed in chapter 1 will guide our analysis, its application to the specific social context of the military requires that we elaborate it somewhat further. So far, we should point out, the model has been formulated irrespective of the characteristics of specific social contexts in which conflicts arise.

Therefore, with regard to the participants in the social structure of the military, we shall have to define how the social goods of class, status and power may be expected to appear in this context. The application of the model, subsequently, will lead to hypothetical formulations of the alternatives open to the participants in their competition for shares of social goods. We repeat here that the argument will focus on one specific outcome: the military coup.

2 Relative shares and reference groups

The act of evaluating the justness of one's share of social goods involves a process of comparison, both internal within the context of a person's total assortment of relative shares, and external, that is to say a comparison with the shares of other persons. This process of comparison is explicitly referred to in my definition of status, but my position will be that the assessment of a person's class position and

31

power involves a similar process. The application of the theoretical framework to the specific social context of the military requires that I define some of the relevant reference groups.

In this connection, we want to emphasize that for the assessment of rank equivalence and mobility on the part of the actors, reference group behaviour is the crucial instrument. Reference groups provide the standards for this assessment rather than any 'absolute' values of the social goods of class, status and power. We would be ill-advised if we conceived of these social goods as reified or monolithic in any sense. Rather, they constitute analytic aspects of an individual's position *vis-à-vis* others; they only assume specific values through comparison with those others. This consideration in itself would contradict an assumed homogeneity of the goods. The assessment of their value depends critically on the reference groups chosen. Thus rank inequivalence can occur in the assessment of the value of only one such good, as soon as various reference groups are involved in the assessment. It need not, therefore, of necessity be linked with value differences among a person's shares of all three of the social goods.

With regard to status, one can distinguish, first, internal status, as defined and enforced within the military itself. The distribution of status closely follows the well-defined military hierarchy of roles, although an increase in the scope and complexity of the military will tend to undermine any clear-cut distribution of status and may lead to a struggle for greater shares. Second, there is an external dimension of status: the esteem in which the military profession is held by society at large, relative to the esteem granted other occupations and careers. Third, there is a sense of national status which may be particularly acute among military men. The relevant reference group here is the international forum of nations who, among themselves, develop a certain consensus as to their relative status. Finally, it is presumed that the status of a person's social origin may have an impact on the assessment of his present status, especially in situations where occupation and social background correlate highly.

With regard to power, similar distinctions can be made. First, differences in power can be perceived within the military in the sense of differences in access to military centres of decision-making. Second, differences in external power refer to the differential access to the authoritative structures of the political system; relevant reference groups here are especially non-military social interest groups that compete with the military at large. Again, the assessment of a nation's international power may be an over-riding concern of that nation's military. In the absence of a well-defined international decision-making arena, it may be wise to conceive of power in this context in more traditional Weberian terms, power being a nation's capacity to have things go its way against the opposition of other nations. Finally, the power of the *milieu* of origin of military men may be a relevant dimension.

As to class, I should like to point out that the definition I gave the term already implies the outcome of a process of comparative evaluation. Both internal and external market position refer to a net balance between investments and rewards. The outcome of the comparison of both these net balances may link a person more or less closely to the organization in which he finds himself employed. Class position in this sense, as a summary statement of both internal and external market position, will be rated positive if the internal market position is better than the external market position, and negative in the opposite case. Even so, however, a class position may be perceived as relatively good or bad when compared with the shares of this social good that other groups have. These may be groups either within or outside the organization, depending on whether or not the individual has chosen the organization as his principal frame of reference.

Again, apart from class position in these terms, I shall insert into the model the class position of the *milieu* of origin as a separate dimension. I shall, however, refrain from considering separately the dimension of what might be called national class position, since this dimension appears to be inextricably interwoven with the power potential of a nation that I referred to earlier.

As a final remark in this context, I should like to point out that the time dimension in the evaluation of a person's relative shares deserves separate attention. A class position, for instance, may be 'high', but subject to a downward trend or pressure due to increased competition of rival groups. In the schemes that I shall use shortly, these trends or pressures will be indicated by upward- or downward-pointing arrows, whereas the high-low categories will be indicated by $(+)$ or $(-)$ signs.

3 Different socio-political arenas[2]

In order to determine some crucial parameters of the structural situation in which the competitive struggle for a person's or a group's share of social goods goes on, I shall use a pair of concepts that Huntington has developed, for instance, in his *Political Order in Changing Societies*.[3]

He focuses on the relationship between the level of participation in the political process, on the one hand, and the level of institutionalization of this process, on the other. Participation brings the pressure of demands of rival interest groups to bear on a political structure. The way a political structure copes with this pressure can be distinguished in two main types, civic and praetorian polities. The central distinction between these arenas can be formulated as follows.

33

Whereas in civic societies the access of social interest groups to the political arena is characterized by the fact that established channels of access as well as established means of pressure and, within a certain range of variations, an established balance or order of influence among rival interest groups exist, in praetorian societies, by contrast, it is this very structuring (or institutionalizing) of the political game that is at stake. It may take the shape of the cautious mutual probing in order to size up the opponent that Lipset and Rokkan investigated in democracies of Western Europe on the eve of the introduction of the general franchise and which, according to them, in some countries has led to the institutionalization of mutual distrust in the form of proportional representation.[4] It may also correspond more closely to the violent connotations of the word praetorian. In that case the rival interest groups go all-out in the struggle for political power.

Irrespective of the level of participation, polities can be either praetorian or civic. In the following analysis I shall investigate the operation of the theoretical model in three arenas that are praetorian and are, respectively, on a low level of participation (oligarchical arenas), on a medium level (transitional arenas)[5] and on a high level of participation (mass arenas), and finally, in one arena that can be classified as civic on a high level of participation (a participant arena).

4 The model applied

One methodological point should be raised before we go into the analysis of the model. It is a matter of research strategy which groups within the army we consider relevant parties in the competition for higher shares of social goods when the focus is on one possible outcome of this competition—the military coup. It might seem self-evident to centre attention on the officer corps down to the level of tactical officers and leave out the common soldiers or enlisted men altogether. A note of warning should be struck, however. It appears to be a rather general distinction between officers and enlisted men that the first can avail themselves of the opportunity to orient themselves permanently towards groups outside the army, to engage in non-military contacts and to gather information on developments outside the army, opportunities that are lacking for the enlisted men. Where the enlisted men are thus a group that is kept fairly isolated from the surrounding society, they constitute no independent factor to be reckoned with in a struggle that ultimately aims at political power. The only arena where enlisted men should enter into strategic calculations is within the military, in so far as the distribution of social goods within the army might cause disobedience or mutiny. Though relevant from the point of view of the general theoretical framework, mutiny, as a phenomenon strictly confined within the army, falls outside the scope of this chapter.[6]

It may be evident, however, that as soon as the isolation of the enlisted men from the surrounding society becomes less rigid and their general level of information and sophistication rises, they may be an independent check on or support for preparations for military intervention in politics. Some of the implications of this development will be dealt with in the analysis of a participant arena. In the analysis of the other arenas we shall limit our perspective to the officer corps and focus on the differences and similarities in interests that occur among what we shall broadly refer to as senior and junior officers.[7]

1 An oligarchical arena

In an oligarchical arena the only contending parties are rival factions within the oligarchic elite. They have to watch nobody else but themselves. The ensuing game might fruitfully be described in terms of Kaplan's analysis of the rules underlying a balance of power system.[8] The rival parties are essentially equals, warily measuring slight shifts in either's class, status or power positions and trying to restore the balance through the formation of countervailing alliances.

In this game a coup, or, more properly, a palace revolution,[9] is one among several means of shifting the balance in one's favour. It is clear, however, that the theoretical framework that was developed earlier is not particularly fit for the analysis of such a situation. Terms we used such as mobility, achieved and ascriptive criteria, all involve the presence of essentially inequal parties in the arena. Therefore I prefer to focus on a situation where a rise of industrial and commercial middle classes threatens, initially, the established class position of the oligarchical elite and, eventually, its status and power. I shall first analyse an oligarchical arena on the eve of transition, where the oligarchical elite is still in full command despite the rise of the middle class, and then shift attention to an arena where the middle class has made inroads into the military and is represented in the officer corps. We can schematize the oligarchic arena as in Table 2.1.[10]

TABLE 2.1 *Oligarchical arena—no middle-class representation within army*

Level in army	Class		Status				Power			
	Or.	Occ.	Or.	Int.	Ext.	Nat.	Or.	Int.	Ext.	Nat.
senior	+↓	+	+	+	+	?	+↓	+	+	?
junior	+↓	+	+	+−	+	?	+↓	+−	+−	?

The overall picture is essentially one of shared interests. If we assume, moreover, that the differences which do exist are based on ascriptive criteria such as age and seniority and are properly internalized and therefore non-controversial, due to a common social background and a shared military tradition, these differences, therefore, are highly unlikely to spur a conflict within the military. We are thus permitted to conceive of the senior and junior level as constituting one group that from the vantage point of the army observes the rising threat to the entrenched positions of the oligarchical elite of which it forms part and parcel. In the struggle for access to the centres of decision-making, centred for instance on the position of a king, the threatened elite will increasingly resort to ascriptive criteria to prevent further encroachments of the middle class on its position. Also, within the army, careers will become linked to explicit ascriptive criteria in order to assure the threatened elite permanent control of the military command structure. A balance, once established in this competition, can hold for a long time, as is illustrated for instance by Norbert Elias's analysis of the French political system through the sixteenth, seventeenth and early eighteenth centuries.[11]

The table developed above may help us find the strategic points where a miscalculation of one of the rival parties may lead the oligarchical elite to mobilize its military resources. I suggest that the external power dimension of the army and also the dimensions of national status and national power are precisely such points.

A policy in which the king aligns himself more openly with the middle class, thereby upsetting the balance of power, directly affects the relative position of the oligarchical elite. This reduction in its share may lead to forceful intervention by the military especially where such additional factors are at work as miscalculations in international politics which the military will perceive as devastating to national status and national power, and very likely will hold against the central authoritative body. As I said earlier, international status and international power are a special concern of the military and are tightly linked to its sense of military honour and its traditional calling to defend forcefully a given territory.[12]

What is brought out in the analysis thus far are strategic options of a military elite that can be characterized as belonging to a radical right on the basis of propositions 1, 2 and 3 and definition 3 (see chapter 1).

We shall now turn to the situation where the middle class has gained access to the military hierarchy.

2 A transitional arena

We assume that the rising middle class we referred to is the recruitment basis for the middle level of the officer corps in particular. The situation can be indicated as in Table 2.2.

TABLE 2.2 *Oligarchical arena with middle-class representation within army*

Level in army	Class		Status				Power			
	Or.	Occ.	Or.	Int.	Ext.	Nat.	Or.	Int.	Ext.	Nat.
senior	+↓	+	+	+	+	?	+↓	+	+↓	?
junior	+− ↑	+−	+−	−	+	?	+− ↑	+−	−	?

Contrary to the previous example, we find here within the officer corps the representatives of two interest groups that in the larger society are opposed in a situation of conflict (definition 3). We expect this state of affairs in society to reverberate within the context of the military. The top level of senior officers will turn to an increased emphasis on ascriptive criteria for recruitment to the military top positions; no longer, it should be added, in terms strictly of age and seniority but of social origin as well. This puts a constraint on the internal market position of the junior officers. The top level of senior officers will seek, moreover, to counteract the decline in power of its social membership group by consolidating its access to the decision-making bodies. The senior officers can again be characterized as representing the radical right within the military.

The junior officers in this example represent a social interest group that is rising in terms of class and power but is still lacking in status. Within the military they are still subject to the repressive action of the top level which respectively affects their career possibilities, their access to the internal power centre and, consequently, the external power centre.

The levels of both the senior and the junior officers are, therefore, subject to radicalizing pressures, as are the larger groups in society from which they are recruited. Although, in principle, each group can avail itself of the coup as a means to decide the competitive struggle in its favour, it will be impossible to say without further information which of the broader social groups will use its leverage in the military to promote its goals.

One piece of useful information here is the strategic alternatives available to the broader social membership groups outside the army. When the main option of the upwardly mobile class for organizing its strength is precisely through its bridgehead within the army as its best equipped vanguard, the likelihood will increase of schemes for a military coup to be contrived. Once more, strategic miscalculations

37

of either party are important here, in so far as they affect the assessment of the opponent's power potential.

Upsets in foreign policy or domestic economic developments, for instance, could impair the position of the top class in both its status and power aspects. In other words, a Parsonian power deflation might occur—social groups will start to withhold support from the top classes and will constitute a reservoir of discontent that might serve to feed in to the power potential of the upward striving social class from whose ranks the junior officers had been recruited. Developments along these lines contain the first reference so far to processes as outlined in proposition 6 (see chapter 1).

Although not precisely in order here, I should like to go briefly into developments which might occur in a transitional arena whose institutional make-up we can call civic. Huntington refers to it as a Whig arena; we might call it a bourgeois-liberal arena, as it occurs prior to full working-class participation in the political system. As to the bourgeois, or mixed aristocratic-bourgeois elite which is still preempting political participation, internal differences of class, status and power have come to constitute an institutionalized system. In so far as an emergent working class manages to organize itself and presents itself as a social and political rival, voicing demands for participation, and is, as such, a threat to the institutionalized order, this situation can be compared with the threat which, previously, the emergent bourgeois middle class had constituted to an oligarchic arena.

We have made separate mention of this historical configuration of forces because we believe it to represent a foremost category of cases of military intervention in politics. To the extent, namely, that the bourgeois-aristocratic elite is in control of the officer corps within the army, and, moreover, the political balance of power threatens to shift drastically on account of the entrance of an organized working class into the arena, we may again expect the threatened elite to mobilize the power potential in order to forestall the impending shifts.

With a view to the internal differentiation according to class, status and power within the elite, however, proposition 2 (see chapter 1) would seem to justify the prediction that those segments of the military in particular will mount defensive actions whose non-ascriptive, external shares are lowest. For indeed, those segments have the most acute interest in countering an impairment of their ascriptive privileges. In reality, we may expect these moves to result in a 'colonels' regime', forcefully upholding an ascriptive order, and composed of military men who, as like as not, tend to have originated from lower middle-class *milieux* and will rank below the military top command. Thus, through a pre-emptive strike, the colonels may hope to keep the working class from razing established barriers of ascription. The recent

Greek colonels' regime might be a case in point. Although the entire dominant elite coalition stood to gain from the praetorian move of the colonels, of all the coalition partners the latter were the ones to show the most striking increase in power, in addition to shoring up the relative position of the social class from which they originated.

3   A mass arena

It may be convenient to focus on conditions in new nations as a specific frame of reference that closely resembles our ideal-type of a mass arena. Several authors, as for instance Apter, Bendix, Shils and Pye,[13] have pointed to the fact that in developing nations the hierarchies of both the military and the governmental bureaucracy constitute important channels of upward mobility. This fact permits us to consider the officer corps as a group that has opted for individual mobility within the system. To use a value-laden word, they are 'class traitors' in the sense that the individual career on which they have set out does not involve a sense of solidarity with a larger group whose life and misfortunes they have escaped through their careers. The access and rapid ascent of the officers is due to the rapid increase in vacant positions following independence.

In this context, several alternatives come to mind that might trigger a process as outlined in our set of propositions. First of all, a group of senior officers may exist who have received their education and training during the waning years of the colonial regime. In a wider societal context this group may be part of a westernized elite that has risen to its position under the tutelage of the colonial power. The elite group of officers may feel its old, established position threatened by the upsurge in mobility spurred by independence. More specifically, it may feel threatened by claims for mobility meant to offset imbalances that result from primary mobility. These may be claims concerning career possibilities, or internal power or access to the political authorities.[14] The reaction on the part of the senior officers may be one of activating ascriptive criteria, such as ethnic background, seniority, or an education at military academies in the former metropolis. This reaction will lead to an increased blocking of mobility, especially of the induced kind. Meanwhile, however, the upsurge in primary mobility through the channels of the military and the governmental bureaucracy has increased the sense of relative deprivation among the non-mobile, the more so as greater numbers have escaped from their midst. Proposition 6 (see chapter 1) predicts that in this case the group whose upward mobility has been blocked will try to mobilize the deprived group of non-mobile.

A similar situation may result in the absence of an established corps of senior officers. Given the fact of all-out competition in society at large for the scarce goods of status, class and power that is implied in the concept of praetorianism, this competition may lead by itself to an overall blocking of the aspirations of the competing groups. No group is able to realize its goals by itself and any of them may seek alignment with groups of relatively deprived in order to consolidate its power basis.

TABLE 2.3   *A mass arena without clear-cut divisions between haves and have-nots*

Level in army	Class		Status				Power			
	Or.	Occ.	Or.	Int.	Ext.	Nat.	Or.	Int.	Ext.	Nat.
senior	↑↓	+	↑↓	+	+	?	↑↓	+	+	?
junior	↑↓	+−	↑↓	+−	+	?	↑↓	+−	+−	?

Outlined here is a competition among vanguards in primary mobility, in which no group has a clear-cut advantage over any other group. In this broader societal struggle the control of the military command structure will appear a big prize which, if won, may give a competing group a decisive boost. Therefore the on-going struggle will reverberate within the army. Senior and junior officers may align themselves with each other on the basis of membership in these wider social interest groups, and de-emphasize the differences that exist between them in terms of military rank. In so far as the social struggle impinges on career opportunities, power, and the like, of groups within the army, these groups are likely to become aware of their common interests. Moreover, we may expect that as long as the struggle goes on, the competing groups will try to buttress their claims with a variety of ascriptive criteria which, at the same time, allow them to define rival claims as unwarranted and illegitimate.

We might summarize this development by saying that the group whose upward aspirations become blocked develops a sense of 'class solidarity'; it may undo its original 'class treason' by abandoning its aspirations of upward mobility within the established system and by re-orienting itself towards the group with which it has small shares in common. The amount of relative deprivation within this latter group may offer the principal leverage for its political mobilization.

The actual composition of the alliance will be a function of the ascriptive criteria that are being used. The upwardly mobile persons that are confronted with the impact of ascription are actually thrown back towards social aggregates with which they have certain characteristics in common. In the process a social identity in terms of these characteristics is developed. Here an important function may be fulfilled by the leadership of such outcast groups, in so far as it is able to conceive of its misfortunes in the more general terms of class, status and power. This wider perspective may allow the leaders to transcend the narrow identity on the basis of ascription which society has inflicted upon them and seek alliances with social groups that on the basis of different ascriptive criteria may have similar small shares of social goods.

As soon as alliances of this kind are established, groups of officers may engage in planning a coup. If the coup succeeds, it works two ways. The subversive officers have removed the obstacles that blocked their upward aspirations, while, through them, their political supporters have gained access to the central authoritative positions.

4 A participant arena

The shift in analytic focus to a civic arena on a level of mass participation has several consequences:

(a) In a formal sense, there no longer exist differences in political participation between segments of a society. Participation itself proceeds along well-established avenues. Both the struggle for an increase in participation and for the specific mode of participation have subsided. Therefore we may expect to find no more reverberations of this kind of conflict within the military. It has stopped being an important parameter of the behaviour of military elite groups.

(b) The homogeneity of elites in terms of social background has decreased. Such unity of action and outlook as can be perceived within sectors of large, complex organizations should rather be explained in terms of shared professional interests and shared career experiences. The increasing professionalization of organizational tasks along with the diversification of required skills has led to an increasing stress on achievement-oriented criteria. Career lines within large-scale organizations such as the military have grown in number and divergence as have the elites and shades of professional outlook that can be found at the top. Therefore the need no longer exists to insert social background as a separate dimension into the model.[15]

(c) Within the military, the ranks of enlisted men can no longer be discarded as being immaterial to military planning. In less-developed political arenas the isolation in terms of contact and communication to which the enlisted men are subjected could be counted upon to perpetuate their limited individual horizons. A participant arena, especially a democratic one, on the other hand, makes for wider individual horizons, for better information and higher sophistication among the enlisted men and for a far less rigid isolation from the surrounding society. Increasingly, soldiers can avail themselves of information in the same way that civilians do; there is an increased concern for the civil rights of enlisted men. The combined impact of these trends has tended to make the enlisted men an independent factor to be reckoned with. Some of the implications of this development will be brought out later.

TABLE 2.4   *A participant arena*

Level in army	Class	Status			Power		
		Int.	*Ext.*	*Nat.*	*Int.*	*Ext.*	*Nat.*
senior	+↓	+	+	?	+	+↓	?
junior	+−	+	+−	?	+−	+−	?
Enl. men	−	−	−	?	−	−	?

First, with regard to class, the position of the senior officers is subject to a permanent downward pressure due to an increased civilian role in military strategy, weapon systems, the analysis of politico-military developments in the international arena, and the like. The education and knowledge of the senior officers is liable to rapid obsolescence. This will be most acute in the case of what Janowitz has called 'the heroic elite'.[16] Both the managerial and the technical elite are able to fend off the threat of rapid technological change by opting for civilian careers outside the military. The heroic elite, however, has no similar external market position; therefore the undermining of its internal market position affects its overall class position.

With regard to external power, the situation is similar. Aside from the fact that finding access to the centre of political decision-making has become a tremendously complex game, again the competition of civilian know-how and expertise serves to further complicate the situation. As exemplified by developments within the Pentagon, there is a long-range trend towards increased power of civilian experts, with short-range variations in the degree of civilian control depending on which party governs and who is Secretary of Defence. The very proliferation, however, in the means of finding access in order to promote the military point of view may counteract the increase in civilian control; whenever one way of access becomes blocked, there are alternative ways. To mention only a few: the direct articulation of interest within the department of defence is one such way; the penetration through pressure groups of the legislature, the possibility to exert pressure through industries whose interests parallel those of the military, the possibility to influence public opinion and to rally it to the cause of the military are other ways.

With regard to status, factual findings[17] seem to indicate a relatively low external status of the officer corps, especially, it would seem, of the middle ranks.

So far the overall picture does not seem to warrant the planning of a coup by any rank within the military. A coup is in a sense a means of last resort the use of which testifies to the fact that none of the non-violent alternatives offers the military sufficient access to the centre of political authority. Even if such a situation did actually occur, which already is highly unlikely, we might expect that only those groups within the officer corps would be seriously affected that have highly identified themselves with the military.

As we saw before, however, especially on the middle level of the officer corps—which, parenthetically, comprises the largest part of the officer corps[18]—possibilities of alternative careers are offered which may reduce the self-identification with the army. Therefore, if a coup is to have a reasonable amount of support within and outside the army, a number of additional developments must occur:

(a) First of all, we may think of developments that directly affect the evaluation by the military of the national power and status, as, for instance, a treaty with a rival nation against the advice of the military.[19] Such a treaty may have been negotiated and ratified on the basis of broad politico-strategic considerations, whereas the military on the basis of military-strategic thinking may brand the treaty as outright capitulation. The inter-related dimensions of national power and national status, status of the military and military self-esteem have all decreased. We may recall the reactions of the French army to the treaty of Geneva and the treaty of Evian.

(b) Social and economic developments may create a reservoir of right radicalism that can be rallied to the support of a military coup. We specifically have in mind economic developments that cause the balance of economic power to shift from small enterprises to large enterprises—a process in which, moreover, the collective bargaining position of organized labour as well as its access to the centre of political authority increases through the power of the unions. Developments of this kind exert a downward pressure on the power and class positions of segments of the population. Furthermore, we can think of political developments which cause the balance of political power to shift from the local level to the central level, a process which may activate all sorts of conflicts along a centre-periphery axis and may result in an increase in right radicalist sentiments.[20]

These and similar developments, as for instance a ruinous inflation, may lead large segments of the electorate to turn their backs on the political system. In such a case, a widespread feeling exists of being insufficiently represented in the established system. The lack of an adaptive response of the system causes it to slip back from a civic to a praetorian state. There are sizeable groups prone to being politically mobilized in an effort to change radically the existing system.

This combination of factors, summarily described as a relapse into praetorianism, might change the balance of relevant factors in favour of a coup.

(c) I should like to make some final remarks about the role of the enlisted men in the interplay of forces as outlined above. In so far as the enlisted men align themselves with the reservoir of radical right sentiments and share the sense of alienation from the established political regime, they simply reinforce the basis of political support for a rightist coup. However, the curious blend of openness and closedness which characterizes the situation of enlisted men in a civic, especially a democratic, arena, may spur developments toward radicalism of the left.

We mentioned earlier that the general level of education and sophistication among the enlisted men has risen. Their position within the army deprives them, however, of whatever shares they had in civilian society of the social goods of class, status and power. This overall reduction, especially perhaps the acute sense of powerlessness, may spur those for whom the reduction is sharpest—for instance college and graduate students—to mobilize their fellow enlisted men for whom the reduction may be smaller or even non-existent.

Within the microcosm of the ranks of the enlisted men we recognize the process that is outlined in the theoretical framework from which we started. This upsurge in GI-radicalism may gather such momentum as to virtually eliminate all possibilities for a successful coup.[21]

The means at the disposal of this radical body within the army are the strike, which virtually paralyses the army; defection, which virtually turns the balance of forces against rightist plots; and mutiny, which might be conceived of as an actual attempt at taking over the military command structure. It may be clear that in this process wider social references are established and alliances occur with non-military groups. This is further proof that society has slipped back to a praetorian state.

5 Summary and conclusion

Let us summarize here the novel elements which this chapter has added to the general argument developed in the previous chapter, and analyse to what extent they have served to qualify it. The central concepts introduced here have been comprised under the labels of civic and praetorian, as well as of level of participation in the political process. We propose to dwell somewhat more at length on these concepts here.

The degree of institutionalization of a socio-political order which, according to our definitions, can be thought to range from civic to praetorian, is a concise reference to what, in the Introduction, we called a guiding theme throughout the book—the shifting balance of forces between the factors working towards the creation of order and maintenance of social structures, and the factors which, at cross-purposes, work towards disintegration and the disruption of institutionalized order. Now by definition, the processes of conflict and radicalization, outlined in the first chapter, are praetorian in nature. The course of conflict represents the disruption of whatever institutionalized order happened to be extant in the distribution of social goods,

Our over-riding concern, therefore, in developing the conflict model, has been to point out how specific groups of participants in the process of social distribution and competition come to reject the institutionalized patterns of competition and how, on the other hand, the opponent comes to conceive of the newly-risen, left-radical demands as unsatisfiable within the existing order. The conflict, thus defined, creates new 'game' patterns that essentially deviate from the previous, institutionalized pattern of competition. For that very reason we are warranted to use the variable of degree of institutionalization as a parameter of the game of social competition: changes in the value of the parameter signal basic changes in the nature of the game of social competition. By itself, however, this parameter would have no explanatory power; rather, it allows us to formulate systematically the question as to how a civic arena comes to disintegrate into a state of praetorianism.

On the other hand, the second variable of the level of participation provides us with a concise description of forces of disruption and does, therefore, add explanatory power to our analysis. It refers to the mobilization of those groups of participants in the process of distribution of social goods which succeed in introducing themselves in the political arena as well-defined interest groups with a set of novel demands. This variable, too, can serve as a parameter value, as this chapter has shown. For, although each drastic increase in participation carries a praetorianizing potential, the impact on the established order differs, depending on whether the order is oligarchic, bourgeois-liberal, or pluralist-democratic. Each of these arenas has characteristically different ways of coping with the challenge of praetorianization and will, therefore, render a different pattern of parties and strategies.

The crucial factor here is the mode of defence chosen in the attempts at fending off the danger of disruption caused by the rise of left-radical demands. If the disruption is to proceed along the lines sketched in the first chapter, the forces of preservation will have to become perverted, and considerations of an orderly response to the demands, as these are voiced, be subverted by the forceful defence of what a right-radical camp has come to define as its inalienable rights.

45

Only then will forces of preservation develop into forces of reaction, thus providing the necessary lee-way for our conflict model to run its course.

Although this drift from preservation to reaction—springing the final roadblock to disruption—is a central consideration in the perspective which guides our analysis, we omitted it from the first three arenas surveyed in this chapter. There we assumed the arenas to be praetorian from the start. Under that condition, it will be understood, the preservation of law and order in the civic sense of the words is of no concern to any of the contending parties. Only our last case—a participant arena—started from the assumption of an institutionalized frame for the competition of social interest groups. Our conclusion there was that a civic arena with a high level of participation has elaborated such a diversity of means for channelling the on-going social competition—competition, we should add, among interest groups whose interests are more specific and limited than in the earlier arenas—as to virtually exclude the likelihood of broad left-radical alliances emerging or any groups having recourse to praetorian means.

In this context it may be illuminating to return to the concepts of pluralism as applied in the previous chapter. Bearing in mind the argument developed above, we can say that in the first chapter we focused on what we might call the sociological dimensions of the concept. There we referred to the multifarious cross-cutting of dimensions of conflict, leading to a sharp limitation of interests on which coalitions might rest, coalitions, moreover, which, measured according to different interests, might well be internally divided. On the other hand, the instance, elaborated above, of a participant arena would seem to highlight those aspects of pluralism which political science prefers to dwell on and which we can summarily describe as the pressure group model of an institutionalized, democratic order, where a plurality of opportunities of access to centres of political decision-making tends to make for a fair processing of conflicts of interests. We believe that our formulation may serve to point out the relationship between both perspectives—the sociological perspective may serve to study and understand the process underlying the emergence of interest groups which, once arisen, the political scientist studies from the point of view of competitive interaction.

Both approaches, taken together, have provided the bulk of the arguments for theories concerning the stability of pluralist political systems. On the one hand, the conflicts which the system has to accommodate are limited in nature; on the other hand, the institutionalized means for accommodation have become so varied as to exclude a recourse to praetorianism on the part of any of the groups involved. Fully-fledged conflict, radical confrontation and praetorianism, according to this view, should be considered deviant cases for the category of pluralist democracies.

Yet, in so far as this chapter has tried to develop a framework for the analysis of praetorianism, these deviant cases in particular require further analysis. A better understanding of them might well reflect on the body of insights into the problems of stability and instability of pluralist societies. Therefore the empirical case to be treated in the next chapter is one of an arena approaching the ideal-type of a pluralist democracy, and confronted by a broadly-based, left-radical movement. Recent history offers a clear-cut category of such cases: that of colonial empires, where the metropolis can be regarded as showing the traits of a participant arena. The revolutionary independence movements in the colonies could profitably be considered an instance of the drastic increase in demands for participation, the impact of which has been analysed in this chapter.

Here, we should add, the demands are of a special, essentially extreme variety, aiming as they are at a complete take-over of power in parts of the empire by the indigenous populace. The example we have chosen is the Dutch colonial empire. Our main interest is in showing how, in this case, a participant arena has managed to maintain its civic character while fending off a virulent, left-radical challenge.

Yet another category might come to mind, of course, of pluralist democracy facing an unforeseen and sudden left-radical challenge: the political activism of the 1960s. In the second part of this book we intend to focus on that subject as it appeared in student radicalism. There, rather than emphasizing the problem of the maintenance of civic order, we shall examine the rise of left-radical forces and try to account for it in terms of our model of conflict.

3 Decolonization and the military: the case of the Netherlands

A study in political reaction[1]

1 Introduction[2]

Title and sub-title of this chapter, taken together, might seem to suggest that the military would have a pre-emptive claim on right-wing political activism. The analysis in the previous chapter, however, may serve to contradict this suggestion. There we reviewed the various possibilities of the formation of alliances between military and civilian circles. In this chapter, therefore, we shall try to indicate, for the specific historical case of the decolonization of Indonesia, what specific groups within the armed forces of the Netherlands had an interest in opposing Indonesian independence, and what strategic alliances they engaged in with right-wing *civilian* circles. In that sense, the subject of this chapter is rather 'underground' civil-military relations, as they existed alongside the level of *institutionalized* civil-military relations. Our analysis, on the one hand, is intended to specify our expectations as to what interest groups within and outside the army tended to align in opposing Indonesian independence and, on the other hand, to characterize broadly the options open to such coalitions for influencing the course of events either in the Netherlands or in the Dutch East Indies. Although our analysis will undeniably tend to focus on the performance of the 'top-dog' team, the opponent will be introduced in the analysis to the extent that his actions and options are necessary for understanding the context of action of the top dogs.

Referring briefly to the set of postulates, definitions, and propositions that concluded the first chapter, I should like to call attention to the following points. As early as 1945, the point at which we shall start our analysis, the conflict had already run through the first four phases of the model. In the ensuing situation of conflict, the left-radical leadership had already embarked on the course of confrontation: it had unilaterally declared Indonesia independent. Our analysis, therefore, will aim mainly at the subsequent strategies employed by both the left- and right-wing radical camps in the pursuit of their conflicting goals (definitions 3 and 4). It is necessary to emphasize that an analysis pretending to bring out all respective phases of the model would have taken a much earlier starting-point, and would have had to begin with the emergence of a nationalist movement in the Dutch East Indies prior to the Second World War.[3]

The guiding theme of our analysis, as we said at the conclusion of the preceding chapter, will be the question of how the participant arena in the Netherlands has managed to maintain its civic character despite the praetorianizing situation of conflict between left- and right-wing radical opponents. Thus this chapter will see the fusion of themes which we have introduced separately in the first two chapters of this book.

2 Analysis of the arena

The struggle for decolonization cannot be considered an instance of what game theorists would call pure conflict. During the period under study—1945 to early 1950—persistent elements of co-ordination did occur which caused the simple dividing line between the Dutch and the Indonesians to be cross-cut by lines of potential or actual alliances. After all, the final outcome was not surrender by either party on the basis of military defeat, but a solution reached through political negotiation and mediation. External pressure, exerted primarily by the US government upon both parties, was surely one of the forces that worked towards co-ordination. But internally as well, recurrent attempts were made by both contending parties to find allies within the sphere of influence of the opponent. In fact, to mention just one example, one of the prime goals in the use of military means by both parties was to win over the bulk of the Indonesian population to their side. However, whereas the shifting balance of co-ordination versus opposition tended to blur the dividing lines between the contending parties, each participated in the 'game' under a fairly distinct set of rules and in a fairly distinct institutional setting. This fact, rather than the basic fact of the confrontation between Dutch imperialism and Indonesian nationalism, allows us to divide the arena into three, rather distinct, segments. One is the context of the emerging Indonesian Republic, another the domestic scene in the Netherlands; finally Dutch colonial society in the East Indies can be discerned as a third context of action. Let us first try to describe the inner structure of the emergent Indonesian Republic.

(a) The emerging Indonesian Republic

The period of Japanese rule in the archipelago had had a strong mobilizing impact,[4] resulting in a novel sense of national identity; it meant shaking-off the traditional self-effacing, submissive attitude towards the colonial elite. A crucial factor for this emergent nationalist-revolutionary sense to take root was the factual power vacuum following Japanese surrender.

In several ways this so-called *bersiap*-period showed all the signs of a collapse of civil order. There were rampage, pillage and murder, devoid of political content. Yet there were also clear signs of an emergent revolutionary order in both military and civilian spheres. The array of military and para-military organizations created by the Japanese regime[5] gave birth to a wide variety of independent revolutionary bands, summarily described as *pemudas* (youths), which operated in the vacuum. Their structure was reminiscent of the prototype of the revolutionary council or soviet. It was forcefully anti-hierarchical, as illustrated by the fact that the bands appointed their own officers.[6] Only at a much later stage did they consent to their incorporation into an all-embracing Republican Army—the TNI.[7] Within the Republican camp this constellation of forces proved a permanent praetorianizing condition, most strikingly illustrated by the kidnapping of Sukarno and Hatta, when *pemudas* forced them into issuing the declaration of independence and, some time later, the abduction of prime-minister Sharir in what amounted to an abortive communist coup.[8] That the unwieldy, and politically hazardous, aspects of this revolutionary potential were clearly perceived within the Republican camp is illustrated, for instance, by Nasution.[9]

The entire process as described here can be considered as an instance of a sudden increase, unstructured and non-incremental, in the degree of political participation. Related developments could be mentioned, such as the fact that under the Japanese regime, Indonesians had penetrated into the command structures of the economy and the polity to an extent that would have been unthinkable under colonial rule. It is here that analytic labels, such as mobility and mobilization, interlock. Where the latter has special reference to the impact of societal processes of change on a political system, this impact tends to be all the more radicalizing (or mobilizing), once gains in mobility risk being impaired by the return of a reactionary regime. At this point left-radical alliances are apt to grow more virulent. Time and again, the array of built-in praetorian tendencies, as outlined here, would serve as a check within the Republican camp on reaching an agreement with the Dutch.[10]

(b) The domestic scene in the Netherlands

Following the breakdown of German rule in the Netherlands, a system of military governance was established to bridge the time till due democratic processes were re-instituted. It lasted from 14 September 1944, to 4 March 1946. Under this cloak a process of political re-orientation and regrouping went on in an attempt to overcome pre-war parliamentary fragmentation due to party divisions along lines of religious denominations as well as class lines in various shades of ideology.

The integrative forces were rallied in the Netherlands' Popular Movement (*Nederlandse Volksbeweging*). Based mainly on this movement the first post-war cabinet was formed. Of rather strong socialist leanings, it was, by Dutch standards, ideologically homogeneous. It lacked, however, an electoral mandate. This should be considered a serious check on its capacity for swift action and substantial decision.

In the hope that forces of integration might crystallize, elections were postponed until 17 May 1946. Contrary to expectation, forces of restoration had proved stronger than those of innovation, as evidenced by the fact that ten parties participated in the electoral contest. Five were denominational, one was socialist, another communist, still another liberal-conservative. The hopes of a progressive breakthrough, embodied in the newly formed Dutch Labour Party (*Partij van de Arbeid*), were frustrated earlier as evidenced by several consecutive opinion polls which showed a rapid decline in support.[11] A coalition cabinet was formed based on the support of Catholics and Labour. It lasted until the elections of 6 July 1948, when the impending Indonesian independence necessitated amendment of the Constitution.[12] Finally, with the aim of rallying as much support as possible for liquidating the issue of decolonization, a cabinet was formed based on four parties: Catholics, Labour, one of the two main Calvinist parties, and the liberals. The other Calvinist party, of old named the Anti-Revolutionary Party, kept aloof from participation in government all through these years. In this party some of the most vocal opponents of any kind of agreement with the Republic of Indonesia at Jogjakarta were assembled, although leadership of its parliamentary party, was in the hands of strict constitutionalists.

Let us now set about the task of analysing the lee-way offered by this arena to praetorian tendencies. The strongest challenge to democratic rules of the political game on the part of the military occurred during the period of military rule. Both in London, the war-time refuge of the Dutch cabinet and of the Dutch titular head of state Queen Wilhelmina, and in Eindhoven, administrative centre of the liberated southern provinces, there had been thoughts of a post-war political system of strong autocratic leanings with a more outspoken role for the Queen.[13] Similar thoughts seemed to underlie the way military rule set about the task of reconstructing the administrative apparatus. The approach seemed to bypass civil politicians to such an extent that, for instance, the socialist minister J. W. Burger left the cabinet headed by P. S. Gerbrandy and a revamping of the cabinet was necessary. These tendencies, however, were short-lived; a return to constitutional procedures was apparent in the first post-war, Schermerhorn-Drees, cabinet. The lack of a parliamentary mandate and the postponement of the election date proved praetorianizing factors in their own right. The first round in the attempts to reach an agreement with the Republican government in Indonesia which culminated in the Hoge Veluwe conference, shortly before the election date, set off an outcry from extra-parliamentary organizations.[14] Although the rules of the game were thus under heavy pressure, the balance of power was such that no independent role of the military was conceivable.

The entire period up to the general election contained praetorian trends in a more general way. Where no political party had a clear sense of its electoral support, the first signs were apparent of a regrouping of conservative forces that would prove an increasingly formidable check on a rapid 'sell-out' to the Republic. The relative obscurity of the balance of political forces in this period paralysed the progressive forces in the government while giving the forces of reaction the opportunity to entrench themselves firmly. An effective weapon in this period of rallying support to one's own cause was the strong link between political leadership and media of mass communication such as the press and the radio,[15] a sure sign of a return to *verzuiling* as the principle of organization of political life. For all practical purposes, the general uncertainty about the strength of the rival parties may actually have served as a substitute for an effective balance of power, thus checking any praetorian tendencies.

Following this survey of factors, either promoting or counteracting praetorianization, we shall deal separately with the dimension of degree of political participation. From the start, in 1945, it was understood that mass participation in politics, reflected in a democratic political process, would be re-instituted. Neglecting the short-lived pre-war de Geer cabinet, there was one novel feature in comparison with pre-war tradition: participation in government by the socialists. Throughout the period under study, the socialists clung to government against a rising tide of political reaction and against diminishing electoral returns. In fact, certain socialist circles[16] considered the penetration to the centre of the political process—for the first time in history—such an important attainment that even though the party became divided against itself during the later stages of the Indonesian crisis, it was loath to give up government responsibility.[17]

The entire period up to 1950 can be considered as an instance of what Lijphart has called 'consociational democracy' at work.[18] Gradually, as the Indonesian crisis grew more acute, political parties closed ranks; the basis of the governing coalition was extended, with the result that, increasingly, opponents of an agreement with the Indonesians were incorporated into government affairs. Thus a counter-constitutional alliance of the radical right was prevented from building up steam. In such matters, however, it is always problematical who exactly is encapsulating whom.

The argument may be summarized as follows:

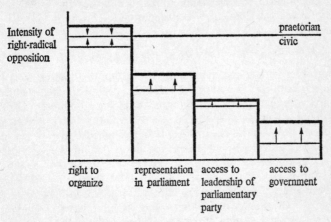

FIGURE 3.1   *Closeness to political centre of various degrees of intensity of right-radical opposition*

When we plot the intensity of right-radical opposition against the dimension of closeness to political centre, and use arrows to indicate shifts through time, we see, at any particular point of time, that where political temper is rising, it finds itself at an increasing distance from the political centre. We further see that, through time, there was a definite trend for any measure of right-wing sentiment to get nearer the political centre. Increasingly, a measure of right-wing influence is incorporated in government; we see that more outspoken opposition was represented in parliament in the one Calvinist party that stayed aloof from government throughout the period under study; we see furthermore that still more radical views are heard either from politicians who were at the ideologic fringe of the Calvinist opposition party and cannot be considered central spokesmen of its parliamentary party, or from splinter parties; the most outspoken opposition, finally, was extra-parliamentary, but enjoyed the freedom to organize itself.

The image of communicating vessels may be appropriate here. It would seem as if once right-radicalism entrenched itself in the established political system, it acquired a stake in the preservation of the system and in countering transgressive tendencies on the part of the extra-parliamentary, right-wing opposition. Although its penetration to the heart of the political system served to raise the level of right-wing sentiment there, at the same time it caused these sentiments among segments of the population to calm down. In conclusion, we may say that an analysis along these lines serves to illustrate the careful manoeuvring, intent on preserving political continuity, which is so typical of consociational democracy.

(c) Dutch colonial society in the East Indies

Between the extremes of the civic nature of the Dutch domestic scene and the praetorian trends within the Republic, each with checks and blockings of its own, the re-emerging colonial regime entered as a third party to the conflict with its own interests and freedom of action.

Here the crucial fact was the incapacity of the Allied Forces for any decisive action immediately after the capitulation of Japan. Most of the pre-war colonial elite, both civilians and military, were interned in concentration camps. By a change of command shortly before the Japanese surrender, the archipelago fell under the South-East Asian Command of Admiral Mountbatten who did not have sufficient troops for a quick occupation of the area. Whereas in the Eastern part of the archipelago Australian forces through swift actions managed to disarm the Japanese forces, enabling the Dutch to take charge of administration of the area as of January 1946, on the main islands of Java and Sumatra only a few strongholds were taken by British troops. General Christison, in factual recognition of the Republican regime, requested that it should maintain law and order in its sphere of influence, while refusing to let Dutch troops enter the islands. The regime lasted more than one year before the Dutch could take over, on 1 December 1946. In the meantime, many Japanese arms had been passed on to the Indonesian forces while an unknown number of Japanese troops had deserted to them.[19]

It is a widely held view that the confrontation with the Republic was territorially confined to Java and Sumatra. This view is unwarranted. At the time of the arrival of Australian troops on islands such as Borneo and Celebes, there too a Republican administration was being set up. Here a policy of 'rolling-back' the Republic with military means started as early as October 1945.[20] Towards the end of 1945 total Dutch forces numbered 20,000 troops, mainly in the eastern part of the archipelago,[21] whereas shipment of troops on a large scale from the Netherlands brought the total number of forces up to 91,200 by 30 November 1946, of which 55,650 were in the narrow corridor on western Java stretching from Batavia (now Jakarta) to

Bandung. They reached a maximum of over 100,000 at the time of the first expedition against the Republic—July 1947.[22] In that period, too, internees, especially on Sumatra, had flocked to these small strongholds, thereby exerting a tremendous pressure on available means of existence. While the Republic maintained a blockade against these strongholds, the Dutch navy countered by a blockade of Republican territory in order to prevent the Republic from buying arms and selling the large stocks of Indonesian staple products.[23]

In this context two distinct policy objectives were pursued by the Dutch government and the Dutch colonial administration. The Dutch government clearly had the initiative in renewed efforts to reach an agreement with the Republic through a fully authorized delegation—the Commission General—whereas the colonial administration, headed by van Mook, led the way in setting up regional entities in those areas where Dutch authority had been restored, with an eye to a future federal structure as envisaged by the Dutch. By the time an agreement with the Republic was reached (March 1947)—an agreement that would prove illusory about four months later—two federal bodies had taken shape, so that the Republic would have been outnumbered by two to one.

In this context what civic channels were open to the military to air its views and have its problems and goals understood? First of all, the highest civil authority in the Dutch East Indies, van Mook, was commander-in-chief of the entire military apparatus in the archipelago. Another link between civil and military authority was the fact that the Army Commander, *qualitate qua*, was head of the Department of War. A smooth functioning of these interlocking positions was evident for instance in the preparations of the first military expedition,[24] whereas, on the other hand, the formal separation of responsibility, especially where van Mook was concerned, created the possibility of using separate channels of information and control.[25]

So, from the point of view of rules of the game and institutionalized ways of access to centres of decision-making, it would appear that the military in the Dutch East Indies by and large worked in a framework of civilian political primacy.

From a balance-of-power point of view, however, the situation appears in a somewhat different light. Van Doorn and Hendrix, in their excellent study,[26] have convincingly shown the harmony of interests between the business and commercial groups and the military, constituting a formidable praetorianizing potential that was only defused by the growing conviction in political circles that military action could no longer be avoided.[27]

3   Interests, alliances and strategies

(a) Interests

As both Messrs P. J. Koets and J. A. Jonkman[28] pointed out in personal communications, an over-riding concern among opponents of appeasement with the Republic was a desire for decolonization along orderly, constitutional lines.[29] To them, the Republic of Indonesia, self-righteously proclaimed in revolutionary turmoil, headed by Hatta and Sukarno who had openly collaborated with the Japanese, was a party unworthy of acknowledgment, and not to be negotiated with. Such a strong ideological (almost religious) factor might resist efforts at an analysis in terms of interests such as status, class and power. Mr Jonkman himself, however, pointed to a curious ambiguity in the Dutch penchant for abiding by the writ, caused by an equally tenacious penchant for binding opponents to one's own interpretation.[30] This shift from writ to interpretation offers plenty of lee-way for an intrusion of interests. Even so, alongside covert influences of this sort, we encounter arguments that openly refer to interests. The list of brochures and pamphlets that were published under the auspices of the NCHR (National Committee for the Maintenance of the Unity of the Empire) states such arguments as the following: Holland could not survive a severing of ties with the colonies (a class argument); the Honour of the Nation and the Army were at stake (a status argument); internationally Holland would be reduced to the rank of a small, powerless nation (a power argument).

It should be clear that even in these arguments—aiming, as they were, at the mobilization of right-wing sentiments on a national scale in the Netherlands—the specific interests of elites among the population remained tacit. These latter interests, in particular, however, may appear from the membership composition of the Committee itself—it offers a vivid illustration of the manifestation of these interests in that many members had clear links with interests embodied in the administration, economy, or army of the colonial empire.[31]

In the Dutch East Indies the case for an analysis in terms of interests is more clear-cut. There we find a colonial society of some 250,000 people[32] who, besides making the colonial area a field of exploitation, gave it the character of a settlement. Many had been born there (in 1930 about 70 per cent),[33] many others had gone there to stay. Their privileged position in terms of class, status and power was about to be wiped away. The threat would dramatically affect the Eurasians who, through the accident of birth, felt superior to the Indonesians and were accorded ample opportunity in the colonial system of dominance to live up to their claims. Their entire self-image, based so predominantly on status, was dependent on the colonial system.

An illustration may be in order, based on data pertaining to the Royal Colonial Army (the KNIL).[34] Of a total of 150 commanding officers,[35] from the Army Commander down to lieutenant-colonel, who were on active duty during the period under study, fifty-eight were born in the East Indies. Of these, twenty-seven were sons of professional soldiers and had been upwardly mobile compared with their fathers. The same holds good for the other twenty-two whose inter-generational mobility we have been able to trace. Most of their fathers' occupations should be classified as middle or even lower-middle: three were teachers in elementary schools, seven were employed by the State Railways, either in white-collar positions or as supervisors, one was a controller in the government bureaucracy, another was employed by the Mail and Telegraph Service (PTT), ten were employed by sugar mills or plantations in supervising or administrative positions. For those who were born in the Netherlands, we have been unable to find similar data. What little information we did find on place of birth and length of residence in the East Indies may serve to supplement the picture. Of a total of ninety-two, sixty-two came from small towns and villages outside the urban concentration in the provinces of Holland, most probably allured by the prospect of a successful career; of the remaining thirty, fourteen came from the Hague, the traditional cross-roads of colonial and domestic society—a city that used to be strongly oriented on the East Indies as a source of social mobility. By far the greater part (sixty-one) had arrived in the East Indies during the years 1919 to 1924. The overall picture of this group of high-ranking officers is one of a group that has staked its life on the opportunity structure of a colonial society.

Just as this group mirrors the situation of the European elite in general, the rank-and-file dramatically reflects the plight of inter-mediate groups who for their positions of relative social elevation were completely dependent on the colonial structure. As a general rule, their ratio was inversely related to rank. The lower ranks of non-commissioned officers and rank-and-file in particular, were mostly filled by Eurasians or Indonesians. Most prominent among the latter were members of Christianized minorities such as the Amboinese and the Menadonese. They clearly epitomized a general strategy under colonial rule where parts of the indigenous population used to be admitted to the exercise of dominance; the price for partial incorporation into the elite hierarchy was a separation from one's ethnic home base, a separation that was either territorial or religious (in so far as recruitment was heavily biased toward Christian minority

57

groups, such as the Amboinese and the Menadonese), or both. We will return later to this strategic device of using the ethnic and social diversity of this large area for the manipulation of tension and conflict.

(b) Alliances and strategies

According to the theoretical model of chapter 1, the most general indication of the strategies deployed by an elite whose shares of social goods are being attacked is a re-activation of ascriptive criteria of distribution. We expect this pattern to show itself most patently and fervently formulated where the ratio of achieved success to ascriptive success is lowest, in the case under study among members of the intermediate layer of colonial society, consisting of Eurasians and those parts of the indigenous population that had been encapsulated[36] in colonial society as well as its structures of dominance. In support of this hypothesis, we find evidence[37] that this reservoir of ideological reaction actually did exist and was militarily 'mobilized', or tapped, by using officers and non-coms of the KNIL to give general instruction about the 'Land and People' of Indonesia to Dutch troops before these were sent overseas. Themes occurred such as the total, innate incapacity of the indigenous population ever to rule itself, being willing only to obey harsh rule and strong will. We ran across this theme elsewhere, as, for instance, in the memoirs of Admiral Helfrich, himself of Eurasian descent.[38] It fits in beautifully, moreover, with another recurrent theme that van Doorn and Hendrix call the centrally justifying argument for the Dutch military presence,[39] the theme of a large co-operative majority of the population being terrorized by a tiny minority of 'evil' elements. In somewhat more civilized disguise, the theme is central to the arguments of those in the vanguard of political reaction; here the unsophisticated factor of 'innate incapacity to rule' is replaced with 'insufficient level of maturity', an argument that smoothly shaded over into the arguments of that vast array of proponents of prolonged, beneficial, paternalistic rule by the Dutch, possibly in co-operation with a Westernized Indonesian elite. This latter version ran strongly through the dominant ideology among government officials and civil servants in Indonesia[40] and was apparent in the policy of setting up federal bodies, resting heavily on Dutch administrative expertise and indigenous feudal elites, especially in those stages of federalization following the first military expedition.

Thus far these strategic answers of a threatened elite are well within the range of normalcy of a civic arena. As was stated earlier, however, transgressive tendencies were strong during the months immediately preceding the first military expedition.

Both in Holland and in Indonesia there were rumours of an impending military putsch, either in the metropolis or in the colony. Thus far, however, I have not been able to substantiate the charges levelled by Mr Slotemaker de Bruine against Gerbrandy,[41] at the time a member of the Anti-Revolutionary Party's parliamentary party, and head of the NCHR.

In Indonesia, van Mook was informed of putschist plans in which the Chief Army Chaplain, who had ties with the NCHR, was said to be involved. Van Mook even requested that the Minister of Overseas Territories fire the Army Chaplain.[42] As several informants assured me these traces of conspiracy were never a serious threat.

One informant confidentially told me that praetorian tendencies were strongest among a group of reserve officers who had been engaged in the right-wing Orangist-Calvinist resistance movement NJV (*Nationaal Jongeren Verbond*) which was officially banned during the German occupation. Unlike the career officers who, for the most part, were deeply imbued with the doctrine of political primacy, this group may have been particularly liable to an intrusion of political orientations of non-military, societal reference groups into their functioning as military men. In a sense, being reserve officers, they were closer to the conflicts and divisions of civilian society than the professional military.[43] As former members of resistance movements, moreover, they may have been less given to civic procedures.

Apart from the coup (the most forceful means of military intervention in politics), other devices were used that imply a transgression of the normatively prescribed role for the military. At the time when a political solution of the conflict was being sought on the basis of the Linggadjati agreement and the swelling ranks of the army were still confined within the strongholds, there was a clear pattern of military violation of the cease-fire, partly in response to Republican infractions, possibly in response to commercial interests, some of them unauthorized by van Mook—all of them, however, a definite contribution to the destruction of what mutual trust did exist.

In this period, too, there is the first large-scale use of a device which might paradoxically be labelled 'transgression institutionalized', namely the use of the Special Forces formula in counter-insurgency on Celebes from December 1946 to February 1947. The forces were mostly Amboinese troops and European cadre. The 'competition for popular support' went on with such atrocity as would resound in the Dutch Parliament as late as 1969.[44]

Starting with the first military expedition, itself a compromise of military and political objectives,[45] new opportunities were open to the military to obstruct political precepts. Circles as high as the Army Commander and the Commander of the Naval Forces exerted strong pressure to extend the scope of the action so as to include Jogjakarta and, bypassing constitutional methods, addressed telegrams to the Queen; van Mook even had to remind the Army Commander of his oath of loyalty to keep him from unauthorized action.[46] Prime Minister Beel, on the other hand, would not have kept van Mook from unauthorized action.[47]

Gerbrandy, member of parliament for the Calvinist Anti-Revolutionary Party, and head of the NCHR, was banned from the radio upon inciting van Mook towards unauthorized action in a speech broadcast on 14 August 1947.[48] By and large, however, military commanders clung to established procedure; even when wanting to continue military action after the order to end hostilities had been issued, they sent telegrams to van Mook, requesting authorization of such action.[49] A second high tide in pressures towards unauthorized action came in the wake of the Van Royen-Rum agreement in May 1949, when some military commanders wanted to continue anti-guerilla actions.[50]

Yet another system of military obstruction of the political process can be discerned. From the start, the Dutch initiative of federalizing the emergent structure of an independent Indonesia offered a possibility as well as a rationale for transgressive military manoeuvring. As early as May 1947, on the eve of the first military expedition, high-ranking Dutch officers as well as colonial civil servants had been instrumental in an abortive coup aiming at a secession of the Pasundan territory[51] from the Republic. Later, when the Pasundan had acquired statehood under the cloak of the Dutch military occupation of western Java, General Engles arrested some members of the Pasundan parliament when, on the occasion of the second military expedition, they took a pro-Republican stand, and he threatened to take stronger measures.[52] After the final cease-fire which was to lead to the solution of the Indonesian issue, and most strongly after independence was formally granted, this strategy of playing the card of territorially-based resistance to the power of the Republic took on desperate features.

This strategy was most dramatically evident in the abortive coups in the Pasundan (this one in January 1950, the so-called 'Westerling putsch'), and on Celebes (the coup by a company commander of the KNIL, Abdul Azis), as well as in the short-lived secession of the Republic of the South Moluccas.

The Westerling putsch had links with the local nationalist-conservative Darul Islam guerillas[53] and, some of my informants asserted,[54] with General Engles, territorial commander of the Dutch troops that still remained in western Java, commander of the '7 December' division that was confined to barracks in Bandung, waiting for repatriation. He certainly did not keep Amboinese KNIL forces under his command, special forces formerly under the command of Captain

Westerling, from deserting to the Westerling forces. One informant was convinced that General Engles was instrumental in the escape of Westerling.[55]

Another source, navy Lieutenant A. J. Schouwenaar, states that the aim of the Westerling putsch was to replace the Republican Minister of Defence with the Sultan of Pontianak, head of the state of West Borneo, colonel of the KNIL, and thus to assure that instead of the Republican Army (the TNI), the former KNIL would be the backbone of the new Indonesian Army.[56] According to Schouwenaar, Vice-admiral Kist must also have known of Westerling's intentions.[57]

In Makassar, Celebes, upon the arrival of troops of the new national army, consisting of former Republican TNI forces, an attempted coup was staged by KNIL company commander Abdul Azis, in the name of defending the state of East Indonesia against the drive towards the unitary state, as promoted by the Federal Government.[58] He was provided with the open support of Amboinese KNIL forces and, as Captain Pielage who was in Makassar at the time and Lieutenant van Gorcum, intelligence officer, have written, secretly spurred by Dutch officers with promises of forthcoming Dutch support to bolster the states in their struggle against centralizing tendencies. Silent support is traced as high as the under-secretaries of the Navy and of the Army at The Hague.[59]

The short-lived attempt at secession of the Republic of the South Moluccas, one of the most dramatic stages of the breakdown of the Dutch-sponsored federal structure, followed the same general pattern. Amboinese KNIL forces, sent back to the isle of Amboyna for demobilization, but left in full possession of their arms, started a virtual terror which was not forcefully countered by Dutch officers at the time; the action was silently condoned by those circles. As Captain Pielage reports, the administrative head of the province was forced into the act of secession by the mutinous troops.

The only instance, to my knowledge, of indigenous KNIL forces choosing the side of the local population and the cause of the unitary state against their own officer corps, occurred in Menado on Northern Celebes. Menadonese soldiers disarmed their officers and fraternized with local pro-Republican forces.[60]

4 A note on rank-and-file dissent

Although the theoretical model from which we started allows us to deal systematically with left-radical tendencies, especially among the rank-and-file, we have not been able to find evidence of 'GI radicalism' to any noticeable extent. A large collection of letters written by Dutch soldiers, which are kept at the archive of the *Partij van de*

Arbeid, centre on such day-to-day problems as the quality of the cigar-ettes and uncertainty as to the date of demobilization. There were instances of draft evasion and conscientious objection, although only a minority, coming from anarchist circles, patently referred to feelings of affiliation with the Indonesian revolution; there were abortive longshoremen strikes when large-scale shipment of troops started. However, no clear pattern emerges of politicization of the rank-and-file, of disobedience movements, of a military-civilian oppositional alliance on the political left.

A comparison with the situation of the US army in Vietnam, where such stirrings did occur, may suggest the following explanation. Whereas among soldiers in Vietnam a feeling had been spreading of risking their lives in what, strategically and politically, was a dead alley, such a feeling did not have time to take root among Dutch soldiers in 1949. Here a similar military situation was brought to an end by the Van Royen-Rum agreement.

5 Conclusion

In the total context of actions taken on the part of Dutch interest groups in their confrontation with the Republic, the part played by praetorianism appears marginal. The most patent instances of the military resorting to praetorianism occurred at the time when the course of events most directly affected the KNIL, especially its indigenous rank-and-file.

When the KNIL as a military structure was disbanded, on 26 July 1950, they had no foreign country to repatriate to and were offered such equally uncertain options as joining the national Indonesian army or joining the Royal Netherlands Army with the risk of a reduction in salary and/or rank.[61]

The heavy investment of Dutch national chauvinism and politico-economic interests in the cause of federalism in Indonesia, made the Netherlands appear a safe ally in praetorian ventures. When no actual support was forthcoming, the days of federalism were numbered. On 17 August 1950, the unitary state of the Republic of Indonesia was officially proclaimed.

The heyday of KNIL power saw no such policy of desperation. The formidable power which the KNIL, however small in comparison with the influx of the Royal Netherlands Army, managed to acquire through monopolizing the military command structure, intelligence and special forces,[62] it acquired along orderly lines without recourse to praetorianism. The harmony of interests in colonial society, the willingness of political circles to rely increasingly on military means and the gradual incorporation of forces of reaction into the political process in the metropolis—all these factors combined in offering lee-way to the KNIL for accumulating power. The height of this development was reached with the replacement of van Mook by Beel, high representative of the Crown, who, contrary to van Mook, was no match for the military.[63]

It will always remain a matter of speculation why no upsurge of praetorianism occurred at the height of anti-guerilla warfare when the military seemed in full sway, but attempts at solving the problem by political means began to prevail.

As a final note, however, we would venture to suggest that a main factor in keeping the military within civic bounds was the united front and relative continuity of rule Dutch politicians managed to maintain in the metropolis.[64]

6 Postscript—The performance of consociational democracy in a situation of crisis

In the analysis of the Dutch political situation earlier in this chapter, we designed a diagram that may serve once again in analysing the characteristic behaviour of consociational democracy in situations of crisis. There we used the diagram for summarizing a verbal argument. Here further analysis of possible patterns which the diagram may show may suggest some further ideas.

If we translate the differences in height between the various bars of the chart in a continuous line of a certain negative slope, we get a picture as in Figure 3.2.

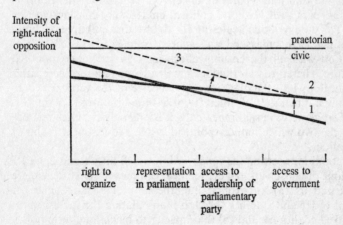

FIGURE 3.2

If we focus attention on the continuous lines 1 and 2, we can note the effects of a policy of broadening the governmental coalition. It allows, on the one hand, a certain increase in the extent to which right-radical sentiments are incorporated in government; on the other, it cools off right-radical sentiments among the populace. In other words: the negative inclination co-efficient of line 2 is smaller than that of line 1. Political leadership, as represented in government, has through this decision gained time for implementing some course of substantial policy, at the cost, however, of greater internal dissension. The considerations underlying the decision to broaden the governmental coalition are in themselves characteristic of consociational democracy, in so far as the assessment of the disruptive potential of political cleavage and civil strife is a permanent parameter of coalition politics.

As such, however, the consideration is one of short-term political wisdom. As we stated above, manipulating the inclusiveness of the coalition tends to gain time for the pursuit of further political objectives. The government's record in this sphere, in the long run, will allow the populace at large, or segments thereof, to measure the effectiveness of the government. One could well imagine the renewed increase in right-radical opposition had the Dutch government, broadly based though it was in 1949, proved unable to settle the Indonesian question (cf. the dotted line 3 in the diagram). This again might have provoked a new wave of considerations of reshuffling the governmental coalition among political elites. For the position of the government, this would have meant a further upward move towards the thin line separating civic from praetorian situations. It indeed appears as if Catholic political circles were considering this option (cf. note 64). Such catering for right-radical sentiments, however, might have unleashed and spurred into action a left-radical opposition with all the ensuing effects of civil strife and political disruption. Therefore we would seem well advised to insert these latter considerations into the diagram and conceive of the vertical axis as indicating a dimension of 'intensity of left- and right-radical opposition'. For, as we have said repeatedly, it is precisely the inter-relatedness of the two which induces political systems to leave the realm of civic politics.

The conditions setting the range within which lines 1 and 2, under conditions of consociational democracy, can move, therefore, can be summarized as (a) an explicit intentness on the maintenance of political order and stability through manipulating the inclusiveness of political coalitions, and (b) the capacity to reach long-term policy objectives. Thus we have stressed both the importance of a specific political culture as expressed under (a), and the role played by the effectiveness of the governmental performance (b). Both factors, if successfully pursued, will bring the populace to extend its mandate to the political system, or, in words suggested by Almond and Verba, the 'output affect' will tend to impinge positively on the 'system affect'.[65]

The absence of an effective realization of goals on the part of subsequent governments throughout the later years of the French Fourth Republic, caused the eventual derailment of the political system and cleared the way for the abrupt penetration of right-radical sentiments to its very core. Only the drastic and efficacious way in which de Gaulle handled the Algerian problem, served to stall those trends, even managed to reverse them and to make for a gradual return to an orderly political process. A similar absence of effective goal attainment in Italy seems to put the system under strong pressure, notwithstanding the dampening effects of factor (a), apparent in the 'opening towards the left' which has been operative during the better part of the 1960s.

In addition to the manipulation of the inclusiveness of political coalitions as a means to prevent radical sentiments from building up steam, we may point to another sphere of strategic action of which the central government can avail itself. It works rather through manipulating the output affect. By taking short-term policy decisions aiming at the temporary satisfaction of oppositional sentiments, the government can bring about a more or less transient reduction of the political fever. At the same time, it will thus have managed to legitimize parallel government actions to quell forcefully the more rabid outgrowths of opposition. The banning of Gerbrandy from the Dutch broadcasting system may serve as an instance of this. It came at a time when right-wing appetites had been assuaged by authorizing the first military action in Indonesia. As we may remember, the use of the alternative strategy of opening up the coalition was to occur somewhat later.

Both strategies, the second of which may be characteristic of consociational democracy, may serve to highlight the range of action of the respective Dutch governments in their attempts to keep the conflict with Indonesia from exploding the civic bounds of the Dutch political process.

part two

Left-wing radicalism among students

4 Student radicalism in the 1960s

1 Introduction

The following two chapters will focus on left-radicalism as it became manifest in the student radicalism of the 1960s. In this chapter we shall try to point out how the general model of conflict can be brought to bear on the subject. The next chapter will be empirical; it will present the results of research into student radicalism inspired by the theoretical viewpoints comprised in the model. The research was undertaken in the spring of 1970.

The immediate task in this chapter is not unlike that of chapter 2, where we laid the ground for an analysis of military intervention in politics. Once more we have to specify the conceptual apparatus in order to be able to apply it to a specific arena of conflict and to come up with specified hypotheses about the rise and course of conflict. For the subject of student radicalism no less than for the analysis of military intervention, this requires that we specify the range of social references which presumably underlie the assessment of relative shares of power, status and class. In that context, too, we shall outline what specific positions in the arena under study might spur the self-conscious realization of interests. The endeavour will specify our expectations as to what conflict parties are likely to arise. Moreover, since we have been using the term 'arena' to refer to the social context in which conflict groups confront one another, we shall have to outline what is to be considered the relevant arena for the case in hand and what are its characteristics in terms of participation and institutionalization.

A final problem in this exercise is the actual issues that set the tone of the dispute. It is a problem that, so far, we have more or less neglected. We have been abstracting from the concrete content of these issues as a theoretical problem on the presumption that, whatever the actual content, conflicts might be reduced to the general label of conflicts about the distribution of class, status and power. In this chapter, however, we shall go into the relation of this general label to the actual content of issues involved in specific conflicts.

2   References, positions and parties

Individuals will experience the distribution of class, status and power in whatever *milieux* and situations they are involved. A recurrent aspect of social structures, ranging from nuclear families to entire societies, is the distribution of social goods. Therefore, along with the number of structures in which an individual is involved, his set of relative shares will increase, as will the likelihood of his shares becoming inequivalent. For that reason, we shall outline a selection of social situations in which each of the social goods is distributed. Underlying this selection is our expectation that, together, they will comprise the main reference points for the individuals under study in the assessment of their shares of social goods.

One such expectation holds that their parental home will constitute an important point of reference. For a large part of the student body the university is the first social terrain where they venture out by themselves upon leaving their parental families and, by themselves, have to cope with a distribution of social goods that may or may not be consistent with what they have experienced and have learnt to expect from their parents. This frontier-like experience may be less apparent in students who have not left home—a fairly common pattern in the Netherlands—and, therefore, face less of a break with high-school life. Yet, even for them, we assume entry into the university to represent some sort of *rite de passage* into the adult world; it symbolizes the end of their apprenticeship *vis-à-vis* their parents. Therefore we have chosen the parental home as a microstructure that provides students with an important yardstick for assessing their experiences in the academic arena.

More than just offering a microcosmic reflection of patterns of social distribution, however, the paternal home will also have served to embed its members in a wider macro-structure. In that sense, the paternal home has served to expose its members to the wider, societal process of distribution of social goods, namely through the shares which the father has managed to acquire in his working role. The perspective on this wider process will, therefore, diverge widely for different socio-economic classes and leave the children with widely divergent images and evaluations. We may expect people of similar social background to use similar yardsticks in their assessment of other areas of social distribution later on in life. Home *and* social background will, therefore, serve as two separate points of reference.

In contradistinction to the reference to past experiences which either of these offers, an additional reference to the future, as expected and anticipated, may be hypothesized. The most ready reference, here, is offered by college and university graduates. They do offer a standard for the assessment of shares of status, class and power which students look forward to. The visibility of this standard and its use for an interpretation of actual deprivation as an investment with a view to future rewards, will depend on whether or not a field of study channels its students to well-defined occupational roles and markets.[1]

In addition to the parental home, the social background and the anticipations of the future, a fourth set of references, is, of course, focused on the university itself. Following the approach of the second chapter, we can discern an *internal* power position of students: the share of power students have within the university structure compared with the shares of other groups within that structure. In addition to that, an *external* power position can be conceived, referring to the structured access to processes of decision-making outside the university. There the students will have to compete with groups of non-students in society, such as categories of age-mates, that may serve as reference groups to students in the evaluation of external power. It may be useful to point out in this context that, in addition to external power as linked with the student's role, students as citizens, as members of a body politic, are apt to experience and assess the distribution of power within that body as well. What interests us here is the possibility that this latter distribution can be a source of grievance and frustrations which students may attempt to transfer to intra-university conflicts for the mobilizing potential such issues may carry. We will return to this strategic option later.

As to status, again an internal and an external dimension can be distinguished. Within the confines of the academic arena status is distributed, in some instances even to the extreme of rank-ordering respective year-groups. Externally, we expect the assessment of relative shares of status of students *vis-à-vis* relevant reference groups to play an important part.

As to class, the application of the definition given in the first chapter, offers some problems. In a strict sense, rather than actually having a definite market position, students should be taken to anticipate one. As students, they are making investments, induced by the expectation of future rewards. Therefore our definition of market position can apply only partially in so far as this investment aspect is concerned. The concept of internal market position would hardly make sense, unless we take the factor of time into consideration. The concept should be taken to refer, then, to the assessment of actual and impending investments against expected future rewards. In the assessment of the students' external market position too, this expectation is involved—here students can be taken to weigh the immediate rewards for their actual investment level on various job markets

71

against the expected future rewards for continued investment. We shall refrain from distinguishing a separate class position for the arena of the parental home, because this would require a further alteration of our definition.

One task remains for this section: to present an outline of potential conflict groups. In general, we can say that the set of reference groups which students use for the assessment of the justness of their shares of social goods and which can be either the object of positive or of negative reference, can for that reason be considered potential allies or opponents. In the case in hand, we can think of year-groups of students, members or non-members of fraternal organizations, the category of non-student age-mates, functional layers within the university, such as faculty and administration, and, finally, seniority levels such as senior and junior faculty. To the extent that parental home and social background are the historic situations that have provided students with standards for the assessment of their present interests, they no longer actively contribute to the reservoir of potential allies or opponents. Similar considerations apply to the reference group of university graduates, in so far as it serves to inspire expectations of future shares of social goods.

3 Institutional characteristics of the conflict arena

For the analysis of these characteristics we may recall Huntington's pair of concepts, used in the preceding two chapters. Again, we expect processes of participation and institutionalization to be prime parameters of the course of competition for social goods. In the second chapter we treated various value configurations of both parameters in their impact on the role of the military as one participant among others in social competition. There our focus was on the behaviour of the military *vis-à-vis* other contenders, rather than on differences in participation and institutionalized opportunities for participation within the military. Since in this chapter we are focusing on one specific component within the larger structure of the university—i.e. on the student body—this shift in analytic focus will be of some consequence for the definition of the arena's boundaries.

To the extent that students have a rather neatly defined position within the university structure, a position which can be thought to entail definite interests, we are warranted in conceiving of the university as constituting the relevant arena within which these interests are voiced and accommodated. Within that structure the need will have arisen for participation and its institutionalization. To the extent, however, that certain student interests spring from authoritative actions outside the university, stemming, for instance, from the central government, the decision-making structures within the university are no longer the appropriate address for filing demands. In other words, to the extent that universities are losing autonomy, the echelon at which demands should aim will tend to move upwards. Thus, the scope of action of student groups from different universities will tend to intersect and coalesce; the attempts at finding access to ever more embracing authoritative structures make for the transcendence of localism in protest. As a consequence, the structural conditions for the rise of extensive student alliances will change drastically. The kind of interest which we have in mind here arises when, for instance, the central government has become the main source of funds for university budgets, the main provider of student scholarships and student facilities, such as housing, and finally, when that government has come to constitute one of the main areas to absorb university graduates.

Thus, in addition to degree of institutionalization and level of participation, the scope of the arena itself has become a crucial parameter.[2] In other words: differences in scope of the arena will tend to correlate with differences in game patterns, most patently patterns of alliance formation.

Yet another structural characteristic of the arena should be inserted into our analytic apparatus: the ecological factor of quantitative 'density'. Variations in the number of students and faculty constitute a separate factor which impinges upon institutionalized processes of participation. It can either tend to facilitate them or be a factor of strain and disorganization. Even if we assume the distribution of objective interests among participants to have remained unchanged, the very fact of an increase in density can dislocate existing procedures for voicing and redressing grievances; it thus, by itself, is able to add to feelings of deprivation and obstruction. Moreover, a marked increase in number and physical proximity of individuals who share certain interests can notably affect the assessment of the power potential of allies and adversaries.[3] For these various reasons, an increase in density is an autonomous development which may spur a course of conflict as outlined in our model. We will return to this point more systematically.

4 Issues

American authors such as Keniston, Flacks and Heist have argued that an important aspect of student activism in the USA is its disinterestedness.[4] Students have acted in support of civil rights, and of students of lesser academic excellence who were threatened by the draft; they have come out against the Vietnam war. They have, in sum, displayed actions whose motivations apparently defy analysis

73

in terms of our model. The latter, we may repeat, does indeed focus on conflict as induced by interests. The divergence, however, may be more apparent than real for two reasons.

First, the very fact that the open profession of a specific point of view, such as opposition to the Shah of Persia visiting West Germany, or resistance against the war of Algeria, may develop into violent conflict with the police, is patent proof that law-enforcing bodies dispute the legitimacy of promulgating specific views at specific times in specific ways. The conflict will then, inevitably, be reduced to the issue of the legitimacy of modes of participation. In other words, the issue is reduced to its power dimensions. The group that is stifled in its attempts at making itself heard will come to realize that it is denied one of the means of finding access to authoritative centres, namely the promulgation of dissenting views. Inevitably, in the relationship of dissent towards a dominant outlook, one of the aspects is that of a power relationship.

Second, this very possibility of conflicts highlighting the bare power aspects of conflictual relations, might suggest an approach that would look beyond the issues at hand and analyse to what extent, for all the apparent diversity of issues in specific conflicts, underlying configurations of interests can be discerned. Issues, in this approach, would acquire a symbolic-expressive function: in the repression which they are apt to provoke against themselves, they serve as vivid images of an underlying deprivation in terms of class, status and/or power. Another suggestive implication here is that issues may carry different meanings for leaders and followers in a protest movement, in the sense that the followers have joined the ranks on the basis of the immediate, intrinsic merits of an issue—they display as it were an *ad hoc* involvement—whereas to the leadership the symbolic-expressive value of the issue may prevail. This difference in evaluation might account for the paradoxical fact that a victory on concrete issues tends to alienate leaders from followers: the followers are satisfied and withdraw from the movement, whereas the leadership, more radical than before, is left behind in a quest for new issues which it hopes will more dramatically and effectively make visible the underlying conflict of interests.

Therefore, to the extent that we shall go into specific issues, we shall do so for their mobilizing function—their function of awakening people to an awareness of their objective interests. In that sense, the sequence of issues that marks off the history of a protest movement offers the learning experiences through which a group comes to a vision of its underlying interests. Accordingly, two main aspects of issues should be pointed out. First, their aspect of mobilizing agents—the leadership of a protest movement that proves unable to come up

with appealing issues will undercut its position and leave the movement to factional strife.[5] The second aspect refers to differences in
scope: some issues will focus on specific cases at specific universities,
whereas others may deal with matters such as the Vietnam war.
For that reason we have chosen to distinguish the role of citizen
from that of student. Experiences of powerlessness in the political
arena, in relation with opposition to prevailing policies, may have a
mobilizing impact on the sense of powerlessness in the more limited
academic arena, and may, therefore, be introduced as an issue
there.

5 Two arenas: traditional and transgressive[6]

In this section we shall compare two arenas—ideal-types, to be
sure—one reflecting a traditional arena of civic quality, the other
an arena as it may be presumed to appear on the eve of student
unrest. Each is intended to illustrate the impact of different configurations of key variables such as numbers and social background
of students, density and scope of the arena, as well as its level of
participation and degree of institutionalization. We may hope to
arrive at a more complete grasp of the process of praetorianization
by offsetting it against the opposite image of civic order. The exercise
will allow us to bring our general model of conflict down to the
empirical level of student activism, and derive a set of expectations
from it as to what changes in student society and in the position
and orientation of several interest groups may help account for the
rise of student activism. These expectations have guided the research
which the next chapter will report on.

Here, as we said, our argument will be conceptual, working down
from a high level of generality to a level of testable hypotheses. The
elaboration will proceed by way of an argument through opposites.
Putting a traditional arena opposite what we shall call a transgressive
arena will serve our goal of conceptual clarification, rather than aiming at historically warranted description. Any suggestion of linear
development from the one conceptual extreme to the other would
be unjustified. As historical research would seem to point out,[7]
student activism is, rather, a cyclic phenomenon. Actual developments, in that sense, can rather be taken to oscillate between our
conceptual extremes.

1 The traditional arena

In its ideal-typical, pure form this arena will contain the following
parties: faculty and the student body, both recruited from the same
oligarchic elite in society. They share the experiences of a similar

75

social background, an elitist view of society, and knowledge pertaining to life chances and a proper course of life. In this configuration, student life is a transitional stage, an apprentice period, carrying expectations on the role of apprentice which the preceding generation too has subscribed to and which the present generation is duly prepared for. The happy congruence of social background and social destiny create a community of interest between apprentice and establishment, whereas, on the other hand, the transient character of divergent interests will keep them from being activated.

The blocking of individual mobility is highly unlikely; on the contrary, on account of ascriptive criteria, students can duly claim eventual access to the elite. This closed system, in which a social elite fills vacancies as they arise from its own progeniture, has never existed in pure form. At all times, there will have been students whose social destination has been superior to their social background. The traditional arena, however, has a variety of means at its disposal to accommodate the potential threat of this situation and to encapsulate it successfully. Fraternal organizations, for instance, as they have been operative in the Netherlands, and which Lammers has called 'frameworks of vertical integration', have fulfilled the function of socializing and integrating newcomers into the system of culturally stylized expectations prevalent among the elite.[8] Even those groups of students who were loath to undergo socialization as practised by the dominant fraternal organization (the 'Corps', as it was called in the Netherlands) and had chosen to set up rival fraternal organizations, were forced to operate in a context that bore the clear imprint of the Corps. Notwithstanding these stirrings of differentiation within student society, the elitist view of society prevailed, even to the extent of pervading the very structure of student society. For, indeed, this society was hierarchical, ordered along status lines, the Corps constituting the pinnacle of power, status and life chances. The very fact of being 'established' accorded the Corps a definite edge in maintaining its power and status.[9] A major factor, of course, to make this situation last, was the equality in social background and destination between Corps members and members of the establishment. This situation made for easy access of Corps members to the establishment in attempts to influence processes of decision-making. Thus the Corps was the born spokesman of student society in a consultative style which, at the time, was known as 'intimate deliberation'.[10]

In addition to insertion into the Corps of the socially mobile, and to the socialization which it offered, other techniques of 'skimming' were used, applying an upward pressure to those students whose set of objective interests was inequivalent and who, therefore, constituted a potential oppositional leadership. The techniques aimed at sustaining their orientation towards individual mobility within the established system. In this context we may think of the institution of the student-teacher which, in the course of their study, offered a premium to those students who had shown signs of excellence and were willing to pass to the side of the establishment. This skimming technique is meritocratic in its very essence; unlike insertion into the Corps—offering a *rite de passage* into the outlook of an ascriptive elite—it focuses exclusively on achievement criteria. In itself, it should be considered an act of wisdom as well as a sign of cunning on the part of the establishment—which history illustrates in a variety of ways. Many ascriptive elites have tended to open their ranks to excellent outsiders.

In addition to this, we should consider that in the traditional arena the very fact of being a student represented an element of skimming: from points of view of class and status, the fact of entering the academic world constituted a definite gratification. The high share of the social good of education was a sure voucher to high future class positions.

With regard to status, we want to make a final remark. The academic arena was relatively small. Students were a small, highly visible elite among their age-group. In addition to this, the position of eminence of the Corps within this arena and the fact that Corps members derived their societal status in large part from their social background, served to create a reservoir of prestige which generously spilled over to tinge the entire student body. Thus, a sensation of upward mobility was created which in itself was experienced as a reward.

The picture of such a traditional arena can be schematized as in Table 4.1 (p. 78). The social goods of status, class and power will be dissected in accordance with the rules laid down in the second chapter. Relevant groups in the arena will be faculty, traditional students, and newcomers. Both categories of students can be operationally discerned by counting as newcomers those students who have non-academic backgrounds. With regard to the faculty, a number of reference points, such as parental home, should be considered of lesser relevance; we have decided to leave the pertinent cells open. For the ensuing scheme, we may refer the reader to Table 4.1 on page 78.

The scheme clearly illustrates the community of interests among faculty and traditional students on the basis of social background and the students' social destination (see the 'future' dimension in the scheme). As to the actual differences between both groups, expectations prevail that these will duly cease to exist following graduation.

The newcomers, in comparison with the traditional students,

77

TABLE 4.1 A traditional arena

Parties	Status					Power					Class		
	at home	social background	in-ternal	ex-ternal	future	at home	social background	in-ternal	ex-ternal	future	social background	in-ternal	ex-ternal
Faculty		++	++	++			++	++	+	+	++	++	++
Traditional students	?	++	+	+	++	++	++	+–	+–	++	++	++	+
Newcomers	?	+	+–	–	+(+)	?	?	–	–	+(+)	+	++	+(–)

TABLE 4.2 A transgressive arena

Parties	Status					Power					Class			
	at home	social background	in-ternal	ex-ternal	future	at home	social background	in-ternal	ex-ternal	future	at home	social background	in-ternal	ex-ternal
Traditional students	+–	++	+	→	++	–	+	+→	+–→	+	++	++	++	+
Potential radical leadership	+		+–	→	+	+–	+–	–	–	+–	+	+	+–	+
Potential radical following	+–	+(–)	+–	→	+	–	–	–	+–	–	+–	+–	+	+–

have similar expectations of high future shares of class, status and power, in addition to having a high actual external status. Concerning internal and external power, we assume student-members of the Corps to have had larger shares than the newcomers. With regard to external market position, a similar assumption holds; on the basis of particularistic prerogatives—such as can be realized through their fathers' 'old boy network'—a traditional student who for one reason or other quits academic life before graduation may reckon to have access to greater rewards than a newcomer who has given up his study. The greater disparity, therefore, between a newcomer's external and internal market position will result in his being more strongly attached to the university as a channel for social mobility and will cause reference groups within the academic world to be of particular relevance to him.

Although, indeed, incongruent interests can be pointed out, such a wide array of opportunities for and expectations of individual mobility exists as to keep blockings of the kind referred to in our conflict model dormant for all practical purposes. No blockings can be thought to exist of central claims which students feel entitled to foster. There is, however, the possibility that, in a somewhat wider perspective, the blocking of claims on positions of power on the part of non-Corps members—due to the Corps' monopoly of power—may have had a slowly-developing effect on the breeding of left-radical, oppositional feeling. Lammers has made an interesting suggestion in this context.[11] The frustration to which, in the traditional arena, the non-Corps members had been subject, did not result in a left-radical movement at the time, due to such factors as relative numbers, the perception of existing power relations, and the differences in status prevailing *among* non-Corps members, effectively keeping them from banding together. For indeed, below the pinnacle of status represented by the Corps, a hierarchy of decreasing status differentiated non-Corps fraternal organizations from one another as well as from non-affiliated students. The latter were allotted the lowest rank. To the extent that the Corps was able to impose a definition of their situation on non-Corps members, it had a definite stake in internally dividing a potential opponent by means of differentially meting out rejection and acceptance. Thus it treated denominational fraternal organizations as closer to the Corps in status than non-denominational fraternal organizations which, more clearly, had been set up in protest against the Corps' dominant position. This strategy, in addition to the lack of numerical strength, apparently forestalled the rise of a protest movement at the time. Yet the blocking of the access to power might have led to a sense of frustration, either individual or shared by small groups, which, over the years, these individuals may have kept alive and transferred to

79

their children. The latter, as second-generation newcomers, may again have introduced this sense of opposition to the Corps' dominant position in the academic arena—an arena, however, which this time showed a markedly different balance of forces and which, for the first time, may have offered a potential following to these dissenters. In Parsonian terms, we might assume protest to have gone through a latency period, in order to gather strength for a renewed emergence into an established integrative structure.[12]

2   The transgressive arena

Pinner uses the word transgression in a dual sense. In his approach, the word refers to that kind of behaviour that aims at changing established situations through the creation of novel roles and positions. Such behaviour can be thought to 'transgress' the bounds of a traditional structure. The second sense of the word also refers to such a transgression, in so far as the behaviour thus depicted may aim at objectives beyond the traditional horizon of a given social arena.[13]

Transgressive student behaviour displays both features. It is novel to the extent that it rejects the traditional structure of student society and the traditional distribution of social goods in it. It is novel also on account of its orientation towards subjects which tradition tends to put outside the students' sphere of interests, such as the transformation of society at large.

It may be useful in this context to bring out one more aspect of the concept of transgression which Pinner does not mention. To the extent that the bounds of a traditional arena are exceeded, an existing institutional structure will have come apart. Unless that order is instantly replaced by a novel institutional order, the attempts at extending participation·will have left an oligarchic, civic arena in a state of praetorianization. Referring to our model of conflict, some broad factors of this set of developments can be pointed out here.

One such factor is the growth of the universities, in student numbers, in numbers of faculty and technical-administrative personnel, as well as in the assortment of disciplines and specializations which are being taught. Irrespective of whether or not those involved in the prevailing oligarchic order agree to such expansion, the factors of scope and complexity of the arena are factors working to upset the rigid bounds of the oligarchic pattern of interest promotion. An institution such as 'intimate deliberation' is contingent upon the existence of a limited, well-structured arena, allowing for unhindered transmission of signals in the particularistic intercourse of oligarchic elites. This essentially non-formalized pattern of intercourse gives way to pressures working towards formalization of intercourse which radiate from extensive, complex organizations.

Developments along these lines tend to have an autonomous influence on the distribution of social goods. They cause the distribution of status, so far clearly perceived and apparently accepted by all those involved, to become problematical. The increased complexity of processes of decision-making makes it harder to influence them, which again impairs whatever access to them groups used to have. The increased complexity of the occupational structure which students will eventually enter, brings uncertainty to the assessment of future rewards for present investments, thus upsetting any clearcut evaluation of the internal market position of students. Thus each of the social goods of status, power and class tends to be affected.

An important factor here is that these developments have not affected every field of study and of occupational career to the same extent. In so far as a field of study attracts smaller numbers of students and offers them a training for more clearly defined occupations and job markets, these fields will more closely resemble the type of our traditional arena; the prevailing institutional order, consequently, will be under less pressure. In this context we can think of traditional, well-established fields of study such as law and medicine; in the first instance, both the factors of fairly limited student numbers and of rather well-defined traditional role expectations are operative, whereas the latter factor in particular would seem to apply in the field of medicine. Disciplines such as the social sciences, on the other hand, are characterized by large numbers of students and markedly diffuse role expectations. In addition to that, in most places the field is relatively young and, if at all, has hardly known oligarchic, civic conditions.

A second factor is the change in the composition of the student body. The very fact of the increase in student numbers implies a marked increase in the number of newcomers lacking academic backgrounds. Further, the traditional over-representation of the higher social strata among the student population will have decreased: lower social strata, for the first time, will have entered the university. We assume this overall trend to have the following effects:

1. gratification effect—we may expect students from non-academic backgrounds to consider the very fact of entering the university a token of success and social mobility. This in turn will sustain their orientation towards individual mobility and success.
2. loss of status—the decreasing over-representation of the top strata in society (in other words, the decreasing correlation between the position of the student and his social background) has caused the external status of students to decrease. This trend may counteract

gratification effects, in the sense that the decrease in external status has served to reduce the total reward to be gained from entering the university. Traditional students too will experience this decline in status.

3. anticipation effect—we expect the gratification effect to diminish for second-wave newcomers, such as second, third or later children from non-academic homes, or second-generation newcomers (children of parents who themselves had been newcomers to the university). For them, the reward has lost the appeal it had to the one first attaining it. To the extent, then, that the power of the gratification effect has been reduced, the likelihood will increase that an orientation towards individual mobility and success will give way to a collective orientation in terms of interests shared with others.

A third factor is trends in family styles of upbringing. We assume that in a large number of families a shift has occurred towards greater equality between parents and children, and towards greater permissiveness.[14] Under those circumstances, the distribution of power and status within the family is no longer based on the ascriptive criteria of sex and age. The further these developments have proceeded, the more abrupt will be the break between experiences in the paternal home and in situations where ascriptive criteria clearly regulate the distribution of power and status.

As in the case of the traditional arena, the transgressive arena can be schematized. We shall concentrate on three groups in the arena: traditional students, a potential radical leadership, and a potential radical following. Our focus will be the situation where, as yet, no actual conflict groups have emerged; the different shares, as indicated in the scheme, have not yet undergone the impact of conflict. Changes in shares or pressure on them will be indicated by arrows, pointing either upwards or downwards. For the scheme, we refer the reader to Table 4.2 on page 78.

Although we have chosen to insert student categories only into the scheme, our assumption is that the shares of social goods of these categories are in part determined by the behaviour of other categories, such as faculty or administrative bodies of the university. This assumption holds in particular where shares of power are concerned.

In the scheme, we have tried to bring out the following overall picture. 'Traditional students' should be thought of as an organized association whose shares of internal and external status as well as of internal and external power are subject to downward pressure, brought about by the increase in density and complexity of the arena which we referred to above. Potential leaders and potential following have a number of interests in common, some of which would rank even on the level of the ones best-off, as, for instance, the shares of external status and the expectations of future status. In addition to these, however, there are interests which clearly mark both categories as the more deprived, as appears from their shares of internal and external power.

Lastly, we assume differences to prevail *between* both categories of leadership and following in the standards they have learned to apply in the context of their paternal homes, in social background (to the extent that the socio-economic background of the leadership is presumed to be higher than that of its following, though not on a par with traditional students) and, finally, in internal and external market position. These latter assumptions need some clarification.

We specifically have in mind students in those fields of study where student numbers are high and role expectations as well as the job market structure are highly diffuse. We assume these expectations to be further limited due to the fact that large numbers of students in these fields reject entire sectors of employment such as business and government as downright unacceptable.[15] Our assumption is that this self-imposed limitation of career opportunities is apt to occur mainly among the potential radical leadership on account of the discontinuity in the style and pattern of distribution of status and power between the parental home and other societal institutions. We, moreover, assume the internal market position of the potential following to be relatively better, for all its diffuseness, due to the absence of this self-imposed limitation.

The external market position, on the other hand, of the potential leadership we assume to be relatively better than that of its potential following. However limited the range of social activities which radical students may deem acceptable, there are such sectors as journalism, media work, or even the recruitment by political parties (European style), or politics (American style), which may attract the leadership of a radical student movement, once arisen, and may lead it to trade its actual investments for rewards outside the academic arena. As we said, for this event to happen, the radical movement should have constituted itself prior to the leadership acquiring the necessary visibility. More generally, with regard to the differences between radical leadership and radical following, we can say that they reflect the underlying difference between vanguard and following, which we can formulate as follows: the balance of deprivations and gratifications will be such as to lean more heavily towards the deprivations for the leadership than for the potential following. Therefore we should conceive of the following as recruited from a wider assortment of students on the basis of successful tarnishing of what, initially, they had perceived as gratifications—a tarnishing, we hold, which to a large extent has been brought about by an activist

83

vanguard. Thus, contrary to what was postulated in the first chapter, for the movement towards a deprived following to occur, the leadership has had to incite and instill these feelings of deprivation first. We shall return to the implications of this change in hypothesis in the final section of the following chapter. Here, suffice it to point out once more that our schematic representation of sets of interests assumes social-psychological states of awareness and reflects definitions of situations rather than any objective reality outside the participant actors. This consideration in particular can help us grasp processes of change in these sets of relative shares.

In this context, too, we should like to tackle the problem of how to project the set of interests of scholarship students and of students who, for one reason or other, are gainfully employed. Both categories have in a way invested in their internal market position; the result is that their study has come to represent a more vivid interest. In the following, we shall assume both categories to be under-represented among the potential radical leadership; they will, however, be a likely object of mobilization for those student actions which directly relate to their specific interests.[16]

The overall picture emerging from the shifts and changes outlined in the two schemes is one of a breakdown of an oligarchic order of civic nature, leaving a constellation of potentially conflicting forces in search of new modes of voicing their demands and pursuing their objectives. Almost any occasion might offset chain-reactions involving ever wider circles of academic society and ever more clearly drawing the lines between opponents and allies. The crucial area that is likely to start this train of events is the area of power. The area itself, on account of a variety of factors, as we have seen above, is in a state of flux, undergoing changes of scope and complexity. At the same time, it has to cope with novel demands for participation in advocacy of the institution of novel structures and channels of participation.

The likelihood arises that demands of this sort are considered such an outrageous infraction on conceptions held by potential opponents concerning the situation as it should be (but certainly is not, or is not any more), as to cause these opponents to mount defensive actions. Again, ascription is a potent instrument here. Attempts will be made to make participation contingent upon the criterion of age, and to make the admissibility of student demands dependent upon more restrained and civil styles of contestation.[17] The clearest case in point may be—in matters concerning professional standards and practices, such as hiring and firing—the granting of an advisory vote to students *as a group*, irrespective of differences in professional achievement among them. This strategy is ascriptive *par excellence*. Other defensive tactics are attempts to increase the opaqueness of the decision-making process through informal, non-public consultation at unannounced times and places.

An emergent radical vanguard will try to mobilize its potential following once conflict has started. In general, these are the problems it has to tackle, and the options it can use:

1. It has to effect the shift from an individual orientation on careers, mobility and success to a more collective orientation. A gratification effect, apt to sustain the individual orientation, needs tarnishing; it should lose its halo of attraction in favour of concentration on the deprivations which a given situation entails.

2. To that effect the leadership can try to weaken existing status gratifications and to cause prevailing status differentials to give way to common interests in terms of power and class position.

3. Moreover, it can try to convey its definition of life chances to its potential following, thus causing a decline in the assessment of the internal market position of the following. In the process deprivation will increase; the basis of common interests will be reinforced.

4. The leadership can try to introduce issues of high symbolic-expressive value, i.e. a value for the illumination of the underlying conflict of interests. It can either choose issues reflecting the structure of interests within the academic arena or come up with issues symbolizing the structure of interests in broader arenas, in the hope of extending its following. In the latter case, as a corollary, it will have to de-emphasize the dimension of external status of the student.

5. The leadership may try to channel its newly mobilized resources through existing avenues of student participation, by 'taking over' representative bodies, or it may set out on novel courses of confrontation through establishing novel media of publication or seeking novel means of expression such as demonstrations to voice its demands.

6. The longer the perceived blocking in this situation of confrontation persists, the longer can the recruitment of a following be pursued. The following will keep growing, the means deployed will grow more violent and the ensuing pattern of confrontation will deviate increasingly from the rules prevailing in a civic arena.

Once conflict has started to take its course, the lines of cleavage will tend to run right through the student body itself. The category of traditional students will perceive the decline in its position of power and status. More than any of the other student categories, it will tend to emphasize status differentials as well as ascriptive criteria, such as social background, membership of certain organizations etc., for the distribution of power. It will tend to reject the use of praetorian measures in conflict, advocating rather the use of the traditionally institutionalized means of a civic arena. Traditional students, moreover, will rather perceive 'the radical students' as their opponents than some higher echelon, such as faculty or administration. The decline in power of the Corps, for instance, will rather be held against the personified rivals among their fellow students than attributed to such causes as structural changes of the arena or the actions of higher echelons. In that sense, then, the conflict will tend to reverberate within the student body; the opposed camps are reflected within its ranks. In the next chapter we will see along what lines this conflict has tended to fan out.

6 Summary

The approach in this chapter is not unlike that of chapter 2. There our main purpose was to elaborate the systematic set of hypotheses concerning conflict and radicalization developed in the first chapter, so as to be able to apply them to the configurations of interests and the patterns of behaviour of right-radical groups. Here our purpose has been, on the basis of the same set of expectations, to develop a framework for the analysis of left-radicalism, as it appeared in the student activism of the 1960s. We have built our argument around a discussion of extreme types, by setting off the transgressive arena in which student radicalism typically occurs, against a traditional arena. Both arenas, as specific elaborations of the general conflict model, are no more than hypothetical constructs. Hopefully, they serve the purpose of highlighting expected configurations of interests; they would acquire explanatory power only if actual research showed these configurations to occur in reality.

What we have done, essentially, is to elaborate the simple diagram of chapter 1, showing four possible configurations of equivalent and inequivalent sets of interests—a combination of two top positions (TT), a combination of one top and one low position (TL and LT), and a combination of two low positions (LL). The basic source of conflict, as we suggested, is the lack of opportunity for TL- or LT-groups to pursue successfully aspirations as induced by primary mobility (cf. chapter 1.8, definition 2). Notwithstanding the more extensive set of interests incorporated in the schemes in this chapter, meant to reflect more realistically the divergent configurations of categories of students, the basic idea is still to project an image of students as subject to the pull of inequivalent interests.

In the traditional arena this inequivalence was not likely to spur radical opposition—small shares of social goods are perceived as transient, as an investment for clearly defined actual *and* future rewards. In the transgressive arena, however, the balance of gratification and deprivation represented by the students' set of interests, has shifted drastically. We indicated a number of possible causes, some structural in nature (caused by changes in the academic situation), some cultural (in so far as groups of students have entered the arena who we presume to have a novel set of standards for the assessment of the legitimacy of small shares, particularly of power). This latter assumption in particular led us to conceive of power deprivations as igniting processes of radicalization rather than deprivations of class or status.

No logical necessity, however, could have kept us from attributing the ignition to these latter deprivations. Yet, on the basis of previous research findings, we have opted for power deprivations. Authors such as Flacks and Keniston have pointed to the acute sense of power deprivation among categories of students. Our assumption, on the other hand, of relatively high shares of class and status in addition to the rather small shares of power, would seem to tie in with conceptions on existential security (or status security, as it is sometimes referred to) which would give radical vanguards the necessary margin of security in their rebellious undertaking. For the radical leadership, according to this view, the odds are fairly limited, due to its position of relative security. Despite the fact that this leadership may come to conceive of its situation as the very epitome of deprivation (cf. chapter 1.8, proposition 4), the basic fact of existential security constitutes a permanent source of distrust in the eyes of those segments of its deprived following which indeed may have nothing to lose but their chains, or rather would not dare risk whatever small shares they have acquired. In spite of professions of solidarity and attempts at the forming of alliances with deprived groups, the leadership may fail in undoing whatever patent elite characteristics it still displays.

In connection with the report in the following chapter on research into student radicalism, we should like to discuss one more point. Our scheme of a transgressive arena referred to *potential* conflict groups; it illustrated the configurations of interests which might cause them to emerge as manifest conflict groups. The piece of research, however, was undertaken at a time (in the spring of 1970) when the fanning-out into rival camps was already in full swing. Therefore we may expect the configurations of interests brought out in the research to reflect the impact of the radical re-orientation which the conflict model refers to (chapter 1.8, propositions 4 and 5). In other words, the processes of activation of deprivations and de-activation of gratifications had been under way for some time. It needs no elaboration that the 'still picture'[18] which the survey technique of research is apt to render is not the most appropriate instrument for the analysis of these longitudinal trends. Yet, as far as possible, we have tried, by the use of retrospective and prospective questions, as well as in our interpretation of the findings, to do justice to the process character of conflict and radicalism.

5 Student radicalism: a survey report

1 Introduction—the research design

In 1970 the author conducted research into radicalism among students at the University of Amsterdam.[1] The main purpose of the research was to gain a better understanding of the rationale of both attitude and action of the left- as well as the right-wings among the student body. A random sample of students would hardly have served this purpose. American research findings in particular clearly show that both wings comprise a very small minority of all students— on the left-wing this minority does not exceed 1·5 to 2 per cent. Therefore two focused samples—or contrast groups—were selected in addition to a regular random sample, the one consisting of left-wing activists, the other of right-wing activists. For the selection of the first contrast group we approached ASVA (General Association of Students) which, at the time of the research, had developed from a politically neutral service organization for furthering and implementing general interests of the student body into a highly politicized, left-wing action centre. From what ASVA itself considered its hard core of activists in the various departments of the university, we obtained the names and addresses of twenty-five students, twenty-three of whom agreed to respond to our questions. For the selection of the contrast group of right-wing activists we approached OBAS (Organization for the Advancement of Student Interests). The year before, OBAS had been set up in response to the politicization of ASVA. Founding OBAS in a sense had been an act of protest against the tide of left-radicalism, enacted by what we might call a deposed elite of student society. The leadership of OBAS came from the traditional fraternal associations, exclusively male or female, that had witnessed a rapid decay of their position of power and esteem among students. Traditionally, spokesmen and representatives of the general student body had been recruited from the membership of these fraternal organizations. Of a total of fifteen student officials of OBAS whose names we had been given, fourteen participated in our research.

In addition to the contrast groups[2] we used a random sample of the total student population of the University of Amsterdam. Of the total 245 students in this sample, thirty-five were non-respondents. The sample served a dual purpose. Findings for the sample as a whole provided us with a yardstick for comparing the responses of the contrast groups. Differences between these groups will stand out more clearly once they are shown to deviate consistently and in opposed directions from findings for a representative sample.[3] In addition to this, we wanted to divide the sample itself into sub-samples, according to their scores on an index of right versus left activism, in order to arrive at a rank order of groups ranging from activist leftists through non-activist leftists, and a neutral middle group, to non-activist rightists and activist rightists. The different response patterns of these groups we compared with the findings for the contrast groups. Thus an element of replication had been built into the research design. The design allowed for yet other comparisons to be made. Since we also interviewed the parents of the student respondents, we could check to what extent differences between contrasted groups of students would hold for their parents. To the extent that our questions covered objective data such as income, occupation, education and voting behaviour of the parents— questions put to both students and their parents—pairing and comparing of the responses gave us a clue as to their reliability.

We propose to structure the following report on research findings around the separate treatment of each of the three social goods of class, status and power. Separate attention will then be given to the reference group behaviour characterizing the left and right activists respectively because, according to our hypothesis in chapter 1 (proposition 6), one of the momentous events in a course of conflict is the radical turnabout of that behaviour. Finally, the research findings allow us to go into the subject of dimensions of radicalism, which may add to the clarity of the profile of left- and right-radicals.

In the report we shall focus on differences prevailing between left- and right-wing activists as these appeared from the responses of the ASVA and OBAS contrast groups; we shall present only those findings, however, which the replication had corroborated. Although actual replication findings may be occasionally inter-spersed in the text, they will be used mainly on a 'stand-by' basis. It is our opinion that the ASVA and OBAS contrast groups are a better reflection of what we have in mind when discussing left- and right-wing activism. They represent groups which actually exist and have actually developed networks of individuals and activities. Our selection of contrast groups would appear to offer a clear advantage over standard survey research techniques where the researcher, on the basis of individual responses, sets out to project categories of respondents which are not likely to reflect precisely actual processes of alliance and opposition formation. These processes, we repeat, are the main object of interest to us. Moreover, in the report we will note that, on the whole, the ASVA and OBAS groups have the most clear-cut profiles and, most outspokenly, as a group 'are of a certain opinion'. This again reflects the fact that in these cases the respondents do have similar backgrounds and do share a network of close relations. For some additional points of methodology, we may refer the reader to Appendix 1, at the end of this chapter.

2 Class position

Each of the following sections will begin with a brief summary of what the author expected to find. Fuller accounts of these expectations, of course, can be found in the preceding chapter, as well as in Table 4.2 on page 78.

Anticipated findings

The left-radical vanguard has a higher social background than the left-radical following or than the average student, though not as high as the right-radical vanguard. In its orientation on job markets and occupational careers it will reject established channels of mobility and success, testifying to its members' inclination to de-activate distributive dimensions on which they rank highly and could expect to rise further (cf. chapter 1.8, proposition 4).

The relationship between radicalism and social background is a matter of persistent scholarly dispute. Research findings here are no more consistent than lay images on the subject.[4] Some findings appear to confirm the image of radical students as an upwardly mobile group that, from non-academic backgrounds, has moved up to reach the university level. Other findings, especially on American radical students, imply the opposite. The radicals, it is found, are rather the best students at the best universities from the best social backgrounds—children from privileged, upper middle-class *milieux* whose fathers are highly likely to have had a university education themselves.

We suggest that the two images are not as inconsistent as may appear at first sight, in that each may be linked to a different stage in the emergence of student activism and student protest. Dutch findings[5] on the initial stage of student protest—what we might call its syndicalist or rather trade-unionist stage—seem to substantiate the first image that we referred to above. Drastic change in the social recruitment of the student body had caused the emergence of novel student interests which the traditional structure of interest aggregation and implementation could not satisfactorily accommodate. The SVB (the Students' Trade Union), founded in response to this novel situation, was an instance of radical innovation, especially in its use of strategy and terminology derived from syndical action in, for example, the economic and political arenas. The emphasis in this stage was on militant advancement of student interests rather than on politicization and political mobilization of the student body. Our hypothesis is that the evident trend towards politicization and the adoption of an emancipist stance during the latter part of the 1960s may well have been accompanied by a change in the recruitment of radical leadership, thus bringing the later stages of student protest in the Netherlands more in line with events in America.

Our research appears to support this hypothesis.[6] A number of separate measurements of social background, such as father's occupation, income of the father, self-ranking by parents and children on a four-point scale, ranging from working class to upper class, consistently gave the following result: both left-wing and right-wing activists had higher social backgrounds than the random sample taken as a whole; left-wing activists slightly lagged behind their right-wing counterparts, although statistically the difference was not significant.

One measure of social background, meant to assess the existence of an academic tradition over three generations, back to the grandparents, rendered results that were not completely consistent, neither internally nor in the context of the other findings. Both grandparents and grandchildren among the categories of left-wing and right-wing radicals had significantly higher proportions of academically trained persons than the sample; the generation of parents of left-wing radicals, however, was significantly below the level of either the right-wing or the sample as a whole.

The pattern of mobility across the generations is one of steady ascension on the social ladder. The ranking on a scale of occupational prestige of grandfather's occupation, father's present and previous occupations as well as the father's assessment of his upward mobility bear this out; the latter measurement most significantly so for fathers of left-wing and right-wing activists. Also, the respondents' subjective ranking of their social background on a four-point scale, similar to the one referred to above, gave consistent results.

The response of the students to a question concerning the expected future position on this scale, however, rendered a pattern that in the context of our argument is highly striking. The upward trend continues for both the sample and the right-wing students; for left-wing students, however, the trend is reversed, due to the fact that a number of them anticipated a future working-class position. A question concerning the expected future income rendered the lowest estimate on the part of the left-wing, estimates being increasingly higher on the part of the sample and the right-wing respectively. Moreover, the left-wing is least likely to call their career opportunities attractive, clear or auspicious. No majority on the left is ever willing to subscribe to any of these labels, whereas clear majorities of the sample and the right-wing think of their opportunities as attractive and auspicious.

In the general pattern of expectation of future mobility, however, the left-wing radicals return to the fold: a majority of each of the three categories anticipates future mobility. As to future mobility in comparison with their fathers' actual position, anticipations are somewhat reduced, notably so for the left- and right-wing radicals—not surprising perhaps, on account of the relatively high ranking of their fathers' actual position. Here, 19 per cent of the left-radicals even anticipate finishing below their fathers' position (compared with 8 per cent of the right-wing and 7 per cent of the sample).[7]

Let us consider these findings somewhat more deeply. The general picture of inter-generational mobility and high social background prevailing among our respondents might cause the emergence of radicalism to appear more difficult to explain than would research findings depicting the leftist radicals as newcomers to academia. In our case, it would seem, the combination of parental mobility and parental achievement of which the students themselves are aware, as their assessment of their social background bears out, would provide the younger generation with a self-assured confidence in its success. Thus, any commitment to a radical movement might seem unwarranted.

One explanation, brought forward by the French sociologist Boudon among others,[8] tackles the problem by focusing on the relatively depressed expectations about future careers and occupations that our research too has established. According to him, the expectation of deteriorating market chances and of future rewards far below the measure of present investments might constitute a powerful explanatory factor of the student protest movement. Leaving aside the point that in our terminology this would rather be an instance of right-radical reaction, our research has produced findings that may suggest a different explanation.

In general terms, this explanation holds that the depressed expectation level of the leftist radicals is not so much a cause of their radical leanings as the consequence of it. They have developed an outlook on the future that is biased by the perspective of an existing radical orientation. The self-ranking on a scale containing terms of high ideological loading such as 'working class' and 'upper class', may especially induce left-radical students, eager to denounce the power structure of capitalism, to refrain from voluntary incorporation into the upper class. Rather, it will provoke them to opt for the more congenial concept of the working class. This we might interpret as evidence of a shift in reference group behaviour that is characteristic of left-wing radicalism—a point we shall elaborate shortly. In contrast to Boudon's thesis, we hold that the reduction of market chances, evident from the responses of the left radicals, is of their own making. Further evidence for this interpretation may be obtained from the order of preference in which our respondents ranked six different aspects of occupations, presented to them as a set of paired comparisons. The aspects were: leadership, prestige, career opportunities, autonomy, high income, and, finally, the opportunity to work according to one's social commitment.

The right-wing accorded priority to autonomy, then to leadership and third to social commitment. The sample and left-wing also selected these aspects as the most important. However, social commitment climbed to second position for the sample and was considered the most important aspect of work by the left-wing. The parents of each of these three groups consistently thought of autonomy as the paramount aspect, whereas social commitment, from a second place for the parents of sample and left-wing students, fell to fourth position for the parents of the right-wing.[9]

These marked differences in preferences seem to corroborate our view that the reduction of market chances for left-wing students has been self-inflicted. Answers to a question concerning the relative attractiveness of fields of work showed a marked rejection by the left-wing of government service and private industry and, relative to the other groups of respondents, a clear preference for politics and journalism. Also, to our question whether the expected income was considered a fair reward for the investment made, the sample as well as the right-wing answered in the affirmative, whereas the left-wing which, one should remember, had given the lowest estimate, said: no, unfairly high! Once more we see to what extent statements on seemingly objective trends and developments are imbued with ideology and political commitment. It would appear as if the assessment of an individual's position in market and class structures, in the eyes of left-wing radicals, is inextricably linked up with their image of an overall societal ordering about which they have come to develop a coherent, oppositional evaluation.

Thus, to our question as to what inequalities in society they perceived, the left-wing consistently responded in terms of social inequalities, referring to differences in income, education, and status differentials; furthermore, they were the only group to refer to differences in power and autonomy. Both the sample and the right-wing, following references to differences in income, education and status, turned to differences of a strictly individual, non-social sort. The left-wing would appear most likely to use a societal frame of reference and to be aware of the social context of things, particularly in terms of inequality. More specifically, their responses would seem to show a sensitivity to power differentials. We will return to this point shortly.

In this section, however, we want to bring in some results of the replication. On the whole, findings in both stages of the analysis were mutually supporting. In one respect, however, the replication gave different results. In contrast to the findings reported above, the replication showed that the socio-economic background of both left- and right-activists within the sample ranked consistently *below* that of the neutral middle group, whatever specific measure we used. Not all measurements were statistically significant; yet the pattern was sufficiently consistent to mention. We may refer the reader to the Notes for specific information on the significance of these differences.[10]

A tentative interpretation of this finding may run along the following lines. When we call to mind what the preceding chapter has assumed to be the characteristic pattern of differences between a left-radical leadership and its following, we may sketch the first outlines of an explanation to be more fully developed later in this chapter—an explanation according to which the ASVA group of left-activists and the replication category of left-activists can be conceived of as representing leadership and following respectively.[11] Certainly we have been warranted in calling the latter group left-activist: it showed both outspoken leftist views and a willingness to act upon its views. Yet, to this group, being of lower social background than the ASVA group of left-activists, the university offered a much stronger lure of drastic upward movement from its social origins—movement along lines of status, income and education. Entrance to the university offered it enticing rewards to a much greater extent than could possibly be the case for the ASVA group. This constitutes a strategic difference of situation. Needless to say, such rewards must have been tarnished and devalued prior to a group's perceiving an acute sense of deprivation and taking a leftist oppositional stance. It is our hypothesis that the mobilizing actions of a vanguard on the left have created the climate in which this shift from a sense of gratification to one of deprivation is likely to occur. The process implies that the impact of the actions of a left-wing vanguard causes a crystallization of antitheses amongst a population that, up till then, may well have shared a sense of gratification. For, surely, the replication category of right-activist respondents must have been as susceptible as the left-activist category to the attractive force of upward mobility. Yet, for this group, less intent by upbringing on power differentials, a sense of gratification has prevailed. Among its favoured aspects of occupations, for instance, the career opportunities have moved up to second position whereas living up to one's social commitment has gone down to a lowly fifth position (see note 9). Moreover, this group is most concentrated in such fields of study as medicine and economics, both channelling into clear, highly rewarded occupational markets. Finally, to an extent significantly greater than the left-activists, they expect to be upwardly mobile in the future. We take this unwavering intentness upon individual mobility, along with the threat that left-wing manoeuvring may constitute to their chosen course in life, to be the main cause of their moving to a reactionary stance.

For a fuller elaboration of this picture we shall have to analyse the balance of gratification and deprivation for the remaining goods of power and status. As in this section, we shall focus on the differences between the ASVA left-wing, the sample, and the OBAS right-wing and explicitly refer to the replication only to the extent that it rendered different findings.

3 Power

Anticipated findings

We expect the left-wing, unlike the sample or the right-wing, to have been reared in families where the style of upbringing and of intercourse are characterized by tolerance, equality and democratic values. As to the perception of power differences, we expect the left-wing to have a keener eye for their incidence than both other groups, in addition to an acute sense of powerlessness where its own situation is concerned.

A number of explanations of student radicalism focus on aspects of generational divergence and generation conflict. Radicalism is sometimes conceived of as the final step towards adulthood, the ultimate emancipation from parental authority. An extreme example is Feuer's analysis,[12] which grants the break with parental authority the dramatic contours of the Oedipal patricide.

An analysis in terms of both generational divergence and similarity, and leading to an altogether different explanation of student radicalism, is encountered in studies by Flacks, Keniston, Heist and Lammers.[13] Research by these authors shows that radical students, rather than rebelling in attitude and action against the parental ethos, actually strongly resembled their parents, although convictions that prevailed among the parents had become more pronounced and accentuated among their children. Just as the left-wing radicals deviate from dominant student opinions, their parents' convictions are to the left of the prevailing outlook among their generation. Moreover, according to Flacks and Keniston, the climate of authority in the parental homes of radical students is different from the climate in which other students have been brought up in the sense that the former have grown up in an atmosphere of greater tolerance and greater equality. Age in their families has not served as the traditional basis for the attribution of authority and status. In other words, in these homes the children have grown accustomed to an equality of rights; they have not been trained to feel automatically subordinated to the authority of those who are older. According to this explanation, previously suggested by Parsons and Eisenstadt,[14] the definite break between the climate of authority in the parental home and that in contexts which the children enter upon leaving their parents causes them to oppose more authoritarian systems of authority. Both with regard to the alleged politico-ideological consensus and the climate of authority in the parental home, our research offers relevant data.

First, we will consider the climate of authority. We asked both parents and children to characterize the styles in which each group had been brought up as well as the style in which the parents had brought up their children. We presented four separate scales to the respondents, ranging respectively from 'democratic' to 'authoritarian', from 'modern' to 'traditional', from 'on equal footing' to 'on unequal footing', and finally, from 'tolerant' to 'austere'. Parents of left-wing students appeared to respond differently from parents of our sample of students and, even more outspokenly so, from parents of right-wing students. In Table 5.1 we indicate both the style in which, according to the parents, the children have been brought up, and (in parentheses) the style in which they were brought up themselves, according to their own account. To a question whether the parents had wanted to bring up their children in a way similar to the one in which they had been brought up themselves, 35 per cent of the parents of left-wing students answered in the affirmative (against 43 per cent for the sample and 64 per cent for the right wing). Among parents who had wanted to bring up their children differently, parents of left-wing students, more often than those of the other categories, referred to an upbringing in a more tolerant, democratic way (34 per cent against 27 per cent and 12 per cent) or to an upbringing in an atmosphere of greater freedom and autonomy (24 per cent against 19 per cent and 17 per cent).

TABLE 5.1 *Style of upbringing of children (and of parents), as characterized by the parents (in %)*

	Sample	Left-wing radicals	Right-wing radicals
democratic	72 (32)	79 (45)	62 (23)
modern	46 (22)	60 (16)	24 (9)
on equal footing	44 (14)	50 (13)	30 (5)
tolerant	66 (34)	87 (37)	45 (18)

(Differences of 14% between right-wing and left-wing are significant on the 20% level; the same condition holds for differences of 12% between right-wing and sample and for differences of 9% between left-wing and sample. Cf. Appendix 1)

The characterization that the students themselves gave of their upbringing exhibits a remarkable pattern (for the replication we may refer to the Notes).[15]

In Table 5.2 we see that those aspects that specifically refer to authority relations (democratic-undemocratic and equality-inequality) lead the left to score lowest! The striking dissonance between the intentions of the parents and the perceptions of the children might be accounted for in the following way. It is plausible to assume that the intentions of the parents to bring up their children democratically and on an equal footing have come across in the sense that they provided the children with a high standard for the evaluation of the actual educational practice. The latter, apparently, fell far below this standard. The patent dissonance, then, would arise from the

TABLE 5.2 *Style of upbringing of children, characterized by the children (in %)*

	Sample	Left-wing radicals	Right-wing radicals
democratic	58	39 (!)	54
modern	36	43	28
on equal footing	47	43	31
(on unequal footing)	25	43 (!)	31
tolerant	60	70	50

(For the significance of the data, cf. Table 5.1)

merciless account on the part of leftist radicals of the educational failure of their parents. Further it would seem that, especially in the portrayal of their upbringing as either on an equal or an unequal footing, two sub-groups emerge within the body of left-wing radicals, groups which we might call Jacobins and Girondists. The former tend to abide uncompromisingly by educational values and norms, the latter are more latitudinarian. We will come across other instances of this divergence shortly.

Next, let us focus on the politico-ideological climate. We asked the students to characterize the political views of their fathers and mothers separately on a five-point scale, ranging from progressive to conservative. 54 per cent of the leftist radicals considered their fathers progressive (against 33 per cent of the sample and 23 per cent of the right-wing); 43 per cent considered their mothers progressive (against 30 per cent and 21 per cent). In response to a similar question, 72 per cent of the parents of left-wing students considered themselves progressive (against 43 per cent and 26 per cent). As to their voting behaviour, 58 per cent of these parents cast their votes for one of the left-wing political parties (the Dutch Labour Party—*Partij van de Arbeid*, a socialist splinter party—Pacifist Socialist Party, and the Communist Party of the Netherlands) against 43 per cent and 26 per cent respectively. Among the students themselves, asked to indicate their present party preference, 78 per cent of the left-wing favoured leftist parties or the 'New Left' opposition wing within the Dutch Labour Party, against 43 per cent of the sample and 8 per cent of the right-wing.

In this context too, we inquired into the exchange of opinions between parents and students on the following subjects: study results, problems relating to the study, and academic problems in a general sense. For the students we cannot discern differences between the radicals and the sample on the first two subjects; on the third subject, however, both the left- and the right-wing engaged in more frequent exchange with their parents than did the sample. The answers of the parents bear out this pattern even more markedly; the frequency of exchange increases for parents of left-wing students as the subject changes from study results to academic problems; for the parents of the sample and the right-wing the frequency decreases in this order. With regard to the similarity of views in these exchanges, 55 per cent of the left-wing students usually disagree with their parents (against 31 per cent and 14 per cent), whereas, on the other hand, 36 per cent usually agree (against 33 per cent and 43 per cent). A majority of the parents of left-wing students declare that they usually agree with their children (53 per cent) against 47 per cent and 68 per cent. Once more, the left-wing student response shows the division between Jacobins and Girondists.[16]

A survey of these results, taken together, warrants an interpretation that preserves elements of each of the contending explanations in terms of generation conflict and inter-generational similarity. Our research clearly shows that, in politico-ideological respects, the left-wing radicals have outspokenly left-wing family backgrounds. As regards the climate of authority, the parents of left-wing students apparently responded in ways that betoken similarity rather than conflict. The way in which these intentions have affected the left-wing students, however, warrants the interpretation that, especially for the Jacobins amongst their number, parental authority has been drastically done away with. Compared with other groups of students, theirs is the only one to reject their own upbringing as a guide for the education of their children; a number among them explicitly refer to the negative experience of an authoritarian upbringing and lack of autonomy.

How do these primary confrontations with the exercise of power in social situations affect the perception and evaluation of the climate of authority of the university? In our research we have tried to answer this question for a variety of reaches of power at the university, ranging from the immediate field of study, through the climate of authority in particular departments, to the decision-making structure of the university at large, affecting the entire student body.

With regard to the immediate field of study, we asked whether, according to the students, their field of study had become more tightly organized. Of the left-wing 77 per cent answered in the affirmative, against 51 per cent of the sample and 43 per cent of the right-wing. To the extent that the question 'tapped' the experience of students of being increasingly regimented, the answers provided us with further proof of the left-wing's inclination to feel powerless;[17] the right-wing, on the other hand, was far less inclined to feel deprived.

This impression finds further support in the answers to a question whether the tighter organization of their field of study made sense to our respondents. To about half the sample and half the right-wing radicals, compared with 83 per cent of the left-wing, it did not. Again, the left-wing, asked to elaborate on its considerations, referred about twice as frequently as the other groups to 'lack of student power', no 'training for independent thinking', no clear 'relevance' to either fields of individual or of social interest.[18]

The somewhat wider domain of power relations at the departmental level, as apparent from the style of intercourse with faculty and the style of decision-making at that level, rendered similar results. The sample and the right-wing did not differ very much in their evaluation of what can be summarily called the climate of authority in the department. It is never the case that a majority characterizes the climate as tolerant, democratic, on an equal footing, or personal. The left-wing, however, is consistently some fifteen percentage points below the scores of the other categories (for the replication, see note 23).

One of our questions, covering a still wider area, asked for the students' assessment of their actual influence as well as their opinions on what measure of influence they desired to have. We presented three areas of influence to our respondents:
(a) their work situation (comprising such aspects as subjects of term papers, course programmes, regulations pertaining to length of study etc.);
(b) student facilities (i.e. 'student interests' in a restricted sense, as measured by influence on student housing policy);
(c) university management.
We tried, moreover, to assess the degree of urgency with which change in the influence of students was desired.

All categories of respondents agreed that student influence in each of these fields was small, most obviously so in the field of university management. The left-radicals scored consistently lowest, the right-radicals highest. As to desired influence, each category insisted on having a majority vote in the area of student facilities. With regard to their work situation, the right-radicals are the most likely to settle on a fifty-fifty share, whereas the others, especially the left-wing, still uphold their desire for a majority vote. A comparison of the groups of respondents according to their estimated sense of urgency shows the radical wings to have opposed priorities. The left-wing accords highest priority to an increase of the influence of students on university management, then to an increase of influence in matters of student facilities and, third, to influencing the work situation. Both the sample and the right-wing, on the other hand, consider the more immediate student interests (both in the work situation and the area of student facilities) to have the highest urgency, whereas influencing the course of events beyond these immediate interests is given far lower priority.

Indeed, these results come as no surprise, considering the fact that OBAS, from which our right-wing radicals were taken, emphatically rejects the trend towards politicization and social commitment that ASVA stands for; OBAS explicitly focuses its activities on the advancement of student interests in a restricted sense.

The answers of the left-wing allow us to make some further comments. On a number of occasions in the answers pertaining to the desired measure of influence, the Jacobins and Girondists appear, *increasingly so as matters of university management are concerned rather than the more immediate student interests*. Specifically in relation to university management the Jacobins appear as maximalists who will not settle for anything less than exclusive student power, whereas the Girondists prefer a proportional student share of power. It would appear as if the 'lust for power' of the Jacobins especially concerns those areas of academic decision-making which have the widest reach and which, moreover, are at the centre of the exchange with other powerful institutions in society; in the eyes of the Jacobins, pure student interests no longer constitute crucial issues or incentives to action.

A further glimpse of the divergent attitudes towards student influence and the power distribution at universities, can be gathered from our respondents' preference for different modes of student participation in decision-making. We asked our respondents to choose from four options: a minimal advisory student voice, representative government with a fixed parity for students and faculty, direct democracy on the basis of one man, one vote, and, finally, a highly decentralized form which we can term a council structure. Large majorities of the left-radicals opted for the council structure (78 per cent) and direct democracy (74 per cent); the sample preferred the council structure (60 per cent) and the fixed-parity structure (56 per cent). On the radical right, finally, none of the alternatives invoked a majority preference; the fixed-parity system received strongest support (43 per cent).

Next, we will turn to the wider, though related, theme of the images of the power structure which the different response groups hold.[19] A first question bearing on this point inquired into the share of power in university management that our respondents allotted to a variety of groups: the board of curators,[20] senior faculty, junior faculty, the student body, the clerical workers, ASVA, private industry. We also inquired into the share that our respondents thought each group should have. Clear differences between left-wing, right-wing and sample emerged.

According to the right-wing, the actual power structure is one in which the board of curators has the largest share of power, closely followed by the senior faculty. The junior faculty is allotted some power, the other groups little to very little. We might conceive of this portrayal as approaching a type of organization which Lammers calls a hierarchy of administrative offices.[21] The board of curators, as the top executive level, is the formal employer and fulfils a watch-dog function in the public interest; the implementation of the central aims of the university, as prescribed by law, are bestowed on the collective body of the senior faculty. With regard to the power structure as it should be, the right-wing more clearly brings out the central function of the university, in that the senior faculty, as main guardian and instrument of this function, is allotted most power; the junior faculty, however, receives only a tiny share. The watch-dog

101

role of the administration, i.e. the board of curators, although markedly reduced, still has a sizeable share of power. Such a power structure we might, borrowing once more from Lammers, take to approach a professional model of organization. Elements of 'noise' in this professional model with its measure of administrative surveillance have vanished on account of ASVA and private industry losing what little power they had been considered to wield.

On balance, the redistribution of power leads to a power deflation, a decrease in the total reservoir which the respondents thought actually existed. Rival powers as well as mutual dependence have been removed from the picture. The senior faculty remains as the one relatively autonomous group.

The response of parents of right-wing students does not replicate this shift from a hierarchy of administrative offices to a professional model. Both the actual and the desired power distribution display the traits of the former model, although once more, on balance, a power deflation occurs. In view of this deflation, it is noteworthy that those groups involved in the exercise of the profession—senior and junior faculty as well as students—are each allotted somewhat larger shares of power.

On the left-wing the picture is strikingly different. The actual power distribution is conceived of as starkly dichotomous. Those in possession of power are firstly the curators, closely followed by the senior faculty and private industry. Little to very little power is wielded by the junior faculty, the students, the clerical workers and ASVA. Such a picture does not allow of description in terms of models of organization or of types of institutional or constitutional power. The image clearly belongs to a tradition of leftist thought which views constitutions as the sham of covert power alliances. We might call it, borrowing from C. W. Mills, a power elite model.

Conceptions of the situation as it should be are in the same vein. The resulting image is one of revolutionary reversal. The established wielders of power, *except the senior faculty*, are completely deposed; the alliance of the previously powerless takes over, with the students as a self-styled proletarian vanguard pre-empting the largest share, leaving large shares to the junior faculty and the clerical workers. About an equal share is allotted to the senior faculty which, not unlike tsarist generals in the Red Army, is maintained by the revolutionary regime.

Responses regarding the increase of power of junior faculty, students and clerical workers repeatedly display the difference, noted earlier, between maximalist Jacobins and proportionalist Girondists. Here, again, the disagreement centres on the organization of power through an effective alliance rather than on the design of a new constitutional order for regulating the struggle between rival powers and interests. Yet the relative stability of the share of power of the senior faculty seems to indicate that the victorious alliance still acknowledges the need for professional expertise whatever the effects in other respects wrought by the revolutionary revamping of the university.

The response of the sample constitutes a mid-point between the ideological wings in that its perception of the actual power distribution betrays the cynical sophistication of the left-wing in unmasking power elites. Again, the picture is dichotomous. The sample's conceptions of the situation as it should be, on the other hand, are more nearly like those held by the right-wing; they approach the model of a professional organization with an amount of administrative surveillance that, compared with the right-wing's position, is still further reduced.

Next, if we compare the overall increase or decrease of power that accompanies the shift from the actual to the desired power distribution, only the left-wing wants an overall power inflation; for the sample the reservoir of power remains approximately the same, whereas the right-wing, similar to its parents in this respect, wants a power deflation. We may tentatively interpret this as evidence that, in the eyes of the right-wing, naked power may be somewhat disgusting and in need of regulation and containment; on the left-wing, however, power exerts an equivocal fascination in the sense that it might be safely inflated once it passes from the hands of the adversary into those of one's own allies.

Parents of left-wing students, finally, do resemble their children in the assessment of the actual power distribution, but, with regard to the desired situation, opt for the professional model with a slight measure of administrative surveillance. The parents of students in the sample, in contrast, hold the actual situation to be one of a hierarchy of administrative offices which they desire to be replaced by a professional model with a strong administrative watch-dog role.

Our research also inquired into the actual and the desired distribution of power in society at large. In general, the findings here reflect the patterns which we have just reported. For the portrayal of what appear to be opposed views of the societal power structure, it may be illuminating to introduce concepts coined in the debate among American political scientists, sociologists and historians between the consensus school and the radicals. The former has advocated the pluralist or, in Dahl's terms, the polyarchical view of the distribution of power in society, whereas the latter have stood for the power elite view, forcefully introduced by Mills.[22]

We asked our respondents to indicate both their perceptions of the actual distribution of power and what they thought should be its distribution among the following categories: big business, political parties, trade unions, religious denominations, agrarian interests, the government, university graduates. The right-wing in our research closely approximates to a pluralist position. Government is allotted the largest share of power, followed by the political parties as the established channel for the input of political support and political demands; big business and the trade unions, each with somewhat smaller shares than both government and political parties, are ordered around the established power system as co-equal interest groups. The image of the situation as it should be is still pluralist, although the naked power of the interest groups has been reduced. On balance, a clear deflation of power occurs. For the parents of right-wing students, the findings are similar.

The left-wing, on the contrary, perceives the actual situation as highly elitist: it allots big business a very large share of power, government and political parties a large share, the other categories small to very small shares. In view of the excess of power allotted to big business, we may rightfully interpret government and political parties as the instruments which serve the interests of a capitalist power elite. The situation as it should be is still conceived of along elitist lines; here, however, the distribution of power is the radical reverse of the perceived actual situation. Trade unions are the one category to be allotted a large share of power, government takes a lame-duck, intermediate position, the other categories are left in possession of small to very small shares of power. On balance, a power deflation occurs, mainly, we suppose, because our list of categories contained too few trustworthy allies for the revolutionary reversal of the power distribution.

The parents of the left-wing students also perceive the actual situation as elitist. Their conceptions of the situation as it should be, however, more nearly approximate to a pluralist model. Here the situation is kept under strong, what we might call working-class surveillance on account of the relative share of power of the trade unions, placed next to the government.

Finally, the students of the sample take the actual situation to be one of domination by a power elite. They too project a pluralist perspective on the situation as it should be; again, it should be kept under working-class surveillance. In both respects, the parents behave in ways similar to their children. In this case, too, for both parents and children, a power deflation occurs.

In conclusion of this section on power position and power images, a few remarks. Our analysis of social background and style of upbringing of left-wing students in the preceding section has led us to emphasize their acute awareness of phenomena of power, their keen perception of power differentials and their inclination to feel more acutely deprived in these respects than other groups of students.

This impression has been substantiated in the present section. Their sophistication in unveiling power structures and in taking a stark view of the exercise of power is coupled with a willingness to acquire power for themselves. We will have occasion to go more deeply into the strategies deployed and the alliances engaged in this endeavour. Here, suffice it to say that their adroitness in competing for power characterizes them more than any of the other categories as 'political animals'. They are the one group that clearly attests to its being politically interested (65 per cent of this group against clear minorities of the sample and the radical right). In the previous section we discussed the point that its sensitivity to and intentness on deprivations of power may have led the radical left to reduce autonomously its market opportunities and to reject 'normal' career patterns. In the following, we propose to analyse whether a similar downward adaptive response can be perceived in the definition of its status position which the radical left holds.

Before proceeding to the next section, however, some comments on the findings of the replication. Except for one result,[23] the replication rendered findings similar to those presented above. One more finding may serve to complement the picture. Both the analysis of the focused samples and the replication showed that a minority on the left, against a majority on the right, tended to affirm questions about whether the respondent anticipated a larger 'say' in his future working life than presently as a student, about whether he expected to have greater autonomy and, finally, more opportunity to voice his opinions. Once more, on the left, the experience of the distribution of power tends to go hand in hand with a sense of deprivation, whereas, on the right, the sense of deprivation is either far more muted or even clearly outweighed by the anticipation of future rewards, as in the case just mentioned. For the group of left-wing activists within the representative sample, tentatively described as a left-wing following at the end of the preceding section, the findings in this section offer strong evidence of the force of deprivations which may work to counter effectively the attraction of opportunities of upward mobility.

4 Status position

Anticipated findings

We expect left-radical students to be more acutely aware of traditional status distinctions and of their deprivations in that respect. More than the other categories, they will show the de-activation of status and prestige.

Let us first try and find out whether the social good of status is relevant at all as a point of reference for our respondents. There is little
use in assessing orientations towards a good which receives only
marginal attention. A question directly tackling this problem showed
that a majority of all groups concerned thought of differences of
prestige as highly unimportant. Yet, among left-wing respondents,
30 per cent attested to their being highly intent on such differences,
against 22 per cent for the sample and 7 per cent for the right-wing.
The display of deference towards others solely on account of their
position, 83 per cent of the left-radicals deemed unjustified, against
61 per cent and 43 per cent.[24] Furthermore, since the ordering of
people in a social context according to differences in prestige
materializes as a set of rules of courteous intercourse, the opinions of
our respondents on these rules offer relevant data. A number of
statements on the positive functions of rules of courtesy for the
functioning of organizations showed marked differences in response,
for both parents and children, between the left- and the right-wings;
a majority on the left disagreed with the statements, in clear contrast
with the right-wing. A contrasting question ('emphasizing rules of
courteous intercourse is one of the means to keep students in their
place') received the approval of 70 per cent of the left-radicals
against 14 per cent of the radical right; for the parents the difference
pointed in the same direction, although majorities on both wings
disagreed.

Let us now proceed to the images of actual and desired distribu-

TABLE 5.3 *Images held by students on the distribution of status in
society at large among a number of academic professions,
reflecting the situation as it is and as it should be
(as appears from the mode on a five-point scale
ranging from 1—very little, to 5—very much prestige,
as well as from the modal percentage, given in
parentheses)*

Professions requiring degrees in:	Sample		Left-wing radicals		Right-wing radicals	
	actual	desired	actual	desired	actual	desired
law	4 (53)	3 (51)	4 (43)	3 (50)	4 (50)	3 (36)
sociology	3 (44)	3 (51)	2 (52)	3 (73)	2 (50)	3 (29)
medicine	5 (72)	3 (45)	5 (74)	3 (68)	5 (71)	4 (50)
economics	4 (50)	3 (50)	4 (56)	3 (77)	4 (64)	4 (50)
Dutch language	3 (48)	3 (57)	3 (48)	3 (73)	3 (64)	3 (36)
chemistry	4 (49)	3 (53)	4 (70)	3 (82)	4 (50)	4 (36)

tions of status which our respondents hold. Of special relevance here may be a question inquiring into such images concerning the differences in prestige between a number of academic professions in society at large. Our questionnaire contained a list of professions requiring degrees in the following fields: law, sociology, medicine, economics, Dutch language and literature, chemistry. Opinions on the actual prestige connected with each of these professions did not vary significantly between sample, left- and right-wing, for both parents and children. The desired order, however, showed interesting differences. The right-wing, both parents and students, slightly retouches the picture but still ends up with a rank order of differences. But the left-wing and, though somewhat less outspokenly, the sample tend to eradicate all differentiation *in the sense that each profession is relegated to the mid-point of the scales where it commands neither much, nor little prestige.*[25] In other words, prestige itself, as a ground of human inequality, is banned. This might relate to a conception among leftist radicals of established status differentials constituting a system of fake rewards in society that keeps men from an awareness of their real interests and from action based on it.

Once more, as in the case of the self-imposed reduction in market opportunities, we see the overbearing impact of the sense of power deprivation. Once this deprivation has come to be the main criterion on which to distinguish allies from opponents, the reduction of market chances as well as of status differentials takes on the strategic character of a razing of barriers between potential allies. This, we hold, is the meaning of the shift in reference group behaviour towards a 'horizontal' oppositional stance; this, too, is what makes it one of the crucial processes in the emergence of radicalism.

In addition to this, we want to point out that the replication, most outspokenly for the category of left-activists, bore out a similar devaluation of the good of social status. This may serve to add final detail to our replication category of left-activists. By now it clearly stands out as a group which, in the assessment of its relative shares, closely resembles the group which we have chosen to consider as a left-radical vanguard. It is, however, different, due to the fact that this assessment, for all its apparent similarity, has required a de-activation of the attractive force of mobility chances far more drastic than was the case for the radical vanguard.

5 Reference group behaviour

Anticipated findings

In so far as the left-radicals constitute a mobilizing vanguard in search of a following, we expect them to show a clear orientation towards deprived groups in society on the basis of similarities which they perceive between their own situation and that of these deprived groups.

In our inquiry into reference group behaviour we made several approaches from different directions. In the first place we attempted to assess the level of participation in student society outside the immediate field of study. Both the left- and the right-wing had much higher levels than the sample. For the right-wing the main factor was its frequency of interaction with classmates beyond the sphere of study as well as with Amsterdam students in different fields of study. In these respects the left also scored higher than the sample; the left scored highest, however, as to the frequency of interaction with students from other universities.[26]

This we may take to be a first, though tentative, sign of the different character of reference group behaviour on the left-, as opposed to the right-wing. For the right-wing, this behaviour might be aptly called local or parochial, oriented to interests as they rise in the immediate province of experience. For the left-wing, the character is rather cosmopolitan,[27] based on an interpretation of interests that transcends one's own province. This distinction is brought out more clearly in the response to a question whether or not the respondents spent most of their time with other students. The right-wing, in large majority (86 per cent), answered in the affirmative against 45 per cent of the sample and 48 per cent of the left-wing.[28] The same picture emerges from the response to a question as to what, according to the respondents, were the two main causes of the existing tension at universities across the country. We presented to our respondents a list of ten options more or less closely related to the institutional context of the university, such as interference from private industry, interference from the Ministry of Education in university affairs, shortage of faculty, the authoritarian posture of professors, the radical students' actions. Once more we established that, moving from left to right, our respondents increasingly tended to seek the causes more close at hand; their horizons increasingly tended to coincide with the reach of their own province. The left-wing tended to choose such causes as interference from industry and the Ministry of Education, whereas the right-wing incriminated the left-wing by choosing 'the actions of radical students'. This lends support to the expectation formulated in section 5 of the preceding chapter.

Part of this first approach was a question concerning the respondents' opinions on the role of representative bodies of student society, in this case ASVA. We mentioned some spheres of action, ranging from simple observance of student interests in a restricted sense to the active commitment to matters of general social relevance. The left-radicals opted for the broadest possible sphere of action in contrast to the right-radicals who wanted to restrict this sphere to pure student interests.[29]

A second approach was explicitly intended to assess the reference towards a number of intra- as well as extra-mural groups. We had composed a list of groups which, at the time of the survey, had been drawing public attention. On the one hand we listed socially deprived groups (such as foreign migrant labour), groups that were highly stigmatized (such as hippies), or emancipation and protest movements. All these groups we may hold to be liable to positive leftist reference. On the other hand we listed groups whose position of privilege was disputed or openly attacked (such as professors who try to turn the tide of student activism or employers who resent increasing interference from the political sphere). These groups we assume to be liable to positive rightist reference.

We asked the respondents to indicate for each group in the list whether they considered their own position to be similar to, different from or non-comparable with that of the listed groups. The left-wing among our respondents was most likely to perceive similarities. Not surprisingly, we may add, these tended to be between its own situation and that of the leftist reference groups. The sample came next; to the extent that it referred positively at all to the listed groups, it made reference to the leftist groups. The right-wing, in contrast, was most likely to consider its own situation non-comparable with that of any of the listed groups. This finding lends further support to the picture of the right-wing's reference group behaviour as parochial.

We then proceeded to inquire to which two groups the strongest positive reference was made. Both the left-wing and the sample selected leftist reference groups. The left-wing, however, appeared to favour groups whose selection of means of resistance was more violent; the sample was more favourably inclined towards groups whose more restricted deprivation issued in specific demands or which, by and large, stayed within the margin of established procedure. Finally, the right-radicals emphasized similarities with professors trying to turn the tide of student activism and with a presumed 'silent majority in the Netherlands'.

A similar question, inquiring into which two groups were perceived as most strikingly different from the respondents' own situation, rendered a pattern that was almost the perfect reverse of the one sketched above.

We next inquired into both the sense of affiliation with groups to which respondents had positively referred, and the active display of this sense. On the left-wing, 87 per cent attested to its sense of

109

affiliation; 61 per cent claimed to have actively displayed this affiliation in one way or another. For the sample, figures were respectively 55 per cent and 35 per cent; for the right-wing, 25 per cent and 17 per cent. Reverse questions, measuring an attitude of rejection towards groups that our respondents had negatively referred to, as well as the active display of this rejection, rendered the following percentages of affirmative answers: 83 per cent and 65 per cent on the left-wing, 67 per cent and 39 per cent for the sample, 71 per cent and 43 per cent on the right-wing. These results appear to bear out that the left-wing as well as the sample behave similarly towards groups to which they either positively or negatively refer. The right-wing, however, appears to be more outspoken in its attitudes and active display of rejection. This is what makes the right-wing literally reactionary. It needs a sense of *ne plus ultra*, a perception of social groups trespassing bounds of orderly behaviour, to provoke it into action. Therefore, it is the true guardian of orderly and gradual change, if not of a *status quo*.[30]

One more question from our survey may be in order here. We presented to the respondents a variety of actions open to students in the case of a breakdown of consultation between students and ruling bodies of the university. These actions ranged from the highly peaceful, such as demonstrations and the use of mass media of communication, to the highly forceful, such as occupying the administration building. None of these actions was condoned by a majority of the right-wing, whereas the left-wing assented to each of them. The ordering of means of action according to the percentage of each group that approved of the respective actions showed striking differences between the left-wing on the one hand, the sample and the right-wing on the other. For the latter, assent decreases as the actions become more forceful and violent. The left-wing approves most strongly of the use of the media and the occupation of the administration building, as well as of occupying classrooms through sit-in actions.[31] It would seem as if the outstanding position of the occupation of the administration building and of sit-in actions betrays two related motives. On the one hand, they are forceful means; they betray a greater distrust in relatively legitimate means of pressure such as mass gatherings and demonstrations. This aspect of the differential evaluation of legitimacy and efficacy will occupy us in the next section. On the other hand, of all the means presented, these are the most spectacular and dramatic, and as such may help us add further detail to the characteristic reference group behaviour of the radical left. The means of action which it prefers may serve its purpose of dramatically communicating to the outside world the sharpness of conflict at the university. They are forceful means which may bully the outside world into taking sides, thus separating supporters from opponents. The choice of forceful means of action along with the use of the media betrays an awareness on the radical left of non-academic publics whose interests may tie in with those on which radical students are ready to act.[32]

This interpretation finds further support in the fact that the left-wing was the only one of the groups under study to show a majority consenting to the participation of non-students in the climactic occupation of the administration building in the spring of 1969. The reasons they gave referred to considerations that the conflict did not centre solely on the university and that students and non-students are involved in one and the same struggle, embracing all of society, and that, by consequence, they confront the same set of opponents.

6 Dimensions of radicalism

We presented a list of seventy-three statements to all our respondents which they could either agree or disagree with. The statements cover a limited range of subjects which we hold to reflect important dimensions of the phenomenon of radicalism. The reduction of the statements to this limited set of meanings was effected firstly according to the meaning which these statements represented to us; it was validated with both a cluster analysis and an analysis of the consistency with which the statements separated left- and right-radicals (cf. Appendix 2 of this chapter). The dimensions which this set of procedures produced can be summarized as follows.

A number of statements referred to the *maturity* of students, to their ability to be involved in matters of university administration as well as their ability to assess their situation autonomously, irrespective of limitations of age and life-cycle. A second set of statements referred to the differential evaluation of the *functions of forms of civil intercourse* in society. We referred to these above. In connection with this set, a third was intended to measure the value accorded *efficiency* and efficacious functioning of organizations in society, particularly the university. Under the heading of *praetorianism* we subsumed statements concerning the admissibility of a variety of means for student actions. Moreover, we measured the incidence of a *reference to the world outside the university*. Next, we distinguished three dimensions, of *political radicalism* in a broad sense, *politicization* (referring to the penetration of politico-social engagement in the academic arena), and *democratization*. Finally, that which may constitute the keynote of radicalism, the point from which the other dimensions can be thought to radiate, we termed *the radical creed*. All these dimensions allowed us to analyse differences between left- and right-radicals, as well as inter-generational differences and similarities. Let us first examine the radical creed.

Two statements can be considered as indicative of the radical creed. These are, respectively: 'the prevailing social system, rather than human nature, should be held responsible for aggressiveness and violence'; and: 'man will never be able to build the ideal society'. The left-wing, in majority, tended to consent to the first statement and to reject the second, whereas the right-wing showed the reverse pattern. Both statements together may illuminate the underlying rationale of the left-wing position. Once social wrongs are deemed attributable to human action as instituted in social systems and, at the same time, it is considered within man's capacity to create a 'good' society, we have uncovered the basic dimension of an optimistic creed which serves to project cohesive meaning on the other dimensions of radicalism. Moreover, it will be possible to translate differences between the left- and the right-wing, and between the generations, in terms of the basic opposition of an optimistic versus a pessimistic outlook.

In that context one thing is immediately apparent—the rift between left-radical students and their parents. Although parents of left-wing radicals are still more prone than parents of right-wing radicals to subscribe to the optimistic creed, yet a definite majority of both groups asserts the inability of human beings ever to build an ideal society. At this point, on the left-wing, generations part company—the optimism of the young is not (or no longer?) shared by the grown-ups.

Let us first set about analysing the internal consistency of the left-wing outlook. Given their acceptance of the radical creed— pertaining to human society in its entirety—it is small wonder that left-radicals score highly on dimensions which reflect a fluidization of societal compartments. When actions aim at the transformation of society as a whole, 'dominant' conceptions on societal compartments and boundaries would interfere unacceptably with this endeavour. Hence the trend towards politicization—towards the introduction of urgent social problems within the confines of academia; hence, moreover, the striking reference to and impulse towards alliance with non-university groups of dispossessed. Given the immediate, urgent task at hand, furthermore, as great a margin of action as possible is required *vis-à-vis* positions of authority— hence the rejection of precepts of deferential behaviour as these are enjoined and enforced 'from above' for positions of subordination in society, positions as, for example, that of student (apprentice) or youngster. Hence, we may add, the low score on statements justifying forms of civil intercourse as well as the demand for full participation as mature members, in spite of their positions of apprentice and youngster. When, moreover, the issue is to take a revolutionary stance towards an established societal structure, considerations of

112

efficiency and bureaucratic rationality, prevailing in the established system, have lost their import. It need not surprise, then, that the left-wing radicals do not shrink from the use or advocacy of forceful means such as violence to remain true to their creed. Finally, it would appear as if the most direct reference to the ideal—where the fusion of means and ends occurs—is contained in the dimension of democratization.

Such an impetuous radiance of the radical creed over the entire range of attitudes and convictions would lose its compelling nature once the basic creed is impaired. The pessimism of the parents of left-wing students (quite conceivably the cumulative result of existential experiences) leads them to reject the extreme consequences which their offspring tend to connect with their basic optimism. Thus the parents agree to statements pointing out the dangers of totalitarian coercion and minoritarian terror inherent in politicization. Thus they shrink from justifying violence with an appeal to ideal ends. It finally leads them—and this would appear the most telling sign of generational divergence—to let their children down when these proclaim their maturity.

In its greatest consistency these implications of the basic sense of pessimism appear in the positions taken by the right-wing respondents. Pessimism has been referred to earlier as the underlying outlook of conservatism;[33] it comprises a fundamental distrust of the pretensions of the 'sorcerer's apprentice', in addition to a sense that the regulation and restraint of human behaviour, as traditionally established, is a good unto itself, worthy of preservation. This would allow us to depict right-wing radicalism as more than just the negative reflection of the left-wing image. We can add more positive traits. Right-radicalism would seem to be characterized mainly by its tendency to subscribe to established processes and structures—structures of authority as well as of submission and deference, linked traditionally with criteria such as age, experience, maturity. An additional characteristic would be its tendency to value the efficient functioning of human organizations as a good unto itself, serving as a crucial standard for the evaluation of left-radical actions. Closely connected with this is the distrust of democratization, of the unbridled bridging of gaps separating government from governed. Once again the picture emerges of right-radicalism as a guardian of the *status quo* as well as of incrementalism, incited into action by the provocation of left-radicalism.[34]

7 Summary and conclusion

In this section of the book we have tried to project an image of left-wing radicalism among students along the lines suggested in the

113

theoretical first part of this book. There, for radicalism to emerge, we postulated the existence of a specific configuration of inequivalent shares of social goods in combination with the incidence of obstructions blocking the realization of those aspirations which had been induced by the initial pattern of inequivalence. The conflict model suggested how groups that are subject to this obstruction tended to show a characteristic shift in reference group behaviour in which a 'vertical' orientation on mobility within the established system of distribution is given up for a radical alliance with groups of more generally dispossessed in an attempt to effectuate drastic transformations of the distributive system (see phases III and IV of the model, chapter 1.8).

Here, in the summary of the research findings presented above, we shall first indicate which configurations of inequivalent shares we have uncovered for the various groups under study, and summarize the interpretation which these findings have inspired. Then we shall go into the relation between the left-wing radical vanguard and its following and ask ourselves whether this relation can be duly considered an instance of the relation between a radical vanguard and a generally dispossessed following as postulated in our model.

As our research findings showed, the shares of social goods of the left-radical vanguard displayed the following pattern. As to social background, of which only two dimensions had been measured, those of status (as appeared from the prestige accruing to the occupation of the father) and of class (based on the occupation and income of the father, as well as on the education and self-ranking on a stratification scale of both parents), we established that the left-wing vanguard did not differ significantly from the right-wing vanguard. It clearly ranked above the 'average' student and above a category of left-activist students which we have chosen to consider as a mobilized following. As to shares of status and power which the respondents had been brought up to consider normal in their parental homes, both the left-wing vanguard and its following ranked well above the other categories. In their perception of their present power position and status position and in their assessment of future shares of power, however, both left-wing categories scored definitely lower than the other categories. Finally, as to the evaluation of their class position, both left-wing vanguard and following scored lower than the other groups. At this point the replication showed up a marked rift between left-activists and left-non-activists; only 38 per cent of the former considered the opportunities of gainful employment in the future as attractive and auspicious against 54 per cent of the latter considering them attractive and 52 per cent auspicious.

In our interpretation the inequivalence between criteria derived from the style of upbringing and the perception of actual differences in power and status constituted a crucial factor. Naturally, the perception is not independent of these criteria—the familiarity with standards of equality prevalent in parental homes will tend to make an experience of deprivations of status and power more acute. Yet, as we pointed out in the preceding chapter, there are also objective grounds for the increase in feelings of power deprivation among students during the last decade, compared with the preceding, more traditional arena. Structural developments, such as the growth of student numbers and the growth of the universities, are precisely such grounds. These structural factors, in addition to the self-conscious protectionist strategies on the part of the traditional power elite, are potent factors of the obstruction of strivings to undo these power deprivations.

A similar argument would hold for the inequivalence between parental class position and expected future class position, as assessed by the students themselves. The depressed expectations can be considered in part as an outlook affected by a previous radical perspective. Here, too, however, objective factors add confirmation to this outlook. The actual academic arena does indeed comprise fields of study which do not channel into clear occupational markets— the very fields of study, we should emphasize, which show the highest density of leftists. Yet it is hard to assess the relative importance of objective factors and subjective impressions unambiguously, especially in view of the finding that left activists and left-non-activists, although not significantly different in their chosen fields of study, do differ significantly in their assessment of occupational opportunities.

In our interpretation of these divergent sets of interests we have, for the left-radical vanguard, chosen to seek the ignition point of conflict in the blocking of its aspirations to undo power deprivations, along with status deprivations. We have inserted the latter for this reason: to the extent that the novel claims on access to processes of decision-making entail the provocative neglect of rules of courteous intercourse and precepts of a display of deference, this will constitute a set of signals signifying a breach of an established distribution of status.

With regard to the right-radicals, we should like to make the following comments. On almost every dimension measured, the right-wing vanguard tended to score highest. In so far as it did perceive small shares at all, for instance in the realm of student participation in matters of their work situation, university government and student facilities, this sense of deprivation was not heightened, as was the case with the left-radicals, by standards of equality acquired in their parental homes. To the extent that this vanguard, the traditional wielders of power in student society, constitutes a dethroned elite, it will tend to impute the changes of the arena to the actions of those who are, in their eyes, the real opponent—the left-wing students.

On the right-wing, as on the left-, we were able to discern a following, markedly different from the leadership in social background and, therefore, all the more guided by motives of upward mobility. In our interpretation, it was particularly the attempts at tarnishing and undercutting these very lures of mobility, in addition to the interference with a regular course of study, due to the actions of left-wing radicals, which had caused the right-wing following to move to the right. The challenge presented by the left-wing made this group on the right-wing into the natural ally of the deposed elite. Both allies, moreover, tend to be alike in their affirmation of an ascriptive order, as we suggested in the section on dimensions of radicalism. This appeared, furthermore, in the desire of the right-wing to limit the range of action of student protest to matters of immediate interest to students. Contrary to what we postulated in the first chapter, the acceptance of an ascriptive order cannot in this instance be attributed to the fact that ascription serves as the very basis of large shares of social goods. Quite the contrary, the acceptance of an ascriptive order here would rather entail the subscription to subordinate positions as well as the display of deference; the acceptance would seem to be based, however, on the consideration that precisely that type of order guarantees the unhampered pursuit of individual aspirations.

Let us now turn to the second problem that we reserved for treatment in this section. Are we warranted in conceiving of the relation between the left-wing vanguard and its following as an instance of the relation between a thwarted left-radical elite and a following of the largely dispossessed, as indicated in phase IV of our model? We would think not.

As far as the left-wing vanguard is concerned, propositions 4 and 6 (see chapter 1.8) would seem to provide an adequate formulation of the shift occurring in its reference group behaviour. Moreover, in the section on reference group behaviour above, we found that this shift had become manifest in an orientation towards potential allies outside the academic arena whom we can indeed regard as broadly deprived. On the other hand, however, it would seem as if the mobilization of a following from within the student body is rather a series of moves between groups which are both characterized by the inequivalence of their set of shares of social goods. Each group, therefore, will have to show evidence of what, in the first chapter, we have considered the characteristic behaviour of a left-wing vanguard: the de-activation of the attractive force of mobility along certain distributive dimensions induced by the perceived impossibility of realizing equivalent mobility along other dimensions. This impossibility constituted the crucial factor in starting the shift in reference group behaviour and direction of orientations. To the extent that leadership groups are those groups who do have something to de-activate—who actually are subject to the lure of primary mobility—both the left-wing vanguard and the following which we have discerned in this chapter can be considered leadership groups. However, there are such marked differences between the two that we seem well-advised to conceive of the left-wing student following as some sort of lower echelon within what, from the perspective of the wider society, may well appear one homogeneous leadership body. For indeed, as our analysis has borne out, this lower echelon has clearly needed the mobilizing efforts of the radical vanguard; the de-activation of gratifications and the activation of deprivations is not self-imposed, as with the radical leadership. On the contrary, it has been induced by the exemplary action of a radical elite. In that sense, the student following is the first in line to present itself to a radical leadership in its quest for support among groups that will be increasingly deprived once this search descends the social ladder. Even so, however, in the eyes of a non-academic potential following, the relation between the echelons of the student radical body may appear as reflecting similarity rather than divergence. And, compounding the gaps in perspective, groups which student radicals may choose to consider a potential following in society may in turn choose to conceive of these radicals as constituting a privileged elite rather than a consort in deprivation. This may go a long way to explain the recurrent frustration of mobilizing efforts of radical students outside the confines of the university.

Appendix 1   A note on methodology

The numbers of respondents—students, their fathers and mothers—constituting our focused samples of ASVA and OBAS were as in Table 5.4.

TABLE 5.4   *Number of respondents in the contrast groups*

	children	fathers	mothers
ASVA	23	18	20
OBAS	14	9	14

For the replication the sample was sub-divided into five categories, ranging from left-activist, through left-non-activist, middle, and

117

right-non-activist, to right-activist. The numbers of respondents were as in Table 5.5.

TABLE 5.5 *Number of respondents per replication category*

	children	fathers	mothers
left-activists	53	34	43
left-non-activists	53	40	41
middle	59	40	47
right-non-activists	40	26	34
right-activists	4	2	2

This categorization was based on an index of ideological position, ranging from left to right, and on an indicator of activism. The index of ideological position consisted of four items which had tended to discriminate strongly between the ASVA and OBAS groups. The items were, respectively:

social and academic reform should be attained exclusively through mutual arrangement and deliberation;

politics should be kept out of the classroom;

the university must be used for experimentation with more direct forms of democracy;

granted that radical students may have legitimate grievances on a number of points, their style of action precludes any understanding with people in positions of responsibility.

The index was cumulative; it based itself on an addition of the respondents' scores on each item. Although initially the items had been presented as five-point scales, ranging from 'strongly agree' to 'strongly disagree', for the construction of the index we reduced the items to three-point scales. The third item was scored in reverse to the other items.

The activist/non-activist distinction was based on an item which was the last of a series that, as a whole, had a funnel structure. We presented a series of groups to our respondents which, at the time of the interview, had been drawing the public's attention—'leftist' and 'rightist' reference groups (see section 5 of this chapter). We asked the respondents to indicate whether they considered their own situation to be rather similar or rather dissimilar to that of the enumerated groups or flatly non-comparable. This set of questions was followed by questions eliciting assessments as to which two groups were deemed most similar and which two groups most dissimilar to the respondents' own situation. Next, we inquired into our respondents' sense of affiliation with those groups they had referred to positively, as well as into their sense of rejection towards those groups referred to negatively. Finally, we asked whether our respondents had *actively* displayed either affiliation or rejection. Of these final two questions we used the one referring to the active display of rejection as an indicator of activism on the ground that research findings had shown the right-wing to tend towards the active display of rejection rather than affiliation (see section 5 of this chapter). This indicator was a rather weak criterion of activism, intended to inflate the number of right-activists as much as possible. As Table 5.5 clearly shows, the attempt was not very successful: we found only four right-activists. Yet it was a weak criterion, as may appear from the fact that only 34 per cent of the group of left-activists thought of themselves as being activists (as compared, we hasten to add, with only 8 per cent, 5 per cent, 0 per cent and 0 per cent for the remaining categories, from left to right). Although weak, the measure was certainly valid with regard to the borderline between left-activists and left non-activists (Blalock's significance of difference of proportions: $p < 0.05$). Further proof was added by the following findings. When asked to indicate at what affective distance the respondents placed themselves from the phenomenon of student radicalism, the five categories appeared to differ significantly (Kendall's $T = -0.59$; $p < 0.001$). Questions dealing explicitly with the participation in certain specified protest actions—such as actions aimed at re-structuring university departments, actions instigated by either of the left-radical student organizations, SVB and ASVA, or the occupation of the administration building in the spring of 1969—all tended to confirm this picture, as shown in Table 5.6.

TABLE 5.6   *Participation in protest actions (in %)*

Type of action	left-act.	left-non-act.	middle	right non-act.	right act.
Departmental re-structuring	34	11	5	2.5	0
SVB- or ASVA- sponsored action	32	17	5	0	0
Ad. building occupation	32	23	10	0	0

(Except for the occupation of the administration building, the differences between the categories are significant on the 5% level; Blalock's diff. prop.—see below in this Appendix.)

On the basis of these findings, we hold the indicator of activism to be valid for the left-wing of the ideological spectrum. We have not been successful, however, in finding an effective criterion for

119

distinguishing right-non-activists from right-activists. If we recall, moreover, that the index of ideological outlook consisted of items strongly differentiating between ASVA and OBAS respondents, the conclusion may seem warranted that, for purposes of replication, we have indeed come up with categories of respondents reflecting the characteristics which we had initially attributed to ASVA and OBAS.

In connection with the problem of validation, let us make somé additional remarks. Our research was essentially exploratory, aimed at uncovering specific value configurations of a number of key variables in empirical material in accordance with previous theoretical expectations rather than at the generalization towards an operationally specific universe. Given that preoccupation, we have tried to create as many opportunities as possible for checking the consistency of our research findings—the internal consistency of findings, acquired with different measuring techniques, as well as the external consistency, acquired by checking our initial findings with those of the replication. Moreover, we have taken into account what we might call the theoretical consistency of our findings, referring to the fit between the array of research findings and the previous set of expectations as to the profile—or the configuration—of interests as well as of social position on both the left- and the right-wing.

Although none of these consistencies has been expressed in a specific measure, our overall procedure would seem to render an impression of 'significance' of research material that we hold to be more relevant than the usual tests of significance. The latter, in fact, assess the chance that findings of one single piece of research are confirmed in subsequent research (namely $1-p$). Actual findings of replicating research, corroborating previous findings, therefore, would seem to provide a more solid basis than the statistical significance of just one single finding, uncorroborated by replication. Arguments along these lines have led some sociologists to refrain completely from applying traditional tests of significance.[35] We have chosen not to take this position, if only in order to give the reader a more precise insight into the differences which, in the absence of a quantitative criterion, could not have been described other than verbally as 'rather strong', 'sufficiently great', 'negligible' and so forth, thus obscuring the criteria for the admission of research evidence in our discussion.

We used the following testing criteria. Considering the relevance which both contrast groups of OBAS and ASVA represented to our research objective—a relevance due to their marked ideological divergence as well as to the fact that both groups represent actual network structures rather than research constructs—we decided to lower the level of significance for the analysis of differences between these groups. We admitted differences between ASVA and OBAS respondents once these were significant at the 20 per cent-level. For the replication we used the more traditional 5 per cent-level. This decision applies to all the findings reported in this chapter, unless otherwise mentioned. All the findings have been subject to one-tailed testing.

As a measure of the significance of differences between the contrast groups of ASVA and OBAS we used Blalock's measure of the significance of differences of proportion (to be referred to as Blalock's diff. prop.);[36] in the replication phase we used either this measure or the significance of Kendall's Tau, in so far as associations of ordinal data were concerned.

Appendix 2 Dimensions of radicalism

The entire set of seventy-three statements used for the assessment of dimensions of radicalism has been subjected to various procedures of data reduction. The first criterion was whether or not the statements did differentiate significantly between the two focused samples on a 5 per cent level of significance. Two statements were excepted from exclusion on this ground—although not yielding significant differences between the students, they did differentiate significantly between their parents. Thus a set of fifty statements was left. These were ordered according to the difference in meaning which these items conveyed to us. In all, we grouped the fifty items under nine different headings, as mentioned in section 6 of this chapter.

In addition to this, we wanted to subject all of the seventy-three items to a different procedure of reduction. For all of the students in our sample, as well as for their parents, two separate correlation matrices were constructed. We decided to drop items from further analysis if, in the case of students, they did not exceed a correlation of 0·45, if only once; in the case of their parents, items were dropped if no correlation higher than 0·35 was attained. On the whole, correlations in the matrix based on the responses of the parents, were lower. Thus, forty-three items remained for the students, compared with forty-one for the parents. Both sets were then separately subjected to the cluster analysis developed by Johnson.[37] The main finding was that for parents and students respectively, the ordering of items in different clusters diverged clearly. Of the total of thirty-two statements which the two sets of items had in common, twelve tended to cluster differently for parents and students. On the other hand, the boundaries between the various clusters cannot be considered too strict, since, for both cluster analyses, in the end all clusters tended to inter-correlate, to the effect that the various clusters should rather be taken to constitute sub-clusters within a wider general factor. This would seem to lend further support to our conceiving the sub-clusters as separate dimensions of the wider concept of radicalism, as we did in section 6 of this chapter.

The analysis as reported in this chapter has been based on the face-value ordering according to various related, though divergent, meanings. The cluster analysis has served as an external check; it did not lead us to drop any further items or move items from one dimension to another.

6 Evaluation: structuralism and phenomenology reconciled

1 Introduction

The argument as presented in the previous chapters leaves many points for discussion, some of which we have chosen for elaboration here. The general argument can be briefly summarized. Our analysis has been inspired by the apparent contradiction between two frameworks for conceiving the causation of social conflicts; we referred to them as the rank equivalence and the rank inequivalence model respectively. Both models tried to reduce the apparent diversity of social conflict to uniform underlying patterns of interests. These interests, in either instance, were conceived of as generated by specific configurations of positions held by individuals or groups of individuals in the overall distributive system of society. Both approaches, therefore, are structuralist—seeking underlying structural configurations, thus transcending the limited and slanted perspectives of the participants involved. If not downright disregarding of the actor's viewpoint, at best both approaches deemed these viewpoints of secondary significance. By turning this inherent set of priorities upside down, we not only managed to reconcile both structuralist views of conflict, but also reconciled structuralism and phenomenology. For, although we labelled the effort at integration 'social-psychological' in its frame of reference, our focus was still on underlying structural configurations—this time, however, as defined and interpreted by the actors involved. The dual nature of the ensuing model of conflict calls for further discussion.

To the extent that both structuralism and phenomenology stand for traditions of sociological thinking which have grown in relative isolation, a fusion of these perspectives may entail the danger of one conceptual framework hampering the full deployment of the other perspective. Tacit connotations of one set of concepts may interfere with those inherent in the other. To the extent, moreover, that the

123

structuralist perspective has tended to be more of an acquired habit of generations of sociologists, and phenomenology has been rather an oppositional minority view, the present author may have been unaware of some of the implications of structuralism when fused with phenomenology. The main implication we have in mind here may be the false impression that structuralism tends to uncover long-term configurations, persistent through whatever epiphenomenal, erratic movements may strike the non-structuralist beholder. The conceptual apparatus of structuralism, focusing on roles, relations, institutions, seems to take a long-range view of society which unduly bypasses the reflection of structural elements in the various definitions of the situation which sets of actors may hold. One of our tasks in this chapter will be, therefore, to analyse carefully to what extent derivations from the conceptual universe of structuralism may be carrying such implications. In other words, we shall have to check what is the precise impact of the invasion of a phenomenological perspective into the conceptual world of structuralism. Here, closer inspection of our comparative case studies may help us grasp the problem of to what extent the model is overly structuralist. In so far as the model contains a set of definitions which borrow heavily from structuralism, the confrontation of model and historical cases may indicate the extent to which the concepts are overly static and unduly long-range in character. They may be so rigid in definition and range of application as to preclude the possibility of adequately formulating shifts and jumps in actors' viewpoints.

On the other hand, the very taking of the actor's viewpoint may suggest that there is such a thing as the experience of enduring, overpowering, well-established social structures. Here, structuralism may well serve to formulate systematically the empirical referents of this experience. Then, the problem is rather to specify the range of historical situations which are appropriately covered by our set of structuralist conceptions. Again, our efforts at comparative analysis of historical cases may inspire our discussion. We propose first to examine the implications of phenomenology for our structuralist concepts and then to deal with the problem of the range of validity of the model.

2 The impact of the phenomenological perspective

Among all the concepts constituting the vocabulary of our conflict model, the central place is taken by the social goods of class, status and power. We have introduced them as brief captions for the various stakes of social competition. To the extent that competition has set the tone of our interpretation of society throughout the preceding chapters, the crucial problem arises of finding a set of concepts for the description of what is at stake in societal competition—a set which, in addition to being unambiguous and appropriate, should be as comprehensive as possible. We hold our set of concepts of class, status and power to fulfil these requirements adequately. We could, of course, have borrowed from different conceptual frameworks. One of the more appropriate could have been some variety of exchange theory, as developed by such authors as Homans, Blau or Gouldner.[1] An analysis of social competition would apparently stand to gain by the application of a theoretical perspective whose very focus is on the assessment of rewards and investments in the consecutive moves in which rival interest groups engage.

This perspective, however, does not differ essentially from ours, in so far as we, in the definitions of the three social goods as well as in their application, have stressed aspects of relative assessment, exchange and some computation of the overall balance. In our definition of class, for instance, we emphasized the assessment of investments and rewards, both present and future. Our definitions of power and status may appear to be less illustrative in this context. We may point out, however, that our use of the concepts has consistently attempted to conceive both concepts in a context of reference group behaviour—a procedure which inevitably directs the attention to processes of assessing positive or negative balances.

It is hard to deny, however, that exchange entails more than just this aspect of relative assessment. The concept of exchange refers to an inter-personal process, whereas the assessment of balances refers rather to individual moments in this process. Yet we would assert that the way in which we have used our concepts has been intended to unveil this process character. Thus, for instance, the process of the radical shifting of reference group behaviour as well as the ensuing shifts in patterns of alliance, as outlined in the conflict model, necessarily implies that the actors involved in these shifts have effected a revaluation and a change in mutual understanding as to the 'price' of the various social goods. The left-radical leadership in particular has arrived at an upgrading of those social goods whose distribution it may attempt to alter through an alliance with groups of broadly dispossessed; it has depreciated goods towards which it was originally oriented. Our entire analysis of the strategies of forming alliances and oppositions presupposes processes of bargaining and exchange which tend to continually feed on and feed back to the assessment of relative shares—of 'balances'. Moreover, we would point out that, for none of the social goods do these processes occur on isolated markets. For instance, our analysis of the traditional student arena clearly showed that the manipulation of the distribution of status by the 'top-dogs' tended to divide the underlying party internally to such an extent that part of it considered its share of status a fair compensation for its relative powerlessness. Thus it had been effectively cut off from potential allies among the underlying groups. What we see illustrated here is the possibility that the various goods can be traded between parties; thus they can be conceived as constituting both a means and an object of exchange. The entire process of competition as well as the ensuing processes of alliance and opposition formation can be aptly described as a continuing struggle to introduce and enforce definitions of the terms of trade. Equilibrium situations in this process, as we pointed out in the first chapter, can result either from consensus or from coercion.

Formulations along these lines would seem to lend considerable dynamism to the seemingly rigid and fixed concept of social goods. The very choice of the word 'goods' may have seemed to introduce an element of reification into the argument. We are of the opinion, however, that the argument presented thus far offers ample evidence that this hazard of naive reification has been effectively contained. We may refer the reader to a formulation given in chapter 2 (section 2): social goods should be taken to constitute analytic aspects of an individual's position *vis-à-vis* others; they only assume specific values through comparison with those others.

In yet a different sense, however, elements of reification may have penetrated into the argument. No matter how strong the emphasis on social goods as aspects of an individual's position relative to others and on processes of relative assessment and of the formation of alliances and oppositions to reflect the changes in weight—or value—accorded these aspects, yet it may seem as if the social goods as such do have unambiguous analytic boundaries. Boundaries, to be sure, which we have determined in our set of definitions and which may appear to remain stable through whatever changes in relative weight may occur. We propose to dwell on this suggestion of stability inherent in defining the concepts of social goods somewhat more at length.

We stated above that as soon as we consider the fact that the various social goods can be traded and exchanged, inevitably these goods have become essentially ambiguous. That is to say, we can conceive of a share of one such good as constituting a potential share of each of the other goods. In other words, to the participants involved, the goods have become mutually convertible.[2] This argument, however, tends to illuminate the ambiguity of the objects of competition by introducing yet another element of apparent unambiguousness—that is, exchange value or price. Inevitably then, the focus is still on the analysis of elements of consensus, if only within each of the oppositional camps of allies. This latter formulation, however, may suggest another aspect of ambiguity of the social goods in the sense that, *to the participants involved*, they may have stopped being mutually convertible. To the extent, namely, that oppositional camps have arisen, this means that processes of exchange have been cut short; the moves of the opposed camps *vis-à-vis* one another can no longer be conceived as intent on the establishing of common terms of trade. In other words, a conceptual framework that aims at formulating this dual ambiguity will have to imply that the definitions of the social goods themselves are apt to shift and move in the process of fanning-out of social conflict. The definitions themselves should be considered as variable in content. Only then will the conceptual framework have been opened up to include the universe of experience of the actors involved in conflict. Only then will justice have been done to the sociology of knowledge aspects of conflict and radicalization.

This may be illustrated by a reference to our analysis of student radicalism. For the description of the competitive game centring on class, status and power in the traditional student arena, our definitions of the social goods, as developed in the first chapter, were quite adequate. Each party involved behaved towards the 'signals' of class, status and power in ways that were understandable to and could be anticipated by the other parties. The meaning these signals conveyed to the participants was similar for all those involved. This common understanding was able to sustain a fairly stable system of stratification; those on the lower rungs of this ladder accepted their relative deprivation, even deemed it legitimized by the expectation of future rewards, which again had a similar motivating power for all parties involved. Inequivalence of rank did occur, but it did not lead to claims which this system could not understand or honour.

The impairment of this traditional arena, as we saw, was effected by such causes as structural changes, most important among which may have been the enlargement of scale of the universities with all this entailed for the smooth functioning of the traditional arena. Thus, autonomously, blockings arose to the honouring of claims, even when these were understandable and legitimate. In addition to this, however, the system was undercut by the emergence of novel patterns of inequivalance and of novel claims and actions, which either met with a lack of understanding or were deemed illegitimate.

This latter instance clearly illustrates the breakdown of mutual understanding: competition around class, status and power had started to proceed in terms which tended to diverge increasingly for the parties involved. This shift may initially have occurred in images concerning power and the exercise thereof. With the increased parting of the opposed camps, however, this shift may have radiated across the entire reach of class, status and power. The research which we undertook at a time that the shift in orientations and reference group behaviour was well under way—the last phase but one of our

127

conflict model—showed the impact on the images of class, status and power as held by the left- and right-wing student radicals. Quite purposely we use the word 'images', as somewhat looser in meaning than 'definitions'; it may help us reach out towards the complex conceptual world of the groups involved in conflict since it pertains to configurations of social inequality in which they find themselves enmeshed. The images which we were able to record clearly illustrated the parting of minds, not just in the conceptual reflection of reality, but also in the related assessments of justice as well as in the willingness to participate any longer in the competitive game on the same old terms—terms, we should add, which the left-wing had come to experience as imposed by the opponent and which were part and parcel of his despicable overall outlook.[3]

If, as may seem plausible from the preceding argument, the three social goods are linked with complex images held by the participants in arenas of conflict, and if these images, in close interaction with the course of conflict, may shift and move, the immediate task at hand is to formulate what specific situation—what phase of our conflict model—our definitions of class, status and power would seem to reflect. In so far as our definitions, most outspokenly perhaps the definition of power, refer to competition along established channels, we may be well-advised to conceive of the definitions as specifically valid for the phase immediately preceding the course of conflict as outlined in the model. That situation, by the way, may be the one most clearly warranting a reification, in so far as the actors themselves may act on the premise of facing an exterior, established system—a crystallized or institutionalized set of rules, opportunities, objectives. These circumstances are clearly reflected in our definition of class in that it refers to an institutionalized system of division of labour as well as of distribution of rewards. It appears also from the definition of power which refers to the institutionalized avenues of access to established positions of decision-making. It may be less apparent in our definition of status, although here as well the definition implies a reference to an established and generally accepted distribution of deference and self-respect according to standards applied by all the participants.

This established system is not simply one of distribution, as we said; it is also a system of opportunities—opportunities for advocacy of interests, for success and mobility. The overall image would seem to reflect the current pluralist model of a democratic society. To the extent that collective actions do occur (and the pluralist model acknowledges this situation, in so far as it is a pressure group model),[4] it concerns alliances which, through collective effort, try to reach the greatest effectiveness in availing themselves of the opportunities offered by the system. The basic premise here is that all participants perceive these opportunities *as sufficiently open to them.*

Now our model of conflict focuses on the situation where groups of participants become aware of their being excluded from equal participation in the established competition around class, status and power. They come to conceive of this competition as a game from which they are excluded and which persistently proceeds in sectors of society to which they have not been able to find access. At this point the model of conflict and radicalism becomes operative. At this point, too, competition turns into confrontation and conceptions about the stakes of the game—the social goods—as well as about the rules of procedure start to move. Conceptions about social goods and conceptions about the rules of the game—the two appear inextricably linked. To the extent that left-radical groups start to disengage themselves from an institutionalized arena in their conceptions about social goods, this inevitably implies a disengagement from established rules. This latter disengagement, it would seem, serves to display brazenly the parting of minds, in so far as the rejection of the rules of the game by definition shows in the behaviour towards the opponent.[5] This development in particular signals the drift from competition to confrontation. A classic example may be the confrontation between a regular Western army and guerilla forces. Guerilla tactics represent such flagrant violation of what is deemed a legitimate response to a regular display of military force that the traditional Western military man cannot but conceive of his opponents as despicable bandits who shrink from open battle. This image of the opponent is fed by the inability (rather than the sheer unwillingness) to understand the motives of the opponent as a complex texture of radically changed images concerning class, status and power as well as the legitimacy of means of confrontation. The evaluations of legitimacy of both opponents have radically drifted apart. Our analysis of the period of decolonization in Dutch history offers another case in point. Even among Dutch politicians of apparent good will, time and again, the *ne plus ultra* in their willingness to understand the opponent was the irregular display of violence by the opponent.[6]

This discussion leaves us with this central problem: if it is true that in the course of conflict images concerning the social goods tend to radically drift apart—if it is true, moreover, that our definitions of class, status and power betray a pluralist perspective, how then are we to formulate the minimal set of characteristics which, despite the shifting images, define class as class, status as status, and power as power? Even in full-blown conflicts, indeed, the opponents share a minimal common focus in that they have set out to confront the adversary for the sake of defending or attacking positions which, apparently, both value highly. If we choose to rank these positions under the headings of class, status and power, we shall have to leave out of our definitions all those aspects relative to which the parties may diverge and only include those aspects which attract them both.

We want to propose the following solution. The entire development from pluralist competition to antagonistic confrontation can be considered:

1. a struggle for *power*, in the sense of a struggle to acquire or enlarge a share in effective decision-making for sectors of a society which may vary in scope. This definition no longer refers to the context of the struggle. The context may well reflect an institutionalized, pluralist arena, where rival interest groups are by and large aware of differences in relative power and, within this balance-of-power situation, deploy tactics of alliance formation and of recruiting and mobilizing their following for the attainment of specific and limited objectives. This situation largely resembles the Parsonian conception of power; here, groups are conceived as organizing their power in order to gain influence in institutionalized processes of decision-making.[7] To the extent that the outcome of the game changes the balance of power, the changes are minor—the objectives of the participant parties are by nature incrementalist.[8] On the other hand, under our definition, the situation of conflict can be praetorian and tend towards the non-pluralist, dichotomous confrontation of adversaries. The objectives are no longer incrementalist. They are rather totalitarian.

Authors such as Elias and Gouldner have pointed out the continuum character of the power concept, to the effect that power can range from situations of interdependence or reciprocity on the one hand to autonomy on the other.[9] Power conceived of as a balance, or in our words, as a relative share, highlights the fact that the stake of the game may aim at the institution of a novel balance on this continuum rather than at the attainment of specific, limited goals under a given equilibrium. What is at stake, then, is rather the definition of the criteria for the distribution of power as well as the societal reach of effective decision-making to be exercised by either of the contending parties. The very fact of violent confrontation testifies to the rift in conceptions as to what the novel balance of power should be like.

Second, the development from competition to confrontation can be considered:

2. a struggle for *class position*, in the broad sense of the share of the social product accruing to individuals or assortments of individuals on the basis of their position in the overall societal division of labour. This definition, too, abstracts from a specific context. It allows, on the one hand, the description of competition around class issues in an institutionalized arena where the distribution of class rewards is

by and large accepted and, on the other hand, competition where the very basis of distribution is at stake. In the latter case, similar to our reformulation of power, once more the possibility is being implied that the criteria for the distribution of the social good of class are in dispute; then again, the stakes of the competitive struggle are no longer incrementalist. The clearest example of this dichotomous confrontation around class position is undoubtedly the Marxist model of revolution where one of the radical camps—the revolutionary proletariat—should aim at the radical destruction of the opponent—the capitalists. Interestingly enough, in this context, Sorel has phenomenologically interpreted this model of revolution as constituting the 'myth' which actually inspires the revolutionary proletariat.

Finally, the drift from competition to confrontation can be considered:

3. a struggle for *status*, conceived of as the assessment of an individual's or group's superiority or inferiority based on the display of deference or disdain by others. Status in this sense is the social component of self-esteem: it brings out the support or lesion which an individual's self-esteem incurs in social intercourse. With reference to the analysis of the social game around status in particular, an approach in terms of symbolic interactionism could be useful. The broadening of the definition once more allows the description of competition around status in arenas characterized by the general acceptance of standards for meting out shares of status—for the attribution of superiority and inferiority—as well as in arenas where these very standards are in dispute and groups of participants no longer want to tolerate the constant lesion of their sense of self-esteem. Through the design of a rival set of standards these groups tend to emancipate themselves from dominant and, in their eyes, traumatic conceptions. In our analysis of student radicalism we found that this emancipation can stop short of the design of novel status criteria, and may just consist in the rejection of dominant criteria. Latter-day emancipation movements of the blacks in the USA, on the other hand, show that these standards, rather than being simply rejected, are being inverted—'black is beautiful'. Later in our discussion we shall examine the various relations which emancipatory conceptions may have to dominant ones.

If we survey the above attempt at purifying our set of definitions of social goods and at shedding elements of structural rigidity, it appears that, as in chapter 1, we have had to use the general concept of *criteria of distribution* in addition to the concept of *social goods*. Perhaps the two concepts constitute the most economical framework for formulating what, in situations of competition or confrontation, commonly attracts the parties involved, as well as for conceiving the various respects in which, along with the drift from competition to confrontation, the opposed camps tend to grow apart. Already in in the first chapter we have linked the introduction of the concept of criteria of distribution with the concepts of *ascription* and *achievement*. It may be useful, here, to try and assess to what extent these concepts too may have been insufficiently reflecting the perspective of phenomenology.

Ascription and achievement

One of the propositions of our conflict model held that, in the course of conflict, the right-radical camp will increasingly come to emphasize ascriptive criteria of distribution in response to the newly-risen demands of the left-radical opponent. The dialectics involved can be more clearly brought out by saying that the demands of the left-wing radicals represent the attempt to extend achievement criteria over terrains where, thus far, they have not prevailed, whereas the right-wing radicals aim at precisely the opposite—extending ascriptive criteria over areas where as yet the criteria have at least been uncertain. That is to say, in the course of conflict, a process of dialectical norm crystallization occurs which leads both camps to a more precise definition of their ideological position.[10]

To what extent have we come across empirical findings in this study to reflect this pattern? Our inquiry into the period of decolonization in Dutch history has rendered clear illustrations of this emphasis on and elaboration of ascriptive themes by elements among the right-wing radicals, the more forcefully and explicitly by those elements whose achieved position was lower.[11] Our research into student radicalism rendered less clear results. The main reason may be that, with respect to an emergent right-radical backlash, our research was limited to the student population, whereas left-radical students tend to locate and defy the opponent to a large extent outside this population. A potential reservoir of right-radical sentiment, therefore, was not incorporated among our respondents. A further reason may be that, unlike what occurred, for instance, at the campus in Nanterre, France, or in Italy, left-wing student radicalism in the Netherlands had not provoked right-wing radicalism into the extreme forms of antagonistic action which our model outlines. Yet, our analysis in the previous chapter of the dimensions of radicalism would seem to bear out that, as far as the left-wing is concerned, outspoken opposition occurred against positions of submission on the basis of ascription, such as age or position of 'apprentice'. The concept of maturity which we introduced there in itself implies hierarchical ranking over the entire reach of class, status and power differentials. Those who are deemed still immature are being ranked below those who deem themselves fully mature; therefore they will be excluded from full participation in processes of decision-making and less well-off with respect to the rewards of a system of division of labour. This formulation may harbour the redefinition of ascription and achievement.

Since the criteria for the assessment of maturity are being formulated by those who consider themselves mature, these criteria will only be socially effective to the extent that the mature have the necessary means at their disposal for making these conceptions prevail, that is, when they are the incumbents of positions of power and are able to manipulate the distribution of rewards among the participants in the social division of labour. Therefore definitions of ascription and achievement should be tied to social interest groups; this would cause the boundaries between the concepts to blur to an extent considerably greater than would appear from our first chapter. We may be well-advised to conceive of an ascriptive frame of mind as roughly similar to the *status-quo* oriented outlook which we regarded as typical of the top-dogs (cf. chapter 5, section 6). Even when these latter do allow mobile individuals admission to their ranks on the basis of achievement, this occurs according to *their* definitions of achievement. It is subject to their conditions, which primarily aim at leaving the *status quo* intact. Therefore ascription is linked not so much to individual characteristics, which are hard, if not impossible, to change, but rather to images of order and persistence prevalent among the elite groups of top-dogs. Ascriptive norms, then, can be broadly defined as the institutionalized conception among an interest group of top-dogs or some alliance of such groups that an established categorial distribution of rewards and productive efforts should form the matrix for future distribution.

Already, in the first chapter, in our elaboration of the conflict model, we found that achievement criteria in particular constitute a revolutionizing element, in so far as they interfere with established ascriptive conceptions. We can perhaps most clearly bring out this insight by tying the definition of achievement to yet another party in conflict—the underlying party or some alliance of such parties. It is this party's 'historic role' to bring a *status quo* into dispute on the basis of what this party itself considers its contribution to the system —its achievement.

This reformulation of the concepts ties in closely with our distinction of primary and induced mobility. Primary mobility is an upward movement within a distributive system which would leave the overall categorial distribution of rewards and efforts unchanged; it may be tolerated or even applauded for its presumed eu-functions for the system. Only when this primary mobility, *in the eyes of the upwardly mobile*, is perceived as an insufficient reward for its 'achievement'—only when it induces claims on secondary mobility—would this constitute an autonomous threat to the system beyond the manipulative control of the top-dogs. Our suggestion, then, is to equate the concepts of achievement and induced mobility and to consider primary mobility, essentially harmless to the *status quo*, as reconcilable with the concept of ascription.

The reader may find this an unwarranted conceptual intermingling. Let us, therefore, make one additional remark. As conceptually opposite to achievement, ascription would seem to preclude requirements of effort and achievement. Nothing would be farther off the mark. It would be totally false to state that, due to the accident of birth—an essentially non-achieved characteristic—some individuals would be entitled to certain positions. For indeed they will only have secured their rights after a demanding, rigorous period of training and education during which they have acquired the intricate pattern of behaviour requisite for the eventual investiture. Elias's analysis of civilized behaviour as the social mark of distinction of privileged groups provides an excellent example.[12] The acquisition of this intricate style of behaviour is certainly an achievement if ever there was one. An achievement, we should add, aimed at preserving a societal *status quo*. Yet, if one considers unacceptable this reduction of the concept of achievement to those efforts which harbour a challenge to a *status quo*, the solution may be to drop entirely the concepts of ascription and achievement and to replace them with the concepts of primary and induced mobility. Following this analysis of the implications of the phenomenological perspective, we propose to proceed to a discussion of the range of validity of our model of conflict.

3 The range of validity of the model of conflict

In this section, as we have stated above, our focus will be rather structuralist. Assuming that actors involved in conflict will have long-range images of social structures in which they are involved and which they may wish to oppose, we have to analyse what range of historic situations is appropriately covered by our conceptual framework. Moreover, to the extent that in our analysis we have transcended the actor's point of view and have rather gone on to the point of view of the 'behaviour of systems', we have come up with structuralist hypotheses concerning the inter-relations of systemic characteristics, constituting the parameter values for specifically varying patterns of conflict. That level of analysis, too, would call for further specification of the range of validity of these statements.

Thus, for instance, in our second chapter, we introduced some such parameter values in order to distinguish between different arenas showing different configurations of participants and rules of the game. The parameter values were, respectively, level of participation and degree of institutionalization. Our analysis there of an oligarchic arena rendered this insight: a fundamental criterion for the applicability of the model is the incidence of social mobility. For, indeed, mobility leads to the emergence of groups holding inequivalent shares of social goods. Thus it represents the basic condition for the model to become operative. We can say that the parameters of participation and institutionalization are powerful indicators of differences in specific conflict patterns, once the model has become applicable, whereas the dichotomous parameter of whether or not social mobility occurs provides us with the basic criterion for judging the very applicability of the model. Let us discuss this basic parameter somewhat more at length.

We have conceived the parameter as dichotomous, allowing us to distinguish broadly between societies with and without mobility. Basically similar distinctions would seem to underlie a variety of studies of macro-sociological change; the distinction is variously described in terms of traditional versus modern, caste versus class societies, and feudal versus post-feudal societies. Galtung, in an excellent article,[13] suggests a number of formulations which we can fruitfully use here. He distinguishes feudal from non-feudal societies according to two criteria: rank concordance and interaction dependence. Rank concordance is similar to what we, in the first chapter, called rank equivalence; under that condition the set of interests of each member of society is internally balanced. Assuming the tendency towards rank equilibration, this situation is apparently in stable equilibrium due to the absence of motives for mobility. The concept of interaction dependence Galtung uses to refer to the tendency for interactions to become more frequent, the higher the rank positions of the persons involved. A feudal society, according to this view, is characterized by high degrees of rank concordance and interaction dependence. This society, in other words, tends to be highly stratified; the frequency of interaction tends to be highest at the top, lower between the top and subordinate strata and very low or absent at the base. The resulting picture is one of a differentially segmented society; the segmentation, indeed, tends to differ for different social strata, in the sense that 'society', as perceived by the social actors, tends to shrink as these actors are embedded in lower strata of society. The picture is one of lord and serf; or, as anthropologists would label the configuration, it is one of patron and client.[14] Isolated islands of clients are stably subordinated to patrons between whom broad social intercourse occurs.

It goes without saying that this societal configuration does not lend itself to analysis in terms of our conflict model. Crucial variables are absent, such as motives for upward mobility, rank discrepancies, and achievement norms, as well as the ensuing interference of the latter with norms of ascription. Instead of the menace of radicalism potentially disturbing the system, we encounter factors reinforcing it, working towards the emergence of what Galtung has termed generalized underdog roles and generalized top-dog roles, due to the fact that, irrespective of the social context or the specific content of the relation, members of different social strata tend to meet in a similar setting of stable super- and subordination.

It is equally apparent that, if the model of conflict and radicalism is to be applicable at all, societies have to grow away from this feudal extreme through changes in the criteria both of rank concordance and of interaction dependence. How, specifically, this change may have been effected is a problem beyond the analytic scope of our discussion, in so far as our theoretical model does not contain references to factors which are to bring about its very applicability. These developments, from the perspective of the conflict model, are autonomous. If we may, however, venture to suggest an explanatory framework, we could, for instance, bring to mind Stein's *The Eclipse of Community*, where the author, under the headings of urbanization, industrialization and bureaucratization discusses a number of factors which tend to disturb both the rank concordance and interaction dependence of feudal societies. All three of these general factors work to upset the internally integrated, and differentially segmented, patron-client structures. Once these developments are under way, however, there will occur a moment where trends as described in our model of conflict themselves start to independently affect the interaction dependence of the system. To the extent, namely, that, for a left-wing radical vanguard, the change occurs in its reference group behaviour and it starts to orient itself towards the mobilization of a following, this very effort implies that it has actively set out to increase the frequency of interaction among previously isolated groups of underdogs. Thus it aims at breaking through the monopoly of information and legitimation of the top-dogs and at introducing novel images and interpretations of society through the institution of novel channels of interaction. We can say that this endeavour is essentially emancipist.

Thus we have introduced a term which the reader may have considered earlier. For indeed the model of conflict, in its analysis of left-radicalism is an emancipation model. It describes the attempt of groups which have come to conceive of their situation in terms of deprivation, to transcend this state through the redefinition of a given societal distribution in terms of justice and injustice, as well as through the active organization of their power potential as they perceive it. Emancipation in this sense would seem to constitute a

136

set of historical developments, representing a victory over two contrary forces—the forces of assimilation and of what we might call self-colonization.

Of these, assimilation may be considered the historic alternative to emancipation, in that assimilation too represents a rise from positions of deprivation, albeit through individual mobility which leaves a given system of societal distribution unaltered. Mobility in this case requires the adoption of—or the assimilation to—the rules which govern the established system. In our model of conflict both alternatives have been built in, in consecutive order, we may recall. The initial frustration of demands for mobility in a context of individual assimilation led the mobile vanguard to a radical reappraisal, intent on collective emancipation. The other contrary force—that of self-colonization—differs from both assimilation and emancipation in that it reflects processes which tend to keep those in lowly positions from an orientation towards social mobility altogether.

The processes referred to in this instance can appear in different configurations. In the first place we can think of the generalized underdog role, referred to above. The self-conception of the underdogs, as well as its display in their behaviour, reflects the low esteem in which dominant groups hold them. The behaviour of the underdogs abounds with the ritual display of self-rejection, humility and worthlessness. It betrays a self-image whose internalization may differ in its compellingness and its traumatizing effects. Indeed, variations in the general theme of the underdog role are possible, offering greater or lesser protection from the effects of adopting a self-image of abjection, as is illustrated, for instance, by Pettigrew or by Den Hollander.[15] The underlying mechanism is, however, clear, as Elias and Scotson state in *The Established and the Outsiders*: ' . . . *this internalization by the socially inferior group of the disparaging belief of the superior group as part of their own conscience and self-image powerfully reinforces the superiority and the rule of the established group.*'[16]

This indeed is the basic mechanism of self-colonization; it is colonization to the extent that the privileged position of one group entails the lesion of pride and self-esteem of another group—it is self-colonization to the extent that this latter group has come to perceive itself, as it were through the eyes of the dominant group, as inferior to it. The very choice, however, of words such as 'colonization' and 'traumatization' may have unduly emphasized one way of experiencing this constellation, either on the part of the underlying parties, or on the part of the outside observer. If we recall the picture which we drew above of a feudal society with its paternalistic patron-client relations, the experience may well be one of a benevolent and just, albeit hierarchical order, where the patron justifies his claims

137

on eminence through his functions of protection and interest promotion for clusters of clients. The display of deference towards the patron on the part of the client, in that case, is freely exchanged for the protection of interests offered in return.[17] It is rather this constellation and this world of experience which is apparent in the analysis by the Lynds of Middletown on the eve of industrialization and in the study by Warner and his associates of Yankee City prior to its disruption by industrialization and bureaucratization.[18] This same constellation figures in the discussion in England around the theme of the 'working-class conservative'—the worker who, though ranking himself as a worker, in his political behaviour subscribes to an established hierarchical order.[19]

This very subscription to an established order with the consequent gratification of feeling respectable which it offers the working-class conservative, is shown *a contrario* in the rejection of any group which is not up to these standards of respectability. The respectables tend to draw a sharp line between themselves and the 'roughs' below them.[20] This illustrates the incidence of status differentials—of the attribution of inferiority in support of a group's sense of superiority—which may work to eclipse potential harmony of interests in terms of power and class. The divisive effects of the distribution of status, which we referred to earlier, would appear one of the most potent instruments of self-colonization. The situation of the working-class conservative *vis-à-vis* the roughs, here described, no longer reflects a generalized underdog role, however, but rather a second configuration of self-colonization.

A series of English community studies highlights this second configuration. The basic pattern here is one of a stratum of traditional workers which, in the course of industrialization, has got to face the intrusion of newly-arrived labour, as a novel and disturbing element, into the integrated traditional community. Time and again, the pattern has been uncovered of the traditional workers aligning themselves with their masters in opposition to and rejection of the newly-arrived groups. Studies by Elias and Scotson and by Stacey offer good cases in point.[21] The lure of relative status gain, as well as of the conservation of what shares of power they had, has effectively kept the traditional workers from aligning themselves with the immigrants on the basis of common class interests. The immigrants become the objects of ostracism and stigmatization which, if internalized by the latter, leads to the traumatizing variant of self-colonization. The traditional workers, on the other hand, while playing a pivotal role in the maintenance of a quasi-colonial situation, would rather appear subject to the non-traumatizing, gratifying variant of self-colonization.

This behaviour *vis-à-vis* outsiders apparently shows yet another mechanism which we should mention; borrowing from Myrdal, we may describe it as the 'inverse rank order of discrimination'.[22] It refers to the tendency to apply behavioural norms with a rigidity and neglect of standards of leniency, as well as of mitigating factors, which increases as the groups under scrutiny are lower in the social hierarchy. In that sense the traumatic self-colonization and the inverse rank order of discrimination are mutually reinforcing. The inability on the part of the outsiders to live up to social tenets in all their absoluteness inculcates the sense of inferiority all the more powerfully.

Finally, a third pattern of self-colonization would appear to manifest itself in American studies of Negro sub-cultures. Hannerz, for one, in his excellent study *Soulside*,[23] has analysed the attempts to overcome the traumatizing impact of the generalized underdog role through innovative shifts in status criteria for the assessment of self-esteem. He refers to criteria such as masculinity or cool self-control in the use of hard drugs. This latter criterion in particular, however, carries associations with Marx's indictment of religion as opium for the people. The struggle thus defined for sustaining self-esteem as well as a sense of identity is nothing but a fake which leaves the traumatizing opponent unchallenged. It consistently keeps the people involved from a consideration of their interests in a societal framework—of the community of interests with others; finally, it keeps them from the organization of their power potential through alliance formation. Only under these conditions would our conflict model become operative.

Myopic declarations of solidarity on the part of a self-styled radical sociology, tending to conceive of this opiate and deviant sub-culture as carrying opportunities for cultural innovation, if only we stop to look at it from the point of view of established, middle-class culture,[24] fully neglect the considerations presented above. Innovation and the victory over inhuman deprivation can only be attained through emancipation, through a radical reorientation transcending the 'false consciousness' of an opiate sub-culture. A trend along these lines towards greater political awareness is, for instance, illustrated by Janowitz's analysis in his *The Social Control of Escalated Riots*;[25] he uncovers an unfolding pattern of race riots, ever since the beginning of this century, towards an increased consciousness of deprivation in a societal context as well as of the opponents to be held accountable.

At this point the discussion draws to an end. The assessment of the range of validity of our general model of conflict has gone through the definition of an absolute condition of applicability—the breakdown of feudal society—to an outline of forces which might continue to keep the model from unfolding. To the extent that these are the

139

forces of self-colonization, whatever their specific configuration, we may add that, essentially, they represent remnants of feudal structures interfering with post-feudal structures. Assimilation and emancipation in these latter structures would appear as actual alternatives; which of these will gain the upper hand at any given point of time depends on what opportunities a given system may offer to satisfy expectations which it has engendered in its members.

References

Introduction

1 For this discussion see Demerath and Peterson, 1967. For a more recent contribution to the discussion, Gouldner, 1971.
2 Dahrendorf, 1959. For a similar approach, cf. Horton, 1970.
3 Elias and Dunning, 1966.
4 Elias, 1969.

1 Conflict and radicalism: a two-stage model

1 Earlier versions of this chapter have been published as Kroes, 1969 and Kroes, 1970.
2 Cf. Dahrendorf, 1959, concluding chapter.
3 See, e.g., Schumpeter, 1947, ch. 2 in which he deals with the tautological aspects in Marx's analysis.
4 In the case of some social goods, such as power, the zero-sum conditions may seem to make more sense than in the case of other goods such as income. However, a short-run analysis of macro-economic equilibrium explicitly holds that national income has a certain, set value to the effect that no one particular group can increase its relative income without, by the very fact, reducing that of other groups. Under short-run conditions of full employment, processes of negative feed-back such as inflation act to restore a short-run equilibrium in the distribution of income. On the other hand, dependent on the way the concept is defined, power can be conceived as subject to zero-sum conditions; cf. Parsons, 1967, pp. 332ff.
5 This definition is similar to the one given by Weber (1921): 'Kampf soll eine soziale Beziehung insoweit heissen, als das Handeln an der Absicht der Durchsetzung des eignen Willens gegen Widerstand des oder der Partner orientiert ist' or the one given by Boulding (1963, p. 5): 'Conflict may be defined as a situation of competition in which the parties are aware of the incompatibility of potential future positions and in which each party wishes to occupy a position that is incompatible with the wishes of the other.'

6 In connection with the problem of definition one further point deserves mention. The word conflict tends to bring to mind movie-like associations with demonstrations, strikes, police action and the like—associations that do not seem warranted on the basis of our definitions of a situation of conflict. We referred, however, to the strategic options that are open to the parties in conflict. The concept of strategy implies a series of decisions on a range of subsequent actions, aiming at a certain goal, with due regard to the possible reactions on the part of the adversary. Strikes and demonstrations can be considered such strategic options; they are means to achieve an end against adverse action of a rival party. The analysis of such strategies is essentially a short-run analysis—one that evaluates alternative actions *within a given structural context*. Studies on this field are, e.g., T. C. Schelling, 1960, and Boulding, 1963. It may be useful, therefore, to distinguish conceptually between a *situation of conflict* and a *course of conflict*.

7 See, e.g., Parsons, 1967. Also Etzioni, 1968: particularly ch. 13, 'Power as a Societal Force'.

8 See, e.g., Dahrendorf, 1959. For recent use of the concept by a political scientist, cf. Dahl, 1967. Pluralism in this sense should not be confused with labels describing ethnically heterogeneous, segmented societies. For this use, cf. Hoetink, 1961; pp. 148ff.

9 Guetzkow, 1955.

10 Kaplan, 1957; particularly ch. 5, 'The Integrative and the Disintegrative Processes'.

11 See, e.g., Galtung, 1966.

12 Coser, 1956.

13 Coleman, 1957. Also Davis, 1966.

14 For the following argument I am heavily indebted to Galtung's excellent article (Galtung, 1966).

15 This definition of pluralism differs from the one Galtung suggests. In his computation of optimal criss-cross in the distribution of individuals over the four cells of the matrix, he does not take account of any external constraint. We, on the other hand, start from a given distribution of the population along the separate dimensions and analyse how these distributions intercorrelate. There would seem to be a definite advantage in this approach, as we shall illustrate shortly, in that it can reveal the fact that a distribution over the high and low positions of one dimension can exert an independent influence on the degree of criss-cross.

16 This procedure would also produce a value of 1 in the opposite case where the cells TT and LL are empty. Galtung points out, that, although taken at face-value this would seem to be a situation of criss-cross, the opposite cells have no positions in common, whereas this, according to pluralist theory, is the crucial element in analyses of conflict.

17 This does not necessarily lead to a reduction in the total conflict potential in a society, as we shall point out in our analysis of the rank inequivalence pattern.

18 L. Coser, 1956, last ch. Dahl, 1967.

19 Coser, loc. cit.

20 E. A. Ross, 1920, quoted in Galtung, 1966.
21 It is these characteristics of conflict which Dahrendorf treats at length in Dahrendorf, 1959. See also Coser, 1956.
22 Galtung has already pointed out this condition, Galtung, 1966.
23 A. Lijphart, 1968.
24 Ibid., p. 104.
25 Ibid., p. 93.
26 Ibid., pp. 88ff.
27 This will come out even more clearly if we take into consideration, along with the socio-economic and religious dimensions, a third one to represent the opposition of centralism vs. regionalism or centre vs. periphery, to use terms that Shils introduced (E. Shils, 1961). Along this axis interests can be ordered that are connected with the geographical position of segments of the population towards central authoritative bodies. The 'objective' conflict of interests which is inherent in this situation has been systematically treated by Lipset and Rokkan (Lipset and Rokkan, 1967), while, for a more theoretical formulation of the sources of conflict in the relation of sub-systems to a wider system Gouldner's article may be illuminating (Gouldner, 1959; pp. 242ff). The consideration of this additional dimension in an analysis of the Dutch social system would—were all Catholics or a majority of them to live in the southern provinces—lead us to assert that conflict on the basis of religion would be reinforced by regional interests. The addition of this dimension, however, again produces the criss-cross pattern: the majority of the Catholics, as a matter of fact, live *outside* the southern regions of apparent high Catholic density, as Goudsblom points out (Goudsblom, 1967).
  It is a problem in its own right how many and what specific distributive dimensions should be considered in an analysis of real-life situations. We shall return to this problem in the sixth section of this chapter.
28 Galtung, op. cit., pp. 152, 153. Our formulation differs slightly from the one he gives without, however, changing the thrust of the argument where the dual interpretation of *shared* positions is concerned.
29 We should point to the fact that in later publications Lijphart tends to accept the autonomous, conflict-reducing effects of the pluralist pattern. Cf. Lijphart, 1971.
30 Berting, 1965. Also Galtung, 1966; Davis, 1966; and Zelditch and Anderson, 1966.
31 Benoit-Smullyan, 1944.
32 See, e.g., Davis, 1966, where this interlinking is achieved. Also Newcomb, 1961. A related, though separate, problem concerns the tendency for this equilibrating force to focus on specific rank positions and to neglect others. In this context Berting points out that the selection of rank positions used in the assessment of equivalence or inequivalence is itself normatively determined (Berting, 1965). Also Sampson, 1963, where the author proposes aiming the analysis of status congruence at the level of congruence of expectations and fulfilment of expectations. These expectations, again, may be conceived as normatively structured. We shall go into this more extensively.

33 For a fully elaborated theoretical formulation in terms of investments and rewards, see Homans, 1961. Also Runciman, 1960.

34 Of course, it is an important question whether, in the absence of the American yardstick, the English situation would have been experienced as internally disproportional. The terms 'structural gap' or 'disproportionality' may seem to be more absolute than the actual situation would warrant. It does seem to be an undeniable fact, however, that given the American yardstick, higher education, especially, in England instils a level of expectation in its students which American society is able to meet *to a larger extent* than English society.

35 For an analysis of the force of such expectations in social situations, see J. Berger, B. P. Cohen and M. Zelditch Jr, 'Status Characteristics and Expectation States', in Berger *et al.*, op. cit.

36 Galtung, 1966; Goffman, 1957; Goldthorpe, Lockwood, Bechhofer, and Platt, 1967; Jackson, 1962; Lenski, 1956.

37 See especially: Lenski, 1954; Lipset, 1960; Bell, 1963.

38 Cf. the instance of Disraeli, as cited in Kroes, 1962.

39 Runciman, 1960.

40 In the context of this chapter it does not seem appropriate to deal with the subject at any length, but we should like to suggest that, applied to the rising tide of negro-radicalism in the USA, this proposition might allow us to evaluate a range of facts and make us aware of the inter-relationships between them.

41 Runciman himself designs a model on the basis of these variables which shows a trend towards increased solidarity and emerging leadership (Runciman, 1960); Merton, too, points out this relationship (Merton, 1957, pp. 266ff, 293). See also Zelditch and Anderson, 1966, especially propositions 10.3 and following.

42 Runciman, 1960, p. 36. Lockwood, 1958, pp. 13–17. Dahrendorf, 1959, pp. 165ff.

43 Runciman, 1960, p. 233. An interesting point in this context has been suggested by Hofstadter: depending on the phase of the economic cycle, class politics and status politics tend to alternate. This would imply a qualification of our statement. Cf. Hofstadter in Bell, 1963.

44 Dahrendorf, 1959.

45 Cf. section 5 of this chapter.

46 An interesting argument in this context can be found in Dahrendorf's Noel Buxton Lecture of 1967. There he disengages himself from the conflict model he had developed in the late 1950s, based on the centrally explanatory value of power differentials. Latter-day industrialized society would hold so many opportunities for individual gratification as to keep individuals from an assessment of lowly power positions they might share with others (cf. Dahrendorf, 1967).

47 A good case is the history of the Zengakuren movement in Japan. Tightly linked with the Communist Party, the movement set out on a course in more democratic directions. Parts among the following considered this treason and left to set up more radical groups. Cf. *Nieuwe Rotterdamse Courant*, 17 November 1969.

48 Dahrendorf, 1959.

49 My set of inter-related definitions of the class concept has been inspired

by Lockwood, 1958, and by Runciman, 1966. An interesting operationalization of the concepts of class, internal and external market position can be found in Benoit, 1965.

2 Military intervention in domestic politics: a framework for analysis

1 Earlier versions of this chapter have been published; cf. Kroes, 1969b and Kroes, 1970b.
2 We choose the word arena in order to emphasize the element of competition among interest groups in social situations.
3 Huntington, 1967; esp. pp. 78–93 and ch. 4.
4 Lipset and Rokkan, 1967.
5 Huntington labels this arena 'radical'; we choose the term transitional, however, on account of the different denotation we gave the term 'radical' in the first chapter.
6 In the analysis of a civic arena at the end of this paper we shall deal briefly with the phenomenon of mutiny.
7 The exact location of this boundary would seem to vary with the concrete cases at hand. Conceivably, in empirical cases, differences in class position could be the crucial criterion; the boundary then would be between the rank of colonel as regimental commander and the rank, immediately above, of brigadier-general. The superior educational requirements for the latter rank—in the Netherlands, e.g., *Hogere Krijgsschool* (Higher War School) in addition to the *Koninklijke Militaire Academie* (Royal Military Academy)—apparently limit mobility from the lower to the higher rank. For different historical cases, however, the boundaries might well operate horizontally, separating territorial commanders from military power centres; potential conflict dimensions are rather the differences in power which this situation entails. These too can serve as the crucial criterion setting off shifts in reference group behaviour, as outlined in our conflict model.
8 Kaplan, 1957.
9 Indeed, the palace revolution is the characteristic variety of the *coup d'état* in oligarchic arenas (cf. Huntington, 1967, p. 201). Within the oligarchic elite changes tend to occur in that faction which is in power at any particular point of time, without these changes having any noticeable impact on the wider society. As Huntington has it: 'The top leadership is changed but no significant changes are made in the scope of governmental authority or the scope of political participation.' (Ibid., loc. cit.)
10 For an account of our selection of different dimensions, cf. section 2 of this chapter: 'Relative shares and reference groups'. Large, medium or small shares of each of the various social goods are referred to as +, + −, − ; downward pressure on shares is indicated with downward arrows, upward pressure with upward arrows.
11 Elias, 1969. Also Moore, 1967; ch. 2.
12 On this point cf. Janowitz, 1960; ch. 2 and *passim*.
13 Apter, 1965, chs 4 and 5. Bendix, 1964. Shils, 1962, p. 17. Pye, 1962, pp. 83, 84.

14 See especially Janowitz, 1964, pp. 70ff, where he mentions this inter-generational cleavage of junior versus senior officers. He suggests that the promotion system based on differences in internal status may act as a check on the disrupting effects of the cleavage. It is a common theme in Marxist social critique that differences in status are a powerful device used by the classes in power to disperse their potential class opponents. Surprisingly, Apter makes a statement to this effect: 'Whereas class tends to promote solidarity among its members, status tends to drive individuals apart and to isolate them in an infinitely extended system of small-scale differences that become the basis of competition' (Apter, op. cit., p. 125).

It is a fact that status as a social good lends itself towards more refined distribution and may be used to keep social groups with low class or power positions from forming alliances. According to our propositions, however, differences in status may be de-emphasized as soon as mobility along class and power dimensions is perceived as thwarted. Moreover, a refined set of status differentials within the context of an organization such as the army need not stand in the way of much cruder external status differentials, so that these latter may well fall in line with class and power differentials.

15 On this essentially Mannheimian point, see Janowitz, 1960, p. 7. Modern technology has produced such a high level of specialization that men are likely to think of themselves as members of a specific skill group, rather than as members of a social class. See also Lang, 1965, p. 841.

16 Janowitz, 1960, ch. 2 and *passim*. P. 21 gives the following description: 'The heroic leader is a perpetuation of the warrior type, the mounted officer who embodies the martial spirit and the theme of personal valor.' In addition to the heroic elite, Janowitz distinguishes a managerial and a technical elite, both reflecting more recent traditions of leadership within military organizations.

17 Janowitz, 1960, pp. 225ff.

18 Ibid., pp. 64ff.

19 An interesting 'study' of the planning of a military coup provoked by such a development, is offered in the film *Seven Days in May* by John Frankenheimer, based on a script by Rod Serling.

20 See, e.g., the analysis of right radicalism in America in Agger, Goldrich and Swanson, 1964. Also Lipset and Raab, 1971.

21 See, e.g., *New York Times*, 'The Week in Review', 'Army Dissent. It raises knotty problems for the military', 20 April 1969. Also *New York Times Magazine*, 'Must the Citizen give up his Civil Liberties when he joins the Army?', 18 May 1969, p. 25.

---

3 **Decolonization and the military: the case of the Netherlands. A study in political reaction**

1 Earlier versions of this chapter have been published; cf. Kroes, 1970c and Kroes, 1971.

2 I wish to express my gratitude to the following people who have been willing to respond to my request to discuss the role of the military

during the Indonesian crisis: Messrs R. de Bruin, L. J. M. Beel, J. A. W. Burger, J. A. A. van Doorn, W. Drees Sr, F. Goedhart, M. van der Goes van Naters, L. de Jong, J. A. Jonkman, P. J. Koets, D. R. A. van Langen, H. Martinot, J. Ozinga, C. Smit, G. H. Slotemaker de Bruine, F. C. Spits, A. Spoor, P. van 't Veer, J. Verkuyl, S. van der Wal, W. F. Wertheim, W. Wierda. I have greatly profited by their inside experience and expert knowledge. Further, I wish to thank the *Partij van de Arbeid* for admitting me to its archives on the Indonesian crisis. This research has been greatly furthered by the co-operation of the Section on Military History and the Stamboek Officieren KNIL of the Ministry of Defence. I wish also to thank Dra. Schmüller of ANP (General Netherlands Press Bureau) for giving me access to its archives. Finally, J. M. Pluvier has been most helpful by lending me his chronological collection of newspaper reports and comments from the period 1945–1950.

3 Good material for study on this subject would be Blumberger, 1931 and Pluvier, 1953.

4 Van Doorn and Hendrix, 1970, pp. 26ff.

5 One survey among many others is given by Dootjes, 1948, p. 93. Also Anderson, 1967.

6 Van Doorn and Hendrix, 1970, p. 35.

7 Smit, 1962, p. 61.

8 De Kadt, 1949, p. 137. Van Doorn and Hendrix, 1970, p. 35.

9 A. H. Nasution, 1965. Smail, 1964.

10 For a brief sketch, see Van Doorn and Hendrix, 1970, pp. 89ff. Also Smit, 1962, p. 110 and *passim*.

11 *Het Parool*, 23 February 1946; *Het Parool*, 14 May 1946. Socialist support fell from 46 per cent to 34 per cent!

12 Amendment of the Constitution, according to Dutch constitutional law, requires both a general election and a qualified majority of two-thirds of the votes of members present in both Houses of Parliament. This second condition especially should be borne in mind as a serious check on the room for manoeuvring of a Dutch cabinet in matters that require constitutional amendment.

13 See, e.g., de Jong, 'Koningin Wilhelmina in Londen, 1940–1945'.

14 Though there was no regularly elected parliament at the time, there was a provisional parliament which derived its mandate from the last pre-war elections of 1937. Its ranks were further filled by people who had deserved well in war-time resistance movements.

15 This point is most strongly proved by the combination of positions of editor-in-chief of a Catholic newspaper and head of the Catholic Parliamentary Party in the person of C. P. M. Romme. Similar links existed both on the political left and on the right, although these were not as tight.

16 Most outspoken was the party leader, K. Vorrink.

17 Other prominent socialist leaders, such as Prime Minister W. Drees, had different, though related, motives for maintaining the coalition. Socialist participation was considered a necessary check on the political right in the painful process of decolonization.

18 Lijphart, 1969.

19 See Van Doorn and Hendrix, 1970, where the authors refer to several thousand troops.

20 Personal communication by Prof. S. van der Wal, based on his government-authorized research of source-material. Also *Vrij Nederland*, 5 July 1947, where reference is made to a petition, signed by 450 radjahs, adat-heads and leaders of several spheres of life as well as civil servants, that was handed to the Australian commander on 4 January 1946. In the petition that should have been forwarded to the United Nations, but never was, it was requested that freedom to join the Republic be granted.

21 Smit, 1962, p. 26.

22 Van Doorn and Hendrix, 1970, p. 122.

23 Through Japanese archives the Dutch were perfectly informed of where these stocks were concentrated. See, e.g., *Het Economisch Weekblad voor Indonesië*, 1946, 1947, where E. de Vries published several reports on the location of stocks.

24 Personal information from J. Ozinga in a letter of 14 July 1970.

25 As, for instance, at the time of an unauthorized action on the eve of the signing of the Linggadjati agreement, when van Mook insisted on having a report through civilian channels. Personal information from P. J. Koets, at the time head of the cabinet of the Governor-General.

26 Van Doorn and Hendrix, 1970.

27 There might, however, be an element of contamination in the argument of Van Doorn and Hendrix. The strongholds where the Dutch military found itself confined after the departure of the British troops were the main urban, commercial centres along the coasts, where the density of concentration camps was greatest (the relief of internees being one of the express commissions of the British forces). At the same time, however, concentrations of European colonists meant concentrations of industrial and plantation interests (mining, oil, sugar, tobacco, rubber, etc.). Whenever the military undertook actions across the confines of the strongholds, it might seem a foregone conclusion that the area it entered was of high commercial interest.

   The empirical correlation need not warrant the conclusion that the military acted mainly in protection of those interests. This fact was pointed out to me in a personal conversation with R. de Bruin.

28 Minister of Overseas Territories in the second post-war cabinet.

29 As Dr Jonkman pointed out, ever since 1795 the subject of the colonies had been incorporated in the Dutch Constitution, thus causing a subject of essentially foreign-policy nature to be subject to procedures of amending strictly Dutch constitutional law. This juridical fiction was never accepted by the United Nations, which, from the start, in its deliberations acknowledged two parties to the conflict: the Netherlands and the Republic of Indonesia, while excluding representatives of the two federal structures.

30 As evidenced most dramatically by the attempt to bind the Republic to the Dutch interpretation of the Linggadjati agreement and, most hilariously, by Gerbrandy, who, on the eve of the Round Table Conference that was to bring an end to the Indonesian crisis, accused the government of infraction of the Constitution and threatened that, in

the face of this infraction, a minority of the Dutch people might take the law into its own hands. (*Handelingen Tweede Kamer*, 16 August 1949, *Avondvergadering*; sheet 482, pp. 1,840ff.)

31 As confidentially pointed out by several of my informants. From the publications we might mention the following: van der Ende, 1946; Feuilletau de Bruijn, 1949.

32 Van Doorn and Hendrix, 1970, p. 40.

33 Ibid., p. 41.

34 Data gathered in *Stamboek Officieren KNIL* at the Ministry of Defence in The Hague as well as in address-books of the Dutch East Indies.

35 All but three of them were Europeans.

36 Apart from groups that we have already referred to, such as the indigenous rank-and-file of the Colonial Army, we should think of elite members of the pre-colonial feudal structures that had been upheld by encapsulation in the colonial system of rule.

37 Van Doorn and Hendrix, 1970, p. 129.

38 Helfrich, 1950, part 2, p. 231.

39 Van Doorn and Hendrix, 1970, pp. 73, 74.

40 Personal communication by Dr Koets.

41 G. H. Slotemaker de Bruine was interviewed in *De Volkskrant*, 28 June 1969. According to him, a meeting was convened of alarmed socialist leaders which he attended. He was unable to remember what was discussed at the meeting. As W. Drees informed me, he could not find an entry in his agenda referring to this meeting, nor could he remember anything relating to it.

42 Confidential information.

43 Cf. Teitler, 1969/70.

44 See 'Regeringsnota inzake Optreden Nederlandse Militairen voorafgaande aan Overdracht Soevereiniteit Indonesië', in *Handelingen Tweede Kamer*, no. 10,008. Cf. n. 20.

45 The socialists would consent only to a restricted action that would not reach Jogjakarta, centre of the Republic. *Notulen Partijraadvergadering* of 19 July 1947; source: archives of the *Partij van de Arbeid*. Also Smit, 1959.

46 Smit, 1962, p. 88. Smit, 1959, pp. 193, 194, 195.

47 Smit, 1962, p. 91.

48 *Het Vrije Volk*, 5 September 1947.

49 J. Ozinga, in a letter of 14 July 1970, refers to telegrams sent by General de Bruine and Colonel Mollinger asking for authorization to continue action in Madura and near Palembang.

50 As is apparent, e.g., from letters sent by the socialist Lieutenant van Gorcum to the chairman of the Dutch Labour Party. Source: archives of the *Partij van de Arbeid*.

51 M. van Blankenstein in the Dutch weekly *De Stem van Nederland*, 5 July 1947. The Pasundan was to include most of western Java.

52 Van Doorn and Hendrix, 1970, p. 92.

53 One of the few examples of a right-radical movement availing itself of guerilla tactics. As Colonel Wierda wrote in a letter of 19 August 1950 (archives of the *Partij van de Arbeid*), it was beyond doubt that Dutch troops had been providing the Darul Islam with arms.

54 Confidential communication.
55 Confidential communication. See also Westerling's own account in his *Mijn Memoires*, 1952. Also a letter by navy Lieutenant A. J. Schouwenaar of 13 April 1950 (archives of the *Partij van de Arbeid*).
56 Consonant with this interpretation is the ultimatum, sent by Westerling to the governments of both the state of Pasundan and the United States of Indonesia in which he demanded that a private army he had formed (estimates of its strength ran from 4,000 up to 30,000) be recognized as the official forces of the State of Pasundan (ANETA, 9 January 1950; ANP archive).
57 A. J. Schouwenaar, letters of 8 March 1950 and 2 March 1950.
58 The reality of this drive cannot be denied. As early as 12 January 1950 the federal government drafted a law to disband the states of East Java and the Pasundan (ANETA, 12 January 1950; ANP archive).
59 A. P. N. Pielage, letters of 21 June 1950 and 21 July 1950 (archives of the *Partij van de Arbeid*). Also G. C. van Gorcum, letters of 13 April 1950 and 2 May 1950.
60 A. P. N. Pielage, letter of 21 June 1950.
61 At the time the Organization of Non-Commissioned Officers of the KNIL filed a petition with the members of the Dutch parliament (13 February 1950) not to allow any such reductions (archives of the *Partij van de Arbeid*).
62 Van Doorn and Hendrix, 1970, p. 127.
63 This was evident on the eve of the second military expedition when, after the socialist ministers had actually handed in their resignation, they were prevailed upon to stay on, on the condition that the authorization for military action be postponed and a three-day ultimatum be posed to the Republic. In Batavia Beel, influenced by military advisers to believe that, for purely military reasons, no delay of action longer than twenty-four hours could be afforded, self-righteously cut back the ultimatum to less than twenty-four hours (confidential information).
64 Despite indications to the contrary (Smit, 1962, p. 159). In Catholic political circles forces were working towards a complete break with the socialists, which would have meant a cabinet crisis that might have provoked a military-civilian praetorian coup. Cf. the development in Algeria: de la Gorce, 1963, chs. 17–20.
65 Almond and Verba, 1963.

4 Student radicalism in the 1960s

1 On this point, see Lammers, 1968. Also Pinner, 1968, and Boudon, 1969.
2 In addition to degree of autonomy of the university as a variable, we could distinguish, as Weinberg and Walker do (1970), variations in the degree to which students are recruited into national political parties. Such variations give some indication of the degree of institutionalization of channels for student participation in the political process. The importance of this variable will tend to increase once universities have

lost their autonomy to a certain degree and the central government has increasingly developed into the focal point for the voicing of demands and grievances.

3 See, e.g., Kroes, 1968. Etzioni, too, pays attention to this assessment of relative power potentials in the decisions of both parties on their strategies (cf. Etzioni, 1968, ch. 13).

4 Flacks, 1967. Heist, n.d. Keniston, 1967.

5 Pinner refers to the UNEF in France as a case in point (Pinner, 1968). Lammers (1968) also goes into the problem of the effectiveness of leadership—the leadership should have a sufficient array of strategies at its disposal.

6 See Pinner, 1968. The concepts used here will be elaborated shortly.

7 Cf. Lipset, 1972.

8 Cf. Lammers, 1968. Also Pinner: 'socializing organizations educate their members so they will be prepared for their future roles in society. . . . Some socializing organizations prepare the student mainly for his future occupation, while others prepare him for status positions in society' (Pinner, 1968, p. 142).

9 Cf. Elias and Scotson, 1965, for an analysis of the means at the disposal of old, established groups in the defence of their position vis-à-vis newly-established groups. Also Stinchcombe, 1965.

10 Cf. Lammers, 1968.

11 Ibid.

12 For a concise elaboration of these concepts, see Parsons, 1967.

13 Pinner, 1968, p. 142.

14 See especially Flacks, 1967.

15 Flacks, 1967. Boudon dwells extensively on the influence of future job opportunities as well as on the differences in this respect between various fields of study (Boudon, 1969).

16 Both the efforts produced by the gainfully employed students as well as the element of external control accepted by scholarship students can be considered as some sort of investment in the market position of these students; the investment tends to have the highest returns on the market of occupations that require academic degrees. The limited external 'convertibility' of this investment can be fruitfully compared with seniority in that it tends to orient the investor more strongly towards the organization constituting his internal market position. He will, therefore, perceive issues pertaining to extra-academic, political matters as interfering with a regular course of study and withhold active support in these matters. On the other hand, he is liable to mobilization in matters regarding discrepancies between his anticipations of occupational opportunities and interpretations developed by a radical vanguard.

17 See, e.g., Becker, 1970, pp. 8ff: 'The general charge that student demonstrators lack civility has been made repeatedly, and the implication has often been drawn that this is no small matter, that it rather represents a fundamental departure from the norms of civilized conduct and that the barbarians are therefore already inside the gate. . . . It symbolizes, in a way that would seem trivial if it were not for the reaction, students' intention to overturn the existing hierarchy of

academic life, a hierarchy that distributes quite unequally participants' power over one another.'
18 Den Hollander, 1968, p. 58.

5 Student radicalism: a survey report

1 I wish to thank W. van Rossum, research associate at the Sociological Institute of the University of Amsterdam, who collaborated in the analysis of the research material in 1971.

2 We tried to match the focused samples of ASVA and OBAS as best we could in their disciplinary composition. As it turned out, eight fields of study of ten OBAS respondents were represented among ASVA respondents. For the entire ASVA group the distribution over the various disciplines largely reflected that found for OBAS, save for two dense clusters consisting of seven economists and seven sociologists. Even these lumps in the overall distribution are not too much of an impediment; the following argument will show that the departments of sociology and economics in certain respects, such as political climate and occupational opportunities, diverge markedly. Therefore it is a good thing to have a broad range of diversity in disciplinary composition for a group that, as a whole, constitutes a left-radical vanguard. In this connection we might mention that with regard to phase of study neither group of activists clearly diverged from the sample as a whole: 35 per cent of the ASVA group and 23 per cent of the OBAS group were graduate students, compared with 25·4 per cent of the sample.

3 When checked according to such criteria as age, religion, type of secondary education, sex, year of study, field of study, phase of study, regional background and residential characteristics (either living or not living with parents), our 210 respondents were still markedly representative of the overall student body of the University of Amsterdam. Only for year of study did we establish that first-year students were markedly under-represented; with regard to field of study, we found that both science and the literary studies were under-represented (9·1 per cent science students in the sample against 15·7 per cent for the overall population; 15·8 per cent against 21·3 per cent for literary studies).

4 At one point the diversity of lay images even showed up in our research findings. In stark contrast to parents of left-wing students, parents of right-wing students believed that radical students acted the way they did because they had not been brought up in proper anticipation of the rules governing academic life. This statement was rejected by all categories of student respondents. The replication showed that, this time, *all* categories of parents tended to accept the statement, whereas their children by and large rejected it.

5 Lammers, 1970, ch. 2.

6 As regards the question whether in our case the radicals were 'the best students', it appeared that 62 per cent of the left-wing respondents ranked themselves according to intellectual ability among the top 40 per cent of the students, against 71 per cent of the right-wing respondents and 39 per cent of the sample. As to study results and pace of study, however, the left-wing lagged behind the sample and the

TABLE A *Sum of the percentages accorded each of six different aspects of occupations, per set of paired comparisons*

	Students sample	ASVA	OBAS	Parents sample	ASVA	OBAS
autonomy	450	403	436	422	439	388
socio-political involvement	316	433	207	305	370	274
leadership	266	273	386	301	287	331
career opp.	191	118	178	244	188	291
income	175	123	185	110	82	88
prestige	101	150	108	118	134	128

The replication rendered the results in Table B.

TABLE B *Sum of the percentages, for each of the replication categories of respondents, accorded each of six different aspects of occupations, per set of paired comparisons*

Students	left-act.	left-non-act.	middle	right-non-act.	right-act.
autonomy	439	451	461	445	(425)
socio-political involvement	424	395	277	161	(75)
leadership	240	250	290	282	(325)
career opp.	136	157	210	293	(175)
income	128	164	189	226	(275)
prestige	133	83	90	93	(225)

Parents	left-act.	left-non-act.	middle	right-non-act.	right-act.
autonomy	425	430	408	416	(300)
socio-political involvement	370	333	319	181	(350)
leadership	301	276	331	288	(300)
career opp.	227	213	226	302	(250)
income	34	123	104	160	(50)
prestige	143	125	112	153	(250)

(For the right-activists figures are presented in parentheses, on account of the extremely small number of respondents in this category.)

right-wing. The replication bore out that of the left-activists and the left-non-activists respectively 42·3 per cent and 45·1 per cent ranked themselves among the top 40 per cent, against 31·6, 36·9 per cent and 25 per cent for the remaining categories. As to study results and pace of study only the left-non-activists tended to rank above the other categories, who scored more or less alike.

7 The difference between left- and right-radicals is not significant; the difference between left-radical and sample is significant.

8 Boudon, 1969.

9 If we add the various percentages accorded each occupational aspect per paired comparison, we get the results in Table A (the total score which an aspect could conceivably collect is 500).

10 See Table C.

TABLE C *Summary of the significance (Chi-square) of the differences between, on the one hand, left-wing and right-wing and, on the other hand, the middle group as to class position of parental family*

	Students' response	Parental response
Father's income	Not significant	Not significant
Academic education of grandparents	Not significant	Not significant
Academic education of the father	Significant only for right-non-activists and middle	Significant
Academic education of the mother	Not significant	Not significant
Academic education of brothers and/or sisters	Significant for right-non-activists and middle	———
Prestige ranking of father's occupation	Significant for right-non-activists and middle	Significant for right-non-activists and middle
Sector of father's occupation	Significant for right-non-activists and middle	Significant
Self-ranking of students' *milieu* of origin	Not significant	Not significant
Self-ranking of parents' *milieu* of origin	———	Not significant

11 Cf. Pear, 1971, p. 103: 'In the U.K. where 25% of students now come from working class homes, it is not the "working class" Universities like Strathclyde in Glasgow which have been turbulent, but the middle class colleges, like L.S.E., which have given the lead.'

154

12 Feuer, 1969.
13 Flacks, 1967. Heist, n.d. (a). Heist, n.d. (b). Keniston, 1968. Lammers, 1970a, ch. 3.
14 Cf. Flacks, 1967.
15 The replication gave results that were partly similar. Let us compare first the style in which fathers assert they have brought up their children, and (in parentheses) the style in which they say they have been brought up themselves. See Table D.

TABLE D   *Style of upbringing of children (and of the fathers themselves), as characterized by the fathers (in %)*

	Left-act.	Left-non-act.	Middle	Right-non-act.	Right-act.
democratic	76·4 (39·4)	84·6 (33·3)	70·0 (35·8)	76·0 (48·0)	50·0 (0·)
(authoritarian)	(44·1)	(35·9)	(35·8)	(36·0)	(50·0)
modern	53·0 (17·6)	47·5 (10·2)	48·7 (23·1)	42·3 (34·6)	0·(0·)
on equal footing	52·9 (14·7)	47·5 (12·9)	27·5 (12·5)	34·6 (26·9)	0·(0·)
tolerant	70·6 (26·5)	71·8 (28·2)	69·2 (35·9)	61·6 (42·3)	50·0 (0·)

(Differences between the categories of 17% or more are significant on a 5% level. Cf. Appendix 1.)

We should point out that the style in which the fathers say they have been brought up shows a different pattern from what we found for ASVA parents, OBAS parents, and sample parents. The pattern of responses concerning the style in which the fathers say they have brought up their children, however, is similar to the one found before.
The responses of the children themselves give the results in Table E. Once again we see that, whatever the intentions professed by their

TABLE E   *Style of upbringing of children, as characterized by the children themselves (in %)*

	Left-act.	Left-non-act.	Middle	Right-non-act.	Right-act.
democratic	58·5	62·3	55·2	55·0	50·0
modern	35·9	44·2	28·8	40·0	25·0
on equal footing	45·3	44·2	48·3	52·5	50·0
(on unequal footing)	30·1	23·0	27·6	20·0	——
tolerant	62·2	65·4	55·1	60·0	50·0

(Differences between the categories of 17% or more are significant on a 5% level. Cf. Appendix 1.)

parents, the left-activists are the most likely to consider their upbringing as having been on an unequal footing.

16 As to voting behaviour and actual party preference, the replication rendered results similar to the ones found before. Moreover, the characterization of degree of progressiveness of the mother, by children and mothers, again showed a steady decline in progressivism when we moved from left to right. For the fathers, however, the characterization given both by the children and by the fathers showed fathers of left-activists to be less progressive than fathers of left-non-activists—possibly an element of generation conflict that may help account for the shift from left-non-activist to left-activist. The difference, however, is not significant on the 5 per cent level.

In addition to this, the replication showed that, with regard to the exchange of views between students and parents on each of the three subjects mentioned above, all categories referred to study results as the most common subject. Yet, of all the groups under comparison, the left-activists were most likely to refer to university problems as subjects of discussion. The difference, however, is not significant. As to the harmony of views in the discussions on university problems, again we found, this time statistically significant, that the left-activists in greater number tended to disagree with their parents than the other categories (44 per cent against 27 per cent, 33 per cent, 19 per cent and 0 per cent respectively). On the other hand, the percentages of those saying they usually agree, did not differ significantly (± 33 per cent).

17 Although we did not check whether this statement would hold under close scrutiny, controlling for field of study, yet the largely similar distribution of disciplines among our left- and right-radical students would seem to warrant the statement.

18 The replication confirmed this finding. Left-activists and left-non-activists, in significantly larger number, did not conceive of the increasing regimentation of the study as making sense.

19 For interesting comparative material, collected with a similar research format in other survey research in the Netherlands, we refer the reader to the summary given by Lammers (1970b).

20 The board of curators, as it existed at the time of research, was, in its functioning, roughly a blend of the board of trustees and the administration at American universities. On the board, high-ranking individuals from several spheres of life were represented. The body as a whole was entrusted with the exercise of control on behalf of the central government.

21 Lammers, 1970a; ch. 5. Also van Zuthem, 1968.

22 Publications on the subject are prolific. To take two prime examples, see Mills, 1956 and Dahl, 1962. A good summary of the conflicting positions taken by historians is given by Guggisberg (1971).

23 The case of questions concerning the climate of authority at the various departments. The right-wing, to a degree significantly less than the left-wing, tended to respond in terms of the climate being tolerant, on an equal footing, and personal. Right-non-activists and left-activists, however, tended to define the climate as democratic to a degree significantly less than left-non-activists and middle.

156

24 In the replication, 26 per cent of the left-activists and 26 per cent of the left-non-activists indicated that prestige differentials were an object of focal attention, against 15 per cent, 20 per cent and 0 per cent for the middle group, the right-non-activists and the right-activists respectively (a non-significant difference). The display of respect and deference towards others solely on the ground of the position held by the latter, was held unjustified by 90 per cent of the left-activists, against respectively 66 per cent, 56 per cent, 30 per cent, and 0 per cent for the other categories (differences between left-activists and the other categories are significant).

25 Here we based ourselves on the statistical mode. Although for both the sample and the left-wing the mode was in the mid-point of the scales, the 'loading' of this modal position tended to be stronger for the left-wing than for the sample. In the replication this same pattern occurred for both the left activists and their fathers. Their mothers, however, tended to come up with a rank ordering of differences, even for the situation as it should be. This was the characteristic response for the other categories as well, with the sole exception of the middle category which modally tended towards the mid-point of the scale for the situation as it should be.

26 See Table F.

TABLE F *Participation in student society beyond the immediate sphere of study (in %)*

	Sample	Left-radicals	Right-radicals
intercourse with study-mates	47	65	71
intercourse with students from different fields of study	55	65	71
intercourse with students from other universities	18	30	21

(Differences of 9% between the sample and the left-radicals are significant on a 20% level. This same condition holds for differences of 14% between the sample and the right-radicals.)

27 On this point, cf. Merton, 1956. Also Gouldner, 1957, pp. 281–306.

28 The replication did not render this pattern. The reason may be that here the drawbacks of the construction character of the replication categories appear, since we are dealing with actual network structures in which respondents are involved.

29 The replication confirmed this finding.

30 The replication confirmed this finding. Here, too, left-activists and left-non-activists parted company in their second choice. The right-wing categories, however, tended to point to similarities with rightist reference groups only in their second choice. In the replication too, we

157

found that the right-wing tends rather towards feelings of rejection of groups which it considers different than towards a sense of involvement with groups deemed comparable. The left-wing, on the other hand, does not show up this difference. We had to refrain from analysing whether these findings would be reflected in the active display of these feelings, since the relevant question here was used as an indicator of activism in the replication.

31 For all three groups of parents we found an ordering largely similar to that found for the sample and the right-wing, although mass demonstrations and press publications had changed places. Majority support among left-wing parents, however, extended as far as mass demonstrations; parents of students in the sample did not support the means beyond press publications, whereas none of the means was condoned by a majority among the right-wing parents.

32 A clear analysis of this intentness on extra-mural publics as a power factor of strategic importance is given by Donald W. Light (1968).

The replication showed only a faint reflection of this exceptional behaviour of left-wing radicals. All categories come up with rather similar orderings of the various means; the left-wing categories this time do not show the spectacular surge of the more forceful means. A faint echo may be that the left-activists ranked demonstrations in first position, whereas this means was accorded a second place by left non-activists and the middle group and went down to third position for the right-wing. This may be an indication of the greater intentness on non-university publics among the activist left-wing who, through the expressive action of demonstrations, may want to involve these publics.

In addition to this, the replication showed that a majority of left-activists tended to support all of the means, whereas majority support among the right-wing did not reach beyond press publications and mass demonstrations.

33 On this point, cf. Abrahamsson, 1971.

34 Here the replication contained an element of contamination as far as the student-respondents were concerned, since the construction of the replication categories was based on an index of four items which happened to belong to four of the various dimensions of radicalism distinguished above. It need cause no surprise, therefore, that the pattern of differences found for the replication categories closely resembles the one found for ASVA and OBAS respondents. For the parents, however, this objection would seem to be less valid. From their answers, it appears that more often than among parents of ASVA students, left-wing parents tend to diverge from their children's opinions and rather tend towards the opinions held by right-wing parents, most outspokenly so on those dimensions referring to the efficiency and efficacious functioning of organizations and to the functions of rules of civil intercourse.

35 Well-known formulations of this position are: Coleman, 1956; Merton, Reader, Kendall, 1957 (Appendix C); Selvin, 1960; Hirschi and Selvin, 1957. Good summaries of this discussion can be found in Galtung, 1967b, pp. 358–90 and Labovitz, 1970.

36 Blalock, 1960, p. 176.
37 Johnson, 1967, pp. 241–54.

6 Evaluation: structuralism and phenomenology reconciled

1 Homans, 1961; Blau, 1964; Gouldner, 1959.
2 In this context, see Runciman, 1970, ch. 4, 'Class, Status and Power?' He too refers to the possible blurring of boundaries between the three concepts. The elaboration of this thought is not too clear due to the lack of an embracing theoretical perspective on the use and dimensions of these concepts.
3 A similar argument can be found in Berger, 1971. He subsumes the widening rift of perspectives under the image of 'performers' and their 'audience', drifting apart in expectations and standards of evaluation . . . 'for whether they know it or not (and at least some of them clearly do), cultural revolutionaries are practicing ethno-methodologists; break the unstated rules on which civil discourse (hence privilege) is based, and society falls apart. The point is to empty the mind of habitual perceptual categories, of the realities these categories define and the rules they imply.'
4 For an instance of the conception of pluralism as a model of individuals in competition, cf. 'Liberalism and the American Negro—A Round-Table Discussion' with James Baldwin, Nathan Glazer, Sidney Hook, Gunnar Myrdal, and Norman Podhoretz (moderator), *Commentary* 37 (March 1964), pp. 25–6.
5 Howard Becker strongly emphasizes this point and provides amusing examples in his introduction to Becker, 1970.
6 There were, of course, exceptions, such as Logemann, and also Schermerhorn in his more reflexive moments. See, e.g., this statement in his *Diary*: 'The sovereign state, sitting in judgment, has the obligation, in deciding upon the choice of means in order to move back from revolutionary upheaval to a regular situation, to take into account values of various kinds which are at the very root of revolution and account for its persistence' (Schermerhorn, 1970, p. 38—my translation, Kroes). On this same page, reference is made to a similar statement by Logemann. On the other hand, the widespread inclination to conceive of a threatening enemy as the very embodiment of banditry and evil offers crucial leverage for the mobilization of right-radical sentiments. 'Moral outrage' often precedes ruthless retaliatory actions, such as lynchings, colonial wars, and the quelling of prison uprisings. Therefore a separate field of attention in the study of right radicalism should be the variety of ways in which the outrage is fed by selective information and manipulation of the news.
7 Parsons, 1967, chapter 'On the Concept of Political Power'.
8 Kroes, 1969. Dahl and Lindblom, 1953.
9 Elias, 1969. Elias, 1970. Gouldner, 1959. Gouldner, 1971.
10 Kroes, 1971, p. 30, where the author elaborates on these processes of norm crystallization.
11 See ch. 3.
12 Elias, 1969.

13 Galtung, 1967a.
14 For the concepts of patron and client, cf. *Sociologische Gids* 16, 6 (1969), for a variety of applications and elaborations.
15 Pettigrew, 1964. Den Hollander, 1966.
16 Elias and Scotson, 1965, p. 159.
17 An analysis in network terms of these patron-client structures would allow us to describe neatly the 'multi-strandedness' of relations between patron and client, resulting in a multiplicity of links, e.g. in terms of affective attachment, which disappears under conditions of fully-fledged capitalism. Then, the cash nexus, a specific market relation, and a single, specific relation of obedience are the sole ties to remain. For a number of excellent analyses along these lines, see Mitchell, 1969.
18 Stein, 1960.
19 Goldthorpe and Lockwood, 1963, pp. 133–63. Lockwood, 1960, pp. 248–59. Runciman, 1966. Runciman, 1970. MacKenzie and Silver, 1968. From this discussion yet another type of worker emerges, whose attitudes and behaviour can be described in terms of 'embourgeoisement'—the worker who thinks of himself as being middle-class and votes conservative. This case is one of assimilation, reflecting a sense of individual mobility, rather than one of self-colonization.
20 Klein, 1965.
21 Elias and Scotson, 1965. Stacey, 1960.
22 Myrdal, Sterner and Rose, 1944.
23 Hannerz, 1969. Finestone, 1963.
24 For an example of this argument, see Horton, 1970.
25 Janowitz, 1967.

Bibliography

ABRAHAMSSON, B. (1971), *Military Professionalization and Political Power*. Stockholm: Göteborgs Offsettryckeri A. B.

AGGER, R. E., GOLDRICH, D. and SWANSON, B. E. (1964), *The Rulers and the Ruled*. New York: John Wiley & Sons.

ALMOND, G. A. and VERBA, S. (1963), *The Civic Culture*. Princeton University Press.

ANDERSON, B. R. (1967), 'The Pemuda revolution: Indonesian politics 1945–1946' (Diss.). Cornell University.

APTER, D. (1965), *The Politics of Modernization*. University of Chicago Press.

BECKER, H. S. (ed.) (1970), *Campus Power Struggle*. Transaction Book. Chicago: Aldine Publishing Co.

BELL, D. (ed.) (1963), *The Radical Right*. Garden City: Doubleday.

BENDIX, R. (1964), *Nation Building and Citizenship*. New York: John Wiley & Sons.

BENOIT, O. (1965), 'Statut dans l'enterprise et attitudes syndicales des ouvriers' in R. Boudon and P. Lazarsfeld (eds), *Le Vocabulaire des sciences sociales*. Paris: Mouton.

BENOIT-SMULLYAN, E. (1944), 'Status types and status interrelationships', *American Sociological Review* 9.

BERGER, B. M. (1971), 'Audiences, art and power', *Transaction*, vol. 8, no. 7, May.

BERGER, J. A., COHEN, B. P., ZELDITCH, M. JR. (1966), 'Status Characteristics and Expectation States' in J. A. Berger, M. Zelditch and B. Anderson (eds), *Sociological Theories in Progress*. Boston: Houghton Mifflin & Co.

BERTING, J. (1965), 'Status-incongruentie en sociale mobiliteit', *Sociologische Gids* 12.

BLALOCK, H. M. (1960), *Social Statistics*. New York: McGraw-Hill.

BLAU, P. M. (1964), *Exchange and Power in Social Life*. New York: John Wiley & Sons.

BLUMBERGER, J. TH. P. (1931), *De Nationalistische Beweging in Nederlandsch-Indië*. The Hague: Tjeenk Willink.

BOUDON, R. (1969), 'La crise universitaire française: Essai de diagnostic sociologique', *Annales*, 24th year, May-June.

BOULDING, K. E. (1963), *Conflict and Defense. A General Theory* (1962). Harper Torchbook. New York: Harper & Row.

COLEMAN, J. S. (1957), *Community Conflict*. Chicago: The Free Press.

COSER, L. (1956), *The Functions of Social Conflict*. Chicago: The Free Press.

DAHL, R. A. and LINDBLOM, CH. E. (1953), *Politics, Economics and Welfare*. New York: Harper & Row.

DAHL, R. A. (1962), *Who Governs?* New Haven: Yale University Press.

DAHL, R. A. (1967), *Pluralist Democracy in the United States. Conflict and Consent*. Chicago: Rand McNally.

DAHRENDORF, R. (1959), *Class and Class Conflict in Industrial Society*. Stanford University Press.

DAHRENDORF, R. (1967), *Conflict after Class: New Perspectives on the Theory of Social and Political Conflict*. Noel Buxton Lecture, 2 March 1967. London: Longmans, Green & Co.

DAVIS, J. A. (1966), 'Structural Balance, Mechanical Solidarity, and Inter-personal Relations' in J. A. Berger, M. Zelditch and B. Anderson (eds), *Sociological Theories in Progress*. Boston: Houghton Mifflin & Co.

DEMERATH, N. J., III and PETERSON, R. A. (eds) (1967), *System, Change and Conflict*. New York: The Free Press.

VAN DOORN, J. A. A. and HENDRIX, W. J. (1970), *Ontsporing van Geweld*. Rotterdam: UPR.

DOOTJES, F. J. J. (1948), *Kroniek 1941-1946*. Amsterdam: Oostkust van Sumatra-Instituut.

ELIAS, N. and SCOTSON, J. L. (1965), *The Established and the Outsiders*. London: Frank Cass & Co.

ELIAS, N. and DUNNING, E. (1966), 'Dynamics of group sports with special reference to football', *British Journal of Sociology*, vol. XVII, no. 4, December.

ELIAS, N. (1969), *Ueber den Prozess der Zivilisation* (1939). 2nd edn. Berne: Francke.

ELIAS, N. (1970), *Was ist Soziologie?* Munich: Juventa.

VAN DE ENDE, E. C. (1946), *Hoe verder met Indië?* The Hague: C. Blommendaal.

ETZIONI, A. (1968), *The Active Society*. New York: The Free Press.

FEUER, L. S. (1969), *The Conflict of Generations*. London: Heinemann.

FEUILLETAU DE BRUIJN, W. K. H. (1946), *Welk aandeel heeft Dr. van Mook gehad in de gezagsschemering in Nederlands-Indië?* The Hague: W. P. van Stockum.

FINESTONE, H. (1963), 'Cats, Kicks and Color' in R. W. Mack (ed.), *Race, Class and Power*. New York: American Book Company.

FLACKS, R. (1967), 'The liberated generation: an exploration of the roots of student protest', *Journal of Social Issues*, vol. XXXIII, no. 3.

GALTUNG, J. (1966), 'Rank and Social Integration: A Multidimensional Approach' in J. Berger, M. Zelditch, B. Anderson (eds), *Sociological Theories in Progress*. Boston: Houghton Mifflin & Co.

GALTUNG, J. (1967a), 'International relations and international conflicts: a sociological approach', *Transactions of the VIth World Congress of Sociology. Evian.* Geneva: International Sociological Association.

GALTUNG, J. (1967b), *Theory and Methods of Social Research.* London: Allen & Unwin.

GERRETSON, C. (1946), *Indië onder dictatuur.* Amsterdam: Elsevier.

GOFFMAN, E. W. (1957), 'Status inconsistency and preference for change in power distribution', *American Sociological Review.*

GOLDTHORPE, J. H. and LOCKWOOD, D. (1963), 'Affluence and the British class structure', *Sociological Review,* n.s. II.

GOLDTHORPE, J. H., LOCKWOOD, D., BECHHOFER, F., PLATT, J. (1967), 'The affluent worker and the thesis of "Embourgeoisement": some preliminary research findings', *Sociology,* vol. 1.

DE LA GORCE, P. M. (1963), *The French Army.* London: Weidenfeld & Nicolson.

GOUDSBLOM, J. (1967), *Dutch Society.* New York: Random House.

GOULDNER, A. W. (1957), 'Cosmopolitans and locals: towards an analysis of latent social roles', *Administrative Science Quarterly* II.

GOULDNER, A. W. (1959), 'Reciprocity and autonomy in functional theory' in L. Gross (ed.), *Symposium on Sociological Theory.* New York: Harper & Row.

GOULDNER, A. W. (1971), *The Coming Crisis of Western Sociology.* London: Heinemann.

GUETZKOW, H. (1955), *Multiple Loyalties.* Princeton University Press.

GUGGISBERG, H. R. (1971), 'Sozialpolitisches Engagement in der Amerikanischen Historiographie des 20. sten Jahrhunderts', *Basler Zeitschrift für Geschichte,* vol. 71, no. 1.

HANNERZ, U. (1969), *Soulside.* New York: Columbia University Press.

HEIST, P. (n.d.) (a), *Intellect and Commitment: The Faces of Discontent.* Center for the Study of Higher Education, University of California, Berkeley.

HEIST, P. (n.d.) (b), *The Dynamics of Student Discontent and Protest.* Center for Research and Development in Higher Education, University of California, Berkeley.

HELFRICH, C. E. L. (1950), *Memoires.* Amsterdam: Elsevier.

HIRSCHI, T. and SELVIN, H. C. (1967), *Delinquency Research: An Appraisal of Analytic Methods.* New York: The Free Press.

HOETINK, H. (1961), *De gespleten Samenleving in het Caribische gebied.* Assen: Van Gorcum.

DEN HOLLANDER, A. N. J. et. al. (1966), *De plurale samenleving. Begrip zonder toekomst?* Meppel: J. A. Boom en Zoon.

DEN HOLLANDER, A. N. J. (1968), *Visie en Verwoording.* Assen: Van Gorcum.

HOMANS, G. C. (1961), *Social Behavior, Its Elementary Forms.* New York: Harcourt, Brace & World.

HORTON, J. (1970), 'Order and Conflict Theories of Social Problems as Competing Ideologies' in L. T. Reynolds and J. M. Reynolds (eds), *The Sociology of Sociology.* New York: David McKay Co.

HUNTINGTON, S. P. (1967), *Political Order in Changing Societies.* New Haven: Yale University Press.

JACKSON, E. F. (1962), 'Status consistency and symptoms of stress', *American Sociological Review.*

JANOWITZ, M., (1960), *The Professional Soldier.* New York: The Free Press.

JANOWITZ, M. (1964), *The Military in the Political Development of New Nations.* University of Chicago Press.

JANOWITZ, M. (1967), *The Social Control of Escalated Riots.* University of Chicago Press.

JOHNSON, S. C. (1967), 'Hierarchical clustering schemes', *Psychometrika,* vol. 32, no. 3, pp. 241–54.

DE JONG, L., 'Koningin Wilhelmina in London, 1940–1945', *Mededelingen der Koninklijke Nederlandse Akademie van Wetenschappen, afd. Letteren,* No. XXIX, 2.

DE KADT, J. (1949), *De Indonesische Tragedie.* Amsterdam: G. A. van Oorschot.

KAPLAN, M. A. (1957), *System and Process in International Politics.* New York: John Wiley & Sons.

KENISTON, K. (1967), 'The sources of student dissent', *Journal of Social Issues* 23, no. 3.

KENISTON, K. (1968), *Young Radicals.* New York: Harcourt, Brace & World.

KLEIN, J. (1965), *Samples from English Cultures.* London: Routledge & Kegan Paul.

KROES, R. (1962), 'Snobisme', *Sociologische Gids* 9.

KROES, R. (1968), *Lastig Amsterdam.* The Hague: Nederlandse Sociologische Vereniging.

KROES, R. (1969a), 'Conflict and Radicalism: A Two-Stage Model', Working Paper no. 132, Center for Social Organization Studies, University of Chicago, May (mimeo).

KROES, R. (1969b), 'Military Intervention in Domestic Politics: A Framework for Analysis', Working Paper no. 133, Center for Social Organization Studies, University of Chicago, May (mimeo).

KROES, R. (1969c), 'Strategie en Structuur in de Nederlandse Politiek', *Sociologische Gids* 16, no. 4.

KROES, R. (1970a), 'Conflict en Radicalisme: Een Tweetrapsmodel', *Sociologische Gids* 17, 1–19.

KROES, R. (1970b), 'Militaire Inmenging in de Binnenlandse Politiek: Een Kader voor Analyse', *Acta Politica* V, 2.

KROES, R. (1970c), 'Decolonization and the military: the case of the Netherlands', *Mens en Maatschappij* 45, December; reprinted in M. Janowitz and J. van Doorn (eds), *On Military Intervention* (1971). Rotterdam: UPR.

KROES, R. (1971), *Arbeiderskinderen en het Middelbaar Onderwijs.* Meppel: Boom en Zoon.

LABOVITZ, S. (1970), 'The nonutility of significance tests', *Pacific Sociological Review,* vol. 13, no. 3.

LAMMERS, C. J. (1968), *Studentenvakbeweging en universitaire democratie.* Amsterdam: Noord-Hollandse Uitgeversmaatschappij.

LAMMERS, C. J. (1970a), *Studenten, politiek en universitaire democratie.* Rotterdam: UPR.

LAMMERS, C. J. (1970b), 'Democratisering van bedrijf en universiteit' in A.v. Braam (ed.), *Actuele Sociologie*. Assen: Van Gorcum.

LANG, K. (1965), 'Military Organizations' in J. G. March (ed.), *Handbook of Organizations*. Chicago: Rand McNally.

LENSKI, G. E. (1956), 'Social participation and status crystallization', *American Sociological Review*.

LENSKI, G. E. (1954), 'Status-crystallization: a non-vertical dimension of social status', *American Sociological Review*.

LIGHT, D. W. (1968), 'Strategies of Protest: Developments in Conflict Theory', Paper presented at the American Sociological Association Meeting, Boston, 28 August (mimeo).

LIJPHART, A. (1968), *The Politics of Accommodation. Pluralism and Democracy in the Netherlands*. Berkeley: University of California Press.

LIJPHART, A. (1969), 'Consociational democracy', *World Politics*, vol. 21, no. 2, Jan., pp. 207–25.

LIJPHART, A. (1971), 'Cleavages in Consociational Democracies: A Four-Country Comparison', Symposium on Comparative analysis of Highly Industrialized Societies, Bellagio, Italy, 1–7, Aug.

LIPSET, S. M., TROW, M., COLEMAN, J. S. (1956), *Union Democracy*. Chicago: Free Press.

LIPSET, S. M. (1960), *Political Man*. New York: Doubleday & Co.

LIPSET, S. M. and ROKKAN, S. (eds) (1967), *Party Systems and Voter Alignments: Cross-National Perspectives*. New York: The Free Press.

LIPSET, S. M. and RAAB, E. (1971), *The Politics of Unreason*. New York: Harper & Row.

LIPSET, S. M. (1972), *The University in Rebellion*. New York: The Free Press.

LOCKWOOD, D. (1958), *The Blackcoated Worker*. London: Allen & Unwin.

LOCKWOOD, D. (1960), 'The "new working class" ', *European Journal of Sociology*, vol. I, no. 2.

MCKENZIE, R. T. and SILVER, A. (1968), *Angles in Marble: Working Class Conservatives in Urban England*. London: Heinemann.

MERTON, R. K. (1957), *Social Theory and Social Structure* (1949). Second revised edition. Chicago: The Free Press.

MERTON, R. K., READER, G. G., KENDALL, P. L. (eds) (1957), *The Student Physician*. Cambridge, Mass.: Harvard University Press.

MILLS, C. W. (1956), *The Power Elite*. New York: Oxford University Press.

MITCHELL, J. C. (ed.) (1969), *Social Networks in Urban Situations*. Manchester University Press.

MOORE, JR, BARRINGTON (1967), *Social Origins of Dictatorship and Democracy* (1966). Beacon Paperback. Boston: Beacon Press.

MYRDAL, G., STERNER, R., and ROSE, A. (1944), *An American Dilemma*. New York: Harper & Row.

NASUTION, A. H. (1965), *Fundamentals of Guerilla Warfare*. New York: Praeger.

NEWCOMB, TH. M. (1961), *The Acquaintance Process*. New York: Holt, Rinehart & Winston.

VAN NISPEN TOT SEVENAER, O. (1949), *De republiek Indonesia. Haar leiders en haar soldateska. De eer van het leger is de eer van het volk*. The Hague: W. P. van Stockum.

PARSONS, T. (1967), *Sociological Theory and Modern Society*. New York: The Free Press.

PARSONS, T. (1968), 'The Primary Subsystems of Society' in R. Peterson and N. J. Demerath, III (eds), *System, Change, and Conflict*. New York: The Free Press.

PEAR, R. H. (1971), 'Students and the Establishment in Europe and the USA' in A. N. J. den Hollander (ed), *Diverging Parallels*. Leyden: E. J. Brill.

PETTIGREW, T. F. (1964), *A Profile of the Negro American*. Princeton: D. van Nostrand.

PINNER, F. A. (1968), 'Tradition and transgression: western European students in the postwar world', *Daedalus* 97 (Winter).

PLUVIER, J. M. (1953), *Overzicht van de ontwikkeling der nationalistische beweging in Indonesië*. The Hague: W. van Hoeve.

PODHORETZ, N. *et al.* (1964), 'Liberalism and the American Negro— a round-table discussion', *Commentary* 37, March.

PYLE, L. W. (1962), 'Armies in the Process of Political Modernization' in J. J. Johnson (ed.), *The Role of the Military in Underdeveloped Countries*. Princeton University Press.

'Regeringsnota inzake Optreden Nederlandse Militairen voorafgaande aan Overdracht Soevereiniteit Indonesië', *Handelingen Tweede Kamer*, no. 10,008.

ROSS, E. A. (1920), *The Principles of Sociology*. New York: The Century Co.

RUNCIMAN, W. G. (1960), *Relative Deprivation and Social Justice*. London: Routledge & Kegan Paul.

RUNCIMAN, W. G. (1970), *Sociology in its Place and Other Essays*. Cambridge University Press.

SAMPSON, E. E. (1963), 'Status congruence and cognitive consistency', *Sociometry*, vol. 26, no. 2.

SCHELLING, T. C. (1960), *The Strategies of Conflict*. Cambridge, Mass.: Harvard University Press.

SCHERMERHORN, W. (1970), *Het Dagboek van Schermerhorn*. Groningen: Wolters, Noordhoff N. V.

SCHUMPETER, J. (1947), *Capitalism, Socialism and Democracy*. New York: Harper & Row.

SELVIN, H. C. (1960), *The Effects of Leadership*. Chicago: The Free Press.

SHILS, E. (1961), 'Centre and Periphery' in *The Logic of Personal Knowledge*. London: Routledge & Kegan Paul.

SHILS, E. (1962), 'The Military in the Political Development of the New States' in J. J. Johnson (ed.), *The Role of the Military in Under-developed Countries*. Princeton University Press.

SMAIL, J. R. W. (1964), *Bandung in the Early Revolution*. Ithaca: Cornell University Press.

SMIT, C. (1959), *Het Accoord van Linggadjati*. Amsterdam: Elsevier.

SMIT, C. (1962), *De Liquidatie van een Imperium*. Amsterdam: De Arbeiderspers.

STACEY, M. (1960), *Tradition and Change: A Study of Banbury*. London: Oxford University Press.

STEIN, M. R. (1960), *The Eclipse of Community*. Princeton University Press.

STINCHCOMBE, A. L. (1965), 'Social Structure and Organization' in J. G. March (ed.), *Handbook of Organizations*. Chicago: Rand McNally.

TEITLER, G. (1969/70), 'Congruentie en Incongruentie: Het Officierscorps en de Oorlog', *Acta Politica* V, 4.

WEBER, M. (1921), *Wirtschaft und Gesellschaft*. Tübingen: J. C. P. Mohr (P. Siebeck).

WEINBERG, I. and WALKER, K. N. (1969/70), 'Student politics and political systems: towards a typology', *American Journal of Sociology* 75.

WESTERLING, R. (1952), *Mijn Memoires*. Amsterdam: P. Vink.

ZELDITCH JR, M. and ANDERSON, B. (1966), 'On the Balance of a Set of Ranks' in J. A. Berger, M. Zelditch and B. Anderson (eds), *Sociological Theories in Progress*. Boston: Houghton Mifflin & Co.

VAN ZUTHEM, H. J. (1968), *Gezag en Zeggenschap*. Kampen: Kok.

Name index

Abrahamsson, B., 158
Agger, D., 146
Almond, G. A., 64, 150
Anderson, B., 143, 144, 147
Apter, D., 39, 145, 146
Azis, A., 60

Baldwin, J., 159
Bechhofer, F., 144
Becker, H. S., 151, 159
Beel, L. J. M., 60, 63, 147, 150
Bell, D., 144
Bendix, R., 39, 145
Benoit, O., 145
Benoit-Smullyan, E., 14, 143
Berger, B. M., 159
Berger, J. A., 144
Berting, J., 14, 143
Blalock, H. M., 119, 121, 159
Blankenstein, M. van, 149
Blau, P. M., 125, 159
Blumberger, J. Th. P., 147
Boudon, R., 92, 150, 154
Boulding, K. E., 141, 142
Bruin, R. de, 147, 148
Bruine, General de, 149
Burger, J. W., 52, 147

Christison, General, 54
Cohen, B. P., 144
Coleman, J. S., 142, 158
Coser, L., 11, 142

Dahl, R. A., 11, 103, 142, 156, 159
Dahrendorf, R., 1, 5, 19, 20, 24, 141, 143, 144
Davis, J. A., 142, 143
De Gaulle, General, 65
De Tocqueville, A., 5
Demerath, N. J., 141
Doorn, J. A. A. van, 55, 58, 147, 148, 149, 150
Dootjes, F. J. J., 147
Drees, W., 52, 147, 149
Dunning, E., 141

Eisenstadt, S. N., 96
Elias, N., 1, 2, 36, 130, 134, 138, 141, 145, 151, 159, 160
Ende, E. C. van de, 149
Engles, General, 60
Etzioni, A., 7, 142, 151

Feuer, L. S., 95, 155
Feuilletau de Bruijn, W. K. H., 149
Finestone, H., 160
Flacks, R., 73, 87, 95, 151, 155
Frankenheimer, J., 146

Galtung, J., 14, 16, 135, 142, 143, 144, 158, 160
Geer, D. J. de, 52
Gerbrandy, P. S., 51, 59, 60, 65, 148
Glazer, N., 159
Goedhart, F., 147
Goes van Naters, M. van der, 147

Subject index

achievement, 4, 16, 27, 35, 41, 77, 132–5, 136
activism, 119; student, 73, 90; left-wing, 88, 89; right-wing, 88, 89
alliance, 41, 50, 58–62, 73, 87, 90, 102, 103, 114, 125, 128, 139, 146n
anticipation effect, 82
arena, 33, 34, 45, 46, 69, 72–3, 145; praetorian, 25, 33–4, 44–5; civic, 25, 33–4, 41, 44–5, 47, 58, 85, 145n; oligarchical, 34, 35–7, 135, 145n; transitional, 34, 36–9, 145n; mass, 34, 39–41; participant, 34, 41–4, 46, 47, 49; Whig, 38; bourgeois-liberal, 38; scope of, 73, 75; traditional, 75–80, 86, 127; transgressive, 80–7; pluralist, 130
ascription, 4, 16, 17, 21, 27, 28, 37, 40, 41, 132–4, 136
assimilation, 137, 140
ASVA (General Association of Students (Amsterdam)), 88, 89, 90, 94, 95, 100, 101, 108, 117, 118, 119, 120, 121, 152n, 155n, 158n

bersiap-period, 50
blockings, 15–18, 127; structural, 15; normative, 15
bureaucratization, 136, 138

career opportunities, 26, 40, 83, 92, 93
centre, 43, 52, 74, 143n; of decision-making, 36, 42, 46, 55; political, 53, 63
class, 19, 20, 21, 22, 23, 26, 31, 32, 33, 37, 38, 40, 41, 42, 43, 44, 56, 69, 70–3, 77, 79, 81, 89, 90–6, 114, 124, 125, 127, 128, 129, 130, 138, 144n, 145n; definition of, 26; position, 33, 35, 42, 85, 90–5, 130; politics, 144n
cleavage, 11, 64
coalition, 46, 48, 63, 64
coercion, 4
competition, 4, 39, 40, 42, 45, 46, 72, 124, 126, 127, 129, 130, 131, 132, 141n, 145n, 146n
conflict, 1, 2, 3, 4, 10, 11, 41, 45, 46, 58, 69, 74, 123, 127, 129, 141n, 142n; sociology of, 1; models of, 5, 6, 11; definition of, 7; intensity of, 11, 24; theory of, 19, 21; reconciliation of models of, 20–1; expansion of scale of, 21; elaboration and formalization of model of, 21–9; groups, 22, 72; course of, 22, 45, 69, 85, 89, 128, 129, 132; arena of, 24, 25, 69, 72–3, 128; process model of, 25, 26–9; phases of, 25, 27, 28, 49; situation of, 27, 37, 142n; dimensions of, 46; issues, 69, 73–5, 85, 101
confrontation, 4, 46, 48, 49, 85, 129, 130, 131, 132
consensus, 4, 7, 16, 126

171

Routledge Social Science Series

Routledge & Kegan Paul   London and Boston

68–74 Carter Lane London EC4V 5EL

9 Park Street Boston Mass 02108

Contents

*Authors wishing to submit manuscripts for any series in
this catalogue should send them to the Social Science Editor,
Routledge & Kegan Paul Ltd, 68–74 Carter Lane,
London EC4V 5EL*

●*Books so marked are available in paperback
All books are in Metric Demy 8vo format (216 × 138mm approx.)*

International Library of Sociology

General Editor John Rex

GENERAL SOCIOLOGY

Barnsley, J. H. The Social Reality of Ethics. *464 pp.*

Belshaw, Cyril. The Conditions of Social Performance. *An Exploratory Theory. 144 pp.*

Brown, Robert. Explanation in Social Science. *208 pp.*

● Rules and Laws in Sociology. *192 pp.*

Bruford, W. H. Chekhov and His Russia. *A Sociological Study. 244 pp.*

Cain, Maureen E. Society and the Policeman's Role. *326 pp.*

Gibson, Quentin. The Logic of Social Enquiry. *240 pp.*

Glucksmann, M. Structuralist Analysis in Contemporary Social Thought. *212 pp.*

Gurvitch, Georges. Sociology of Law. *Preface by Roscoe Pound. 264 pp.*

Hodge, H. A. Wilhelm Dilthey. *An Introduction. 184 pp.*

Homans, George C. Sentiments and Activities. *336 pp.*

Johnson, Harry M. Sociology: *a Systematic Introduction. Foreword by Robert K. Merton. 710 pp.*

Mannheim, Karl. Essays on Sociology and Social Psychology. *Edited by Paul Keckskemeti. With Editorial Note by Adolph Lowe. 344 pp.*

Systematic Sociology: *An Introduction to the Study of Society. Edited by J. S. Erös and Professor W. A. C. Stewart. 220 pp.*

Martindale, Don. The Nature and Types of Sociological Theory. *292 pp.*

●**Maus, Heinz.** A Short History of Sociology. *234 pp.*

Mey, Harald. Field-Theory. *A Study of its Application in the Social Sciences. 352 pp.*

Myrdal, Gunnar. Value in Social Theory: *A Collection of Essays on Methodology. Edited by Paul Streeten. 332 pp.*

Ogburn, William F., and **Nimkoff, Meyer F.** A Handbook of Sociology. *Preface by Karl Mannheim. 656 pp. 46 figures. 35 tables.*

Parsons, Talcott, and **Smelser, Neil J.** Economy and Society: *A Study in the Integration of Economic and Social Theory. 362 pp.*

●**Rex, John.** Key Problems of Sociological Theory. *220 pp.*

Discovering Sociology. *278 pp.*

Sociology and the Demystification of the Modern World. *282 pp.*

●**Rex, John** (Ed.) Approaches to Sociology. *Contributions by Peter Abell, Frank Bechhofer, Basil Bernstein, Ronald Fletcher, David Frisby, Miriam Glucksmann, Peter Lassman, Herminio Martins, John Rex, Roland Robertson, John Westergaard and Jock Young. 302 pp.*

Rigby, A. Alternative Realities. *352 pp.*

Roche, M. Phenomenology, Language and the Social Sciences. *374 pp.*

Sahay, A. Sociological Analysis. *220 pp.*

Urry, John. Reference Groups and the Theory of Revolution. *244 pp.*

Weinberg, E. Development of Sociology in the Soviet Union. *173 pp.*

3

FOREIGN CLASSICS OF SOCIOLOGY

●**Durkheim, Emile.** Suicide. *A Study in Sociology. Edited and with an Introduction by George Simpson. 404 pp.*
Professional Ethics and Civic Morals. *Translated by Cornelia Brookfield. 288 pp.*

●**Gerth, H. H.,** and **Mills, C. Wright.** From Max Weber: *Essays in Sociology. 502 pp.*

●**Tönnies, Ferdinand.** Community and Association. (*Gemeinschaft und Gesellschaft.*) *Translated and Supplemented by Charles P. Loomis. Foreword by Pitirim A. Sorokin. 334 pp.*

SOCIAL STRUCTURE

Andreski, Stanislav. Military Organization and Society. *Foreword by Professor A. R. Radcliffe-Brown. 226 pp. 1 folder.*

Coontz, Sydney H. Population Theories and the Economic Interpretation. *202 pp.*

Coser, Lewis. The Functions of Social Conflict. *204 pp.*

Dickie-Clark, H. F. Marginal Situation: *A Sociological Study of a Coloured Group. 240 pp. 11 tables.*

Glaser, Barney, and **Strauss, Anselm L.** Status Passage. *A Formal Theory. 208 pp.*

Glass, D. V. (Ed.) Social Mobility in Britain. *Contributions by J. Berent, T. Bottomore, R. C. Chambers, J. Floud, D. V. Glass, J. R. Hall, H. T. Himmelweit, R. K. Kelsall, F. M. Martin, C. A. Moser, R. Mukherjee, and W. Ziegel. 420 pp.*

Jones, Garth N. Planned Organizational Change: *An Exploratory Study Using an Empirical Approach. 268 pp.*

Kelsall, R. K. Higher Civil Servants in Britain: *From 1870 to the Present Day. 268 pp. 31 tables.*

König, René. The Community. *232 pp. Illustrated.*

●**Lawton, Denis.** Social Class, Language and Education. *192 pp.*

McLeish, John. The Theory of Social Change: *Four Views Considered. 128 pp.*

Marsh, David C. The Changing Social Structure of England and Wales, 1871-1961. *288 pp.*

Mouzelis, Nicos. Organization and Bureaucracy. *An Analysis of Modern Theories. 240 pp.*

Mulkay, M. J. Functionalism, Exchange and Theoretical Strategy. *272 pp.*

Ossowski, Stanislaw. Class Structure in the Social Consciousness. *210 pp.*

Podgórecki, Adam. Law and Society. *About 300 pp.*

SOCIOLOGY AND POLITICS

Acton, T. A. Gypsy Politics and Social Change. *316 pp.*

Hechter, Michael. Internal Colonialism. *The Celtic Fringe in British National Development, 1536-1966. About 350 pp.*

Hertz, Frederick. Nationality in History and Politics: *A Psychology and Sociology of National Sentiment and Nationalism. 432 pp.*

Kornhauser, William. The Politics of Mass Society. *272 pp. 20 tables.*
Laidler, Harry W. History of Socialism. *Social-Economic Movements: An Historical and Comparative Survey of Socialism, Communism, Co-operation, Utopianism; and other Systems of Reform and Reconstruction. 992 pp.*
Lasswell, H. D. Analysis of Political Behaviour. *324 pp.*
Mannheim, Karl. Freedom, Power and Democratic Planning. *Edited by Hans Gerth and Ernest K. Bramstedt. 424 pp.*
Mansur, Fatma. Process of Independence. *Foreword by A. H. Hanson. 208 pp.*
Martin, David A. Pacifism: *an Historical and Sociological Study. 262 pp.*
Myrdal, Gunnar. The Political Element in the Development of Economic Theory. *Translated from the German by Paul Streeten. 282 pp.*
Wootton, Graham. Workers, Unions and the State. *188 pp.*

FOREIGN AFFAIRS: THEIR SOCIAL, POLITICAL AND ECONOMIC FOUNDATIONS

Mayer, J. P. Political Thought in France from the Revolution to the Fifth Republic. *164 pp.*

CRIMINOLOGY

Ancel, Marc. Social Defence: *A Modern Approach to Criminal Problems. Foreword by Leon Radzinowicz. 240 pp.*
Cain, Maureen E. Society and the Policeman's Role. *326 pp.*
Cloward, Richard A., and **Ohlin, Lloyd E.** Delinquency and Opportunity: *A Theory of Delinquent Gangs. 248 pp.*
Downes, David M. The Delinquent Solution. *A Study in Subcultural Theory. 296 pp.*
Dunlop, A. B., and **McCabe, S.** Young Men in Detention Centres. *192 pp.*
Friedlander, Kate. The Psycho-Analytical Approach to Juvenile Delinquency: *Theory, Case Studies, Treatment. 320 pp.*
Glueck, Sheldon, and **Eleanor.** Family Environment and Delinquency. *With the statistical assistance of Rose W. Kneznek. 340 pp.*
Lopez-Rey, Manuel. Crime. *An Analytical Appraisal. 288 pp.*
Mannheim, Hermann. Comparative Criminology: *a Text Book. Two volumes. 442 pp. and 380 pp.*
Morris, Terence. The Criminal Area: *A Study in Social Ecology. Foreword by Hermann Mannheim. 232 pp. 25 tables. 4 maps.*
Rock, Paul. Making People Pay. *338 pp.*
●**Taylor, Ian, Walton, Paul,** and **Young, Jock.** The New Criminology. *For a Social Theory of Deviance. 325 pp.*

SOCIAL PSYCHOLOGY

Bagley, Christopher. The Social Psychology of the Epileptic Child. *320 pp.*
Barbu, Zevedei. Problems of Historical Psychology. *248 pp.*
Blackburn, Julian. Psychology and the Social Pattern. *184 pp.*

●**Brittan, Arthur.** Meanings and Situations. *224 pp.*
Carroll, J. Break-Out from the Crystal Palace. *200 pp.*
●**Fleming, C. M.** Adolescence: Its Social Psychology. *With an Introduction to recent findings from the fields of Anthropology, Physiology, Medicine, Psychometrics and Sociometry. 288 pp.*
● The Social Psychology of Education: *An Introduction and Guide to Its Study. 136 pp.*
Homans, George C. The Human Group. *Foreword by Bernard DeVoto. Introduction by Robert K. Merton. 526 pp.*
● Social Behaviour: *its Elementary Forms. 416 pp.*
●**Klein, Josephine.** The Study of Groups. *226 pp. 31 figures. 5 tables.*
Linton, Ralph. The Cultural Background of Personality. *132 pp.*
●**Mayo, Elton.** The Social Problems of an Industrial Civilization. *With an appendix on the Political Problem. 180 pp.*
Ottaway, A. K. C. Learning Through Group Experience. *176 pp.*
Ridder, J. C. de. The Personality of the Urban African in South Africa. *A Thematic Apperception Test Study. 196 pp. 12 plates.*
●**Rose, Arnold M.** (Ed.) Human Behaviour and Social Processes: *an Interactionist Approach. Contributions by Arnold M. Rose, Ralph H. Turner, Anselm Strauss, Everett C. Hughes, E. Franklin Frazier, Howard S. Becker, et al. 696 pp.*
Smelser, Neil J. Theory of Collective Behaviour. *448 pp.*
Stephenson, Geoffrey M. The Development of Conscience. *128 pp.*
Young, Kimball. Handbook of Social Psychology. *658 pp. 16 figures. 10 tables.*

SOCIOLOGY OF THE FAMILY

Banks, J. A. Prosperity and Parenthood: *A Study of Family Planning among The Victorian Middle Classes. 262 pp.*
Bell, Colin R. Middle Class Families: *Social and Geographical Mobility. 224 pp.*
Burton, Lindy. Vulnerable Children. *272 pp.*
Gavron, Hannah. The Captive Wife: *Conflicts of Household Mothers. 190 pp.*
George, Victor, and **Wilding, Paul.** Motherless Families. *220 pp.*
Klein, Josephine. Samples from English Cultures.
1. Three Preliminary Studies and Aspects of Adult Life in England. *447 pp.*
2. Child-Rearing Practices and Index. *247 pp.*
Klein, Viola. Britain's Married Women Workers. *180 pp.*
The Feminine Character. *History of an Ideology. 244 pp.*
McWhinnie, Alexina M. Adopted Children. *How They Grow Up. 304 pp.*
● **Myrdal, Alva,** and **Klein, Viola.** Women's Two Roles: *Home and Work. 238 pp. 27 tables.*
Parsons, Talcott, and **Bales, Robert F.** Family: Socialization and Interaction Process. *In collaboration with James Olds, Morris Zelditch and Philip E. Slater. 456 pp. 50 figures and tables.*

SOCIAL SERVICES

Bastide, Roger. The Sociology of Mental Disorder. *Translated from the French by Jean McNeil. 260 pp.*

Carlebach, Julius. Caring For Children in Trouble. *266 pp.*

Forder, R. A. (Ed.) Penelope Hall's Social Services of England and Wales. *352 pp.*

George, Victor. Foster Care. *Theory and Practice. 234 pp.*
Social Security: *Beveridge and After. 258 pp.*

George, V., and **Wilding, P.** Motherless Families. *248 pp.*

●**Goetschius, George W.** Working with Community Groups. *256 pp.*

Goetschius, George W., and **Tash, Joan.** Working with Unattached Youth. *416 pp.*

Hall, M. P., and **Howes, I. V.** The Church in Social Work. *A Study of Moral Welfare Work undertaken by the Church of England. 320 pp.*

Heywood, Jean S. Children in Care: *the Development of the Service for the Deprived Child. 264 pp.*

Hoenig, J., and **Hamilton, Marian W.** The De-Segregation of the Mentally Ill. *284 pp.*

Jones, Kathleen. Mental Health and Social Policy, 1845-1959. *264 pp.*

King, Roy D., Raynes, Norma V., and **Tizard, Jack.** Patterns of Residential Care. *356 pp.*

Leigh, John. Young People and Leisure. *256 pp.*

Morris, Mary. Voluntary Work and the Welfare State. *300 pp.*

Morris, Pauline. Put Away: *A Sociological Study of Institutions for the Mentally Retarded. 364 pp.*

Nokes, P. L. The Professional Task in Welfare Practice. *152 pp.*

Timms, Noel. Psychiatric Social Work in Great Britain (1939-1962). *280 pp.*

● Social Casework: *Principles and Practice. 256 pp.*

Young, A. F. Social Services in British Industry. *272 pp.*

Young, A. F., and **Ashton, E. T.** British Social Work in the Nineteenth Century. *288 pp.*

SOCIOLOGY OF EDUCATION

Banks, Olive. Parity and Prestige in English Secondary Education: a Study in Educational Sociology. *272 pp.*

Bentwich, Joseph. Education in Israel. *224 pp. 8 pp. plates.*

●**Blyth, W. A. L.** English Primary Education. *A Sociological Description.*
1. Schools. *232 pp.*
2. Background. *168 pp.*

Collier, K. G. The Social Purposes of Education: *Personal and Social Values in Education. 268 pp.*

Dale, R. R., and **Griffith, S.** Down Stream: *Failure in the Grammar School.* *108 pp.*

Dore, R. P. Education in Tokugawa Japan. *356 pp. 9 pp. plates.*

Evans, K. M. Sociometry and Education. *158 pp.*

●**Ford, Julienne.** Social Class and the Comprehensive School. *192 pp.*

Foster, P. J. Education and Social Change in Ghana. *336 pp. 3 maps.*

Fraser, W. R. Education and Society in Modern France. *150 pp.*

Grace, Gerald R. Role Conflict and the Teacher. *About 200 pp.*

Hans, Nicholas. New Trends in Education in the Eighteenth Century. *278 pp. 19 tables.*

● Comparative Education: *A Study of Educational Factors and Traditions.* *360 pp.*

Hargreaves, David. Interpersonal Relations and Education. *432 pp.*

● Social Relations in a Secondary School. *240 pp.*

Holmes, Brian. Problems in Education. *A Comparative Approach. 336 pp.*

King, Ronald. Values and Involvement in a Grammar School. *164 pp.*

School Organization and Pupil Involvement. *A Study of Secondary Schools.*

●**Mannheim, Karl,** and **Stewart, W. A. C.** An Introduction to the Sociology of Education. *206 pp.*

Morris, Raymond N. The Sixth Form and College Entrance. *231 pp.*

●**Musgrove, F.** Youth and the Social Order. *176 pp.*

●**Ottaway, A. K. C.** Education and Society: An Introduction to the Sociology of Education. *With an Introduction by W. O. Lester Smith. 212 pp.*

Peers, Robert. Adult Education: *A Comparative Study. 398 pp.*

Pritchard, D. G. Education and the Handicapped: *1760 to 1960. 258 pp.*

Richardson, Helen. Adolescent Girls in Approved Schools. *308 pp.*

Stratta, Erica. The Education of Borstal Boys. *A Study of their Educational Experiences prior to, and during, Borstal Training. 256 pp.*

Taylor, P. H., Reid, W. A., and **Holley, B. J.** The English Sixth Form. *A Case Study in Curriculum Research. 200 pp.*

SOCIOLOGY OF CULTURE

Eppel, E. M., and **M.** Adolescents and Morality: *A Study of some Moral Values and Dilemmas of Working Adolescents in the Context of a changing Climate of Opinion. Foreword by W. J. H. Sprott. 268 pp. 39 tables.*

●**Fromm, Erich.** The Fear of Freedom. *286 pp.*

● The Sane Society. *400 pp.*

Mannheim, Karl. Essays on the Sociology of Culture. *Edited by Ernst Mannheim in co-operation with Paul Kecskemeti. Editorial Note by Adolph Lowe. 280 pp.*

Weber, Alfred. Farewell to European History: *or The Conquest of Nihilism. Translated from the German by R. F. C. Hull. 224 pp.*

SOCIOLOGY OF RELIGION

Argyle, Michael and **Beit-Hallahmi, Benjamin.** The Social Psychology of Religion. *About 256 pp.*

Nelson, G. K. Spiritualism and Society. *313 pp.*

Stark, Werner. The Sociology of Religion. *A Study of Christendom.*
Volume I. *Established Religion. 248 pp.*
Volume II. *Sectarian Religion. 368 pp.*
Volume III. *The Universal Church. 464 pp.*
Volume IV. *Types of Religious Man. 352 pp.*
Volume V. *Types of Religious Culture. 464 pp.*

Turner, B. S. Weber and Islam. *216 pp.*

Watt, W. Montgomery. Islam and the Integration of Society. *320 pp.*

SOCIOLOGY OF ART AND LITERATURE

Jarvie, Ian C. Towards a Sociology of the Cinema. *A Comparative Essay on the Structure and Functioning of a Major Entertainment Industry. 405 pp.*

Rust, Frances S. Dance in Society. *An Analysis of the Relationships between the Social Dance and Society in England from the Middle Ages to the Present Day. 256 pp. 8 pp. of plates.*

Schücking, L. L. The Sociology of Literary Taste. *112 pp.*

Wolff, Janet. Hermeneutic Philosophy and the Sociology of Art. *About 200 pp.*

SOCIOLOGY OF KNOWLEDGE

Diesing, P. Patterns of Discovery in the Social Sciences. *262 pp.*

●**Douglas, J. D.** (Ed.) Understanding Everyday Life. *370 pp.*

●**Hamilton, P.** Knowledge and Social Structure. *174 pp.*

Jarvie, I. C. Concepts and Society. *232 pp.*

Mannheim, Karl. Essays on the Sociology of Knowledge. *Edited by Paul Kecskemeti. Editorial Note by Adolph Lowe. 353 pp.*

Remmling, Gunter W. (Ed.) Towards the Sociology of Knowledge. *Origin and Development of a Sociological Thought Style. 463 pp.*

Stark, Werner. The Sociology of Knowledge: *An Essay in Aid of a Deeper Understanding of the History of Ideas. 384 pp.*

URBAN SOCIOLOGY

Ashworth, William. The Genesis of Modern British Town Planning: *A Study in Economic and Social History of the Nineteenth and Twentieth Centuries. 288 pp.*

Cullingworth, J. B. Housing Needs and Planning Policy: *A Restatement of the Problems of Housing Need and 'Overspill' in England and Wales. 232 pp. 44 tables. 8 maps.*

Dickinson, Robert E. City and Region: *A Geographical Interpretation* *608 pp. 125 figures.*
The West European City: *A Geographical Interpretation. 600 pp. 129 maps. 29 plates.*
● The City Region in Western Europe. *320 pp. Maps.*
Humphreys, Alexander J. New Dubliners: *Urbanization and the Irish Family. Foreword by George C. Homans. 304 pp.*
Jackson, Brian. Working Class Community: *Some General Notions raised by a Series of Studies in Northern England. 192 pp.*
Jennings, Hilda. Societies in the Making: *a Study of Development and Re-development within a County Borough. Foreword by D. A. Clark. 286 pp.*
●**Mann, P. H.** An Approach to Urban Sociology. *240 pp.*
Morris, R. N., and **Mogey, J.** The Sociology of Housing. *Studies at Berinsfield. 232 pp. 4 pp. plates.*
Rosser, C., and **Harris, C.** The Family and Social Change. *A Study of Family and Kinship in a South Wales Town. 352 pp. 8 maps.*

RURAL SOCIOLOGY

Chambers, R. J. H. Settlement Schemes in Tropical Africa: *A Selective Study. 268 pp.*
Haswell, M. R. The Economics of Development in Village India. *120 pp.*
Littlejohn, James. Westrigg: *the Sociology of a Cheviot Parish. 172 pp. 5 figures.*
Mayer, Adrian C. Peasants in the Pacific. *A Study of Fiji Indian Rural Society. 248 pp. 20 plates.*
Williams, W. M. The Sociology of an English Village: *Gosforth. 272 pp. 12 figures. 13 tables.*

SOCIOLOGY OF INDUSTRY AND DISTRIBUTION

Anderson, Nels. Work and Leisure. *280 pp.*
●**Blau, Peter M.,** and **Scott, W. Richard.** Formal Organizations: *a Comparative approach. Introduction and Additional Bibliography by J. H. Smith. 326 pp.*
Eldridge, J. E. T. Industrial Disputes. *Essays in the Sociology of Industrial Relations. 288 pp.*
Hetzler, Stanley. Applied Measures for Promoting Technological Growth. *352 pp.*
Technological Growth and Social Change. *Achieving Modernization. 269 pp.*
Hollowell, Peter G. The Lorry Driver. *272 pp.*
Jefferys, Margot, *with the assistance of Winifred Moss.* Mobility in the Labour Market: *Employment Changes in Battersea and Dagenham. Preface by Barbara Wootton. 186 pp. 51 tables.*

Millerson, Geoffrey. The Qualifying Associations: *a Study in Professionalization. 320 pp.*

Smelser, Neil J. Social Change in the Industrial Revolution: *An Application of Theory to the Lancashire Cotton Industry, 1770-1840. 468 pp. 12 figures. 14 tables.*

Williams, Gertrude. Recruitment to Skilled Trades. *240 pp.*

Young, A. F. Industrial Injuries Insurance: *an Examination of British Policy. 192 pp.*

DOCUMENTARY

Schlesinger, Rudolf (Ed.) Changing Attitudes in Soviet Russia.
2. The Nationalities Problem and Soviet Administration. *Selected Readings on the Development of Soviet Nationalities Policies. Introduced by the editor. Translated by W. W. Gottlieb. 324 pp.*

ANTHROPOLOGY

Ammar, Hamed. Growing up in an Egyptian Village: *Silwa, Province of Aswan. 336 pp.*

Brandel-Syrier, Mia. Reeftown Elite. *A Study of Social Mobility in a Modern African Community on the Reef. 376 pp.*

Crook, David, and **Isabel.** Revolution in a Chinese Village: *Ten Mile Inn. 230 pp. 8 plates. 1 map.*

Dickie-Clark, H. F. The Marginal Situation. *A Sociological Study of a Coloured Group. 236 pp.*

Dube, S. C. Indian Village. *Foreword by Morris Edward Opler. 276 pp. 4 plates.*

India's Changing Villages: *Human Factors in Community Development. 260 pp. 8 plates. 1 map.*

Firth, Raymond. Malay Fishermen. *Their Peasant Economy. 420 pp. 17 pp. plates.*

Firth, R., Hubert, J., and **Forge, A.** Families and their Relatives. *Kinship in a Middle-Class Sector of London: An Anthropological Study. 456 pp.*

Gulliver, P. H. Social Control in an African Society: a Study of the Arusha, Agricultural Masai of Northern Tanganyika. *320 pp. 8 plates. 10 figures.*

Family Herds. *288 pp.*

Ishwaran, K. Shivapur. *A South Indian Village. 216 pp.*

Tradition and Economy in Village India: *An Interactionist Approach. Foreword by Conrad Arensburg. 176 pp.*

Jarvie, Ian C. The Revolution in Anthropology. *268 pp.*

Jarvie, Ian C., and **Agassi, Joseph.** Hong Kong. *A Society in Transition. 396 pp. Illustrated with plates and maps.*

Little, Kenneth L. Mende of Sierra Leone. *308 pp. and folder.*

Negroes in Britain. *With a New Introduction and Contemporary Study by Leonard Bloom. 320 pp.*

Lowie, Robert H. Social Organization. *494 pp.*
Mayer, Adrian, C. Caste and Kinship in Central India: *A Village and its Region. 328 pp. 16 plates. 15 figures. 16 tables.*
  Peasants in the Pacific. *A Study of Fiji Indian Rural Society. 248 pp.*
Smith, Raymond T. The Negro Family in British Guiana: *Family Structure and Social Status in the Villages. With a Foreword by Meyer Fortes. 314 pp. 8 plates. 1 figure. 4 maps.*

SOCIOLOGY AND PHILOSOPHY

Barnsley, John H. The Social Reality of Ethics. *A Comparative Analysis of Moral Codes. 448 pp.*
Diesing, Paul. Patterns of Discovery in the Social Sciences. *362 pp.*
●**Douglas, Jack D.** (Ed.) Understanding Everyday Life. *Toward the Reconstruction of Sociological Knowledge. Contributions by Alan F. Blum. Aaron W. Cicourel, Norman K. Denzin, Jack D. Douglas, John Heeren, Peter McHugh, Peter K. Manning, Melvin Power, Matthew Speier, Roy Turner, D. Lawrence Wieder, Thomas P. Wilson and Don H. Zimmerman. 370 pp.*
Jarvie, Ian C. Concepts and Society. *216 pp.*
Pelz, Werner. The Scope of Understanding in Sociology. *Towards a more radical reorientation in the social humanistic sciences. 283 pp.*
Roche, Maurice. Phenomenology, Language and the Social Sciences. *371 pp.*
Sahay, Arun. Sociological Analysis. *212 pp.*
Sklair, Leslie. The Sociology of Progress. *320 pp.*

International Library of Anthropology

General Editor   Adam Kuper

Brown, Paula. The Chimbu. *A Study of Change in the New Guinea Highlands. 151 pp.*
Lloyd, P. C. Power and Independence. *Urban Africans' Perception of Social Inequality. 264 pp.*
Pettigrew, Joyce. Robber Noblemen. *A Study of the Political System of the Sikh Jats. 284 pp.*
Van Den Berghe, Pierre L. Power and Privilege at an African University. *278 pp.*

International Library of Social Policy

General Editor   Kathleen Jones

Bayley, M. Mental Handicap and Community Care. *426 pp.*
Butler, J. R. Family Doctors and Public Policy. *208 pp.*
Holman, Robert. Trading in Children. *A Study of Private Fostering. 355 pp.*

Jones, Kathleen. History of the Mental Health Service. *428 pp.*
Thomas, J. E. The English Prison Officer since 1850: *A Study in Conflict.* *258 pp.*
Woodward, J. To Do the Sick No Harm. *A Study of the British Voluntary Hospital System to 1875. About 220 pp.*

International Library of Welfare and Philosophy

General Editors Noel Timms and David Watson

● **Plant, Raymond.** Community and Ideology. *104 pp.*

Primary Socialization, Language and Education

General Editor Basil Bernstein

Bernstein, Basil. Class, Codes and Control. *2 volumes.*
    1. *Theoretical Studies Towards a Sociology of Language. 254 pp.*
    2. *Applied Studies Towards a Sociology of Language. About 400 pp.*
Brandis, W., and **Bernstein, B.** Selection and Control. *176 pp.*
Brandis, Walter, and **Henderson, Dorothy.** Social Class, Language and Communication. *288 pp.*
Cook-Gumperz, Jenny. Social Control and Socialization. *A Study of Class Differences in the Language of Maternal Control. 290 pp.*
● **Gahagan, D. M.,** and **G. A.** Talk Reform. *Exploration in Language for Infant School Children. 160 pp.*
Robinson, W. P., and **Rackstraw, Susan D. A.** A Question of Answers. *2 volumes. 192 pp. and 180 pp.*
Turner, Geoffrey J., and **Mohan, Bernard A.** A Linguistic Description and Computer Programme for Children's Speech. *208 pp.*

Reports of the Institute of Community Studies

Cartwright, Ann. Human Relations and Hospital Care. *272 pp.*
●   Parents and Family Planning Services. *306 pp.*
    Patients and their Doctors. *A Study of General Practice. 304 pp.*
● **Jackson, Brian.** Streaming: *an Education System in Miniature. 168 pp.*
Jackson, Brian, and **Marsden, Dennis.** Education and the Working Class: *Some General Themes raised by a Study of 88 Working-class Children in a Northern Industrial City. 268 pp. 2 folders.*
Marris, Peter. The Experience of Higher Education. *232 pp. 27 tables.*
    Loss and Change. *192 pp.*

Marris, Peter, and **Rein, Martin.** Dilemmas of Social Reform. *Poverty and Community Action in the United States. 256 pp.*

Marris, Peter, and **Somerset, Anthony.** African Businessmen. *A Study of Entrepreneurship and Development in Kenya. 256 pp.*

Mills, Richard. Young Outsiders: *a Study in Alternative Communities. 216 pp.*

Runciman, W. G. Relative Deprivation and Social Justice. *A Study of Attitudes to Social Inequality in Twentieth-Century England. 352 pp.*

Willmott, Peter. Adolescent Boys in East London. *230 pp.*

Willmott, Peter, and **Young, Michael.** Family and Class in a London Suburb. *202 pp. 47 tables.*

Young, Michael. Innovation and Research in Education. *192 pp.*

●**Young, Michael,** and **McGeeney, Patrick.** Learning Begins at Home. *A Study of a Junior School and its Parents. 128 pp.*

Young, Michael, and **Willmott, Peter.** Family and Kinship in East London. *Foreword by Richard M. Titmuss. 252 pp. 39 tables.*
The Symmetrical Family. *410 pp.*

Reports of the Institute for Social Studies in Medical Care

Cartwright, Ann, Hockey, Lisbeth, and **Anderson, John L.** Life Before Death. *310 pp.*

Dunnell, Karen, and **Cartwright, Ann.** Medicine Takers, Prescribers and Hoarders. *190 pp.*

Medicine, Illness and Society

General Editor W. M. Williams

Robinson, David. The Process of Becoming Ill. *142 pp.*

Stacey, Margaret, *et al.* Hospitals, Children and Their Families. *The Report of a Pilot Study. 202 pp.*

Monographs in Social Theory

General Editor Arthur Brittan

●**Barnes, B.** Scientific Knowledge and Sociological Theory. *About 200 pp.*

Bauman, Zygmunt. Culture as Praxis. *204 pp.*

● **Dixon, Keith.** Sociological Theory. *Pretence and Possibility. 142 pp.*

●**Smith, Anthony D.** The Concept of Social Change. *A Critique of the Functionalist Theory of Social Change. 208 pp.*

Routledge Social Science Journals

The British Journal of Sociology. *Edited by Terence P. Morris. Vol. 1, No. 1, March 1950 and Quarterly. Roy. 8vo. Back numbers available. An international journal with articles on all aspects of sociology.*
Economy and Society. *Vol. 1, No. 1. February 1972 and Quarterly. Metric Roy. 8vo. A journal for all social scientists covering sociology, philosophy, anthropology, economics and history. Back numbers available.*
Year Book of Social Policy in Britain, The. *Edited by Kathleen Jones. 1971. Published annually.*

Printed in Great Britain by Unwin Brothers Limited
The Gresham Press Old Woking Surrey
A member of the Staples Printing Group